THE STRATEGIC REVOLUTION
Thoughts for the Twenty-First Century

Also available from Brassey's

IISS
STRATEGIC SURVEY

Leech
HALT! WHO GOES WHERE?: The Future of NATO in the New Europe

Orman
FAITH IN G.O.D.S.: Stability in the Nuclear Age

Pascall & Lamson
BEYOND GUNS AND BUTTER

RIPS
ASIAN SECURITY

Van Creveld
ON FUTURE WAR

THE STRATEGIC REVOLUTION

Thoughts for the Twenty-First Century

NEVILLE BROWN

BRASSEY'S (UK)

(Member of the Maxwell Macmillan Group)

LONDON · WASHINGTON · NEW YORK

UK editorial offices: Brassey's, 50 Fetter Lane, London EC4A 1AA
orders: Brassey's, Purnell Distribution Centre, Paulton, Bristol BS18 5LQ

USA editorial offices: Brassey's, 8000 Westpark Drive, First Floor, McLean, Virginia 22102
orders: Macmillan Publishing Company, Front and Brown Streets, Riverside, NJ 08075

Distributed in North America to booksellers and whole-salers by the Macmillan Publishing Company, N.Y., N.Y.

First English edition 1992

Library of Congress Cataloging in Publication Data
Available

British Library Cataloguing in Publication Data
Available

ISBN 0 08 040721 8 Hardcover

Printed in Great Britain by B.P.C.C. Wheatons Ltd., Exeter

Contents

The Author

NEVILLE BROWN is Professor of International Security Affairs at Birmingham University. He has held Visiting Fellowships at the Stockholm International Peace Research Institute, the Australian National University, and the International Institute for Strategic Studies. From 1965 to 1972, he served as a defence correspondent in Africa and Asia for several leading Western journals. He read Economics with Geography at University College, London, and History at New College, Oxford. From 1957 to 1960, he was a forecasting officer in the meteorological branch of the Fleet Air Arm, specialising mainly in upper air analysis. From 1981 to 1986, he was first Chairman of the Council for Arms Control, a British all-party body committed to the multilateral approach to nuclear peace. He is a Visiting Scholar in the School of Astrophysics at Leicester University and a Senior Associate at the Environmental Change Unit at Oxford. His most recent book, *New Strategy Through Space* (1990), has been widely commended as an overview in depth of the military and civil implications of work in the Space environment. He has lately been elected a Fellow of the Royal Astronomical Society.

Preface

IN MARCH 1991, the Iraqi military machine in and around Kuwait endured a defeat more utterly comprehensive than any suffered in desert war since General Archibald Wavell's tiny army overwhelmed Marshal Rodolfo Graziani's mammoth force in Cyrenaica in the autumn of 1940, taking two-thirds of it prisoner. What makes the comparison the more apt is the evident resemblance between Saddam Hussein and Graziani's master, Benito Mussolini. Each of these fascist dictators is or was totally dedicated to brutal power-broking by whatever foul means. Each was always devoid of any broader wisdom, philosophical or strategic. Each was denied the realisation of his more crass ambitions by lack of a technology base and authentic popular support.

The 1940 desert campaign was a turning point in that it showed Britain still to be capable of major offensive action, not just defence and endurance. The 1991 campaign has yet to be evaluated in its wider context. But already that whole situation seems to epitomise the way in which a concurrence of abrupt or rapid changes in fields as diverse as political practice, ecological stress and military science are transforming global strategy. It has thus provided a vivid backcloth to this study.

About terminology, there is not a lot to say. For purposes of enumeration, Anglo-American units are used interchangeably with metric ones because this is how the relevant literature is spread. One should remember that a metric tonne is slightly over 10 per cent more than an American short ton (2,000 pounds), and also that a kilometre is almost exactly five-eighths of a statute mile.

On the political side, a substitution of the term 'Near East' for 'Middle East' is explored in Chapter 10 and duly adopted. The aim is to seek a deeper historical perspective in our view of the region and to encourage a break with recent patterns of thought about its contemporary condition. Meanwhile, a term that is eschewed throughout is 'third world'. It seems to me to lack both form and consistency; and to be, in any case, blatantly patronising. It dates from 30 years ago and the endeavours of Nikita Khrushchev, all too successful for quite a while, to give the neutralist aspirations of many developing nations a Marxian and pro-Soviet tilt.

★   ★

Once again, the secretarial support of Mrs Jill Wells has been invaluable. Special thanks are also due to my cousin, Dr Michael Brown, for many useful comments on the text. I have also received most helpful comments on particular parts of the analysis from Majeed Alawi, Stuart Croft, Alex Garrard, Roger Machin, David Toke and Erol Yagci. This book is dedicated to Sir Peter and Lady Betty Terry for their friendship and moral support.

Neville Brown
21 August 1991

1

The Quest for Strategy

THE GOVERNMENTS in power in the West in the 1980s by no means worked wonders in every sphere. They came but tardily to a due measure of ecological concern. Some presided over a worsening social malaise, often evident to the most casual observer and confirmed by the statistics for delinquency. The record on urban renewal was patchy.

One thing that was controlled much better than in the previous decade was inflation. The mean rise in world trading prices was below four per cent between 1980 and 1987[1] as against 160 per cent from 1970 to 1978.[2] This improvement came about through the absence of oil price shocks anything like those of 1973–74 and 1979–80; and thanks to a more determined control of money supply all round.

Against this background, however, economic growth was middling in the OECD countries as a whole. Altogether, it was 20 per cent in real terms between 1980 and 1988[3] as compared with 27 per cent between 1972 and 1980. More worrisome, however, was the way the developing world's debt burden worsened year by year from 1982. By the end of 1988, it was estimated by the World Bank at $1,300 billion, a figure equal to almost half the combined Gross National Products of all the developing countries for that year.[4]

As will be argued further below, all these elements bear directly on the quest for world stability and peace. Yet, as of 1991, they are dwarfed by the declared end of the Cold War. Though some long-term consequences are hard to gauge as yet, one at least is clear. The collapse of the Warsaw Pact has more or less ruled out the contingency against which NATO has directed its main effort these last few decades – an overland *blitzkrieg* into Western Europe, the 'dash for the Channel ports'. At the same time, of course, the new situation has undercut what was for long one of Moscow's preferred stratagems in its pursuit of influence in the developing world: the use of Eastern European states as surrogates in its bid to bolster certain regimes and menace others. A conspicuous case in point was the use of the Czech arms industry to export weaponry, usually of Soviet design – e.g. to Israel in 1948, Egypt in 1955, Nigeria in 1967, Cyprus in 1971 and, more recently, semtex explosive to Libya for her to pass on to terrorists in Ulster and elsewhere.

What can also be said with some confidence is that Soviet combat forces (at any rate, conscript ground troops) will henceforward be less dependable as instruments of confrontation and intervention. A sharp deepening of the Soviet nationality crisis is a salient reason for saying this. Another can be that Komsomol, the all-Union youth movement interwoven with the conscript system, was already riven with cynicism and disaffection.[5] Along with decreased arms exports, such changes bode ill for fascisto-Marxist radicals throughout the developing world. A motive behind Saddam Hussein's adventurism in 1990 may have been that he wanted to harvest the fruits of Cold War patronage before that became too much a thing of the too distant past.

Already, the transformation globally has been dramatic. A decade ago, world peace was threatened by a whole series of regional conflicts – Afghanistan, Grenada, Iran, the Lebanon, Nicaragua, Poland. Most conveyed the impression of a Cold War revival against the background of an insistent rise in global stress. Analogies were even drawn with 1914. We were warned not to discount the difficulties faced by a multinational Soviet Union, the way some had too long discounted those of a multinational Austria-Hungary.[6] Likewise, a West German commentator wistfully emphasised the instabilities inherent in a technology-driven arms race, the Anglo-German naval competition being the supreme example before 1914.[7] Another precedent grimly recalled in the Federal Republic was that of the fateful lapses in diplomatic dialogue that occurred during that high summer. Such retrospection made the Helmut Schmidt administration in Bonn all the more anxious to maintain links with Moscow in the wake of the Afghanistan invasion.[8]

This time round, no world war broke out. But soon afterwards there was to be a mass upsurge of Left-wing protest, centred largely in the cities of northern Europe yet extending much wider. Needless to say, the activists were not at one on everything. In fact, they ranged politically from hard fascisto-Marxist revolutionaries to decent constitutional liberals unhappy about how Ronald Reagan reacted to Communism. Very generally, however, they persuaded themselves of the following premises. Compared with the 'nuclear threat' to all mankind, the 'Soviet threat' to the West was either secondary or derivative or non-existent. It was all right to solicit Moscow for mutual nuclear disarmament; but should our entreaties not swiftly yield fruit, we in the West would have to cast off nuclear weapons unilaterally. Though a concurrent dissolution of NATO and the Warsaw Pact might be the ideal outcome, one must stand prepared simply to wreck the former alliance rather than compromise on nuclear rejection. Nor would anything be lost by being quite open about such intentions.

In order to appreciate the import of the debate engendered by this medley of strange propositions, one needs to recognise how acute the Soviet internal crisis had even then become – thanks, in the ultimate, to the nationality dilemma. Many economic and social trends (not least, educational advance and urban growth) were fuelling aspirations for political reform. Yet the rub always was that this 'might allow the germination of secessionist movements that could ultimately split the USSR asunder'.[9] Faced with so horrendous a hazard, it was always on the cards that the *nomenklatura* (the ageing mediocracy that still had too firm a grip on the Soviet polity) would prefer the successor to Leonid Brezhnev to be a fascisto-Marxist despot ready to sublimate the deepening 'contradictions' of the regime by means of warlike opportunism: a more ruthless approach to Afghanistan; pressure on Norway, Sweden, West Berlin, Poland or China; more backing for Marxian 'wars of national liberation' ... Surely, too, the temptation to pitch in that direction would have been strong had the Atlantic Alliance then been in a state of nuclear paralysis if not complete disintegration on account of pressure exerted from within by what, in a surfeit of sectarian zeal, dubbed itself the 'peace movement'.

In fact, we could by now have been near the brink of some nuclear showdown, had not the West been led this last decade by people more committed to collective security through adequate military preparedness than were their domestic political rivals:–

From Ronald Reagan and George Bush to Margaret Thatcher to Helmut Kohl to François Mitterrand to Bettino Craxi to Yasushiro Nakasone, the voters in every major Western nation since 1979 have favoured candidates more strongly committed than their opponents to Western military strength and market capitalism. These conservative governments also adopted at crucial times two policies usually associated with liberals – a crusade for international human rights and democracy, and negotiations with the Soviets to reduce tensions.[10]

The rejoinder of the 'peace movement' would, of course, be that it was only moral suasion from themselves that impelled Rightist governments in such directions as arms control. Yet on balance, the virulence of the anti-nuclear protest may have confounded the politics of the moderate Left more than it reformed those of the solid Right. Granted, the arms control agreement on Intermediate Nuclear Forces in 1987 had its origins in the West's 'zero option' overture of November 1981: the offer not to deploy certain Ground-Launched Cruise Missiles (GLCM) and Pershing 2s in NATO Europe if the USSR withdrew the echelon of SS-20 ballistic missiles it was training on Europe. Granted, too, that neither the White House nor other Western chancelleries were blind to the use of this initiative to upstage simultaneously both the peace movement and the Kremlin. What might also be remembered, however, is that some specialists within the Reagan administration had long wondered how operationally viable the GLCMs or Pershings would be in central Europe; and whether, in any case, they were an essential rung in the ladder of controlled escalation.[11]

The Gorbachev effect

Be that as it may, there is no doubt that the availability of Mikhail Gorbachev to assume Kremlin leadership in 1985 still rates as a huge piece of good fortune for mankind. In what was perhaps the nick of time, historically speaking, he urgently addressed some of the more acute deficiencies in the Soviet system. At the same time, he turned to his adversaries in the West and conceded their victory in the Cold War with grace and even panache. Few statesmen anywhere ever have been possessed of the stature such responses required.

Moreover, History may judge him to have altered the political structure and complexion of Europe at large more profoundly than has any individual since Martin Luther, albeit in an opposite sense. After all, Luther played a focal part in triggering off the Reformation which was, in essence, a very sharp and quite even cleavage of Europe, philosophically and geopolitically, between a sunny Catholic south and a sombre Protestant north. This split, which was to be quite the most dominant fact in European affairs for over a century, took place against the background of the great explosion of information that became the driving force of the Renaissance. Printing was the biggest single factor.

Mikhail Gorbachev went the other way about. He inherited a division of the continent that was well-defined and roughly equal, that between a Moscow-oriented east and an ocean-oriented west: a division resulting from Stalin's paranoia and the general circumstances of Hitler's demise. Soon he set off the chain reaction of barrier demolition that has already ended this dichotomy. He also brought Russia into a European concert and into the world at large more completely than ever did any previous ruler, Peter the Great not excluded. He, like Luther, acted at a time of awesome advance in information exchange, the basis perhaps of another Renaissance. A whole range of technologies, from fax machines to Direct Broadcast Satellites sustain this advance.

Paradigmatic change

All of which poses the question of how far the West might cut its defence expenditure in the course of this decade. It also presents the academic discipline we have come to know as 'strategic studies' with both an opportunity and an obligation to effect what Thomas Kuhn of the University of Chicago would call a 'paradigm change'.[12] Though this term has become one of the great clichés of contemporary academe, certainly among social scientists and cultural historians, Kuhn is regularly criticised for not making clear exactly what he was getting at.[13] In response he has stressed how a professional community of the kind he has depicted may share not merely formal rules but 'examples of successful practice' in such matters as the application of doctrine or experimental method. As and when these fail, a new corpus of experience may quite abruptly displace what has gone before.[14] He has taken the Copernican revolution in astronomy, a signal Renaissance achievement, as the prime instance of such displacement.

Strategic studies emerged as a distinct field of scholarly enquiry rather over 30 years ago. What this 'emergence' involved was the burgeoning of a conviction, during the late 1950s, that strategy was altogether too crucial a subject to remain virtually the academic preserve of a small number of somewhat isolated individuals with backgrounds either in history or else the profession of arms. So what was looked for instead was a large and vibrant community of thinkers hailing from a rich variety of academic milieux (the pure sciences most certainly included) and, indeed, from a diversity of occupational backgrounds; the military and academe, of course, but also the public services, the media, the churches and industry. Links with officialdom soon proliferated but were substantially offset by roots sunk deep and wide within the universities, not least through big teaching programmes.

An indication of what might lie ahead in terms of policy analysis had been afforded by the setting up of the RAND Corporation, not long after the United States Air Force (USAF) became an independent service in 1948. This was and is a non-profit-making body linked closely with the USAF but addressing quite a broad spread of strategic topics. Signs that strategic studies had truly arrived on the world stage came with the establishment of centres outside the Atlantic area. The Institute for Defence Studies and Analyses in New Delhi dates from 1965; and the Institute for Zionist and Palestinian Studies in Cairo from 1968. The latter was renamed the Center for Political and Strategic Studies in 1972.

Still, the biggest institutional landmark had been the foundation in 1958 of the Institute for Strategic Studies (ISS), since 1971 the International Institute for Strategic Studies. During the Kennedy years, this London-centred body visibly became *primus inter pares* in this field. It has remained so ever since.

In fact, the year 1958 stands out as a scene-setter in this whole process of academic development. So we do well to recall what kind of year it was, internationally-speaking. First of all, it was spared anything very savage in the way of international armed conflict. The only confrontations deemed of global import (those in the Lebanon and in the Formosan Straits) were carefully constrained by outside parties, not least the two superpowers. Though the twin phenomena we know as Maoism and Gaullism were getting under way (see Chapter 2), their importance was not immediately apparent. On the nuclear front, however, events visibly gathered pace. America's allies in NATO Europe started to receive from her tactical nuclear warheads, albeit under a 'dual-key' control. Meanwhile, the resumption of the leadership of France by Charles de Gaulle had at the very least confirmed that country's determination to achieve military nuclear status. The previous autumn, the USSR had used a powerful and accurate liquid-fuelled rocket to orbit Sputnik I, the Earth's first artificial satellite. The previous year, too, Britain had exploded the prototype of her first thermonuclear warhead, alias 'hydrogen bomb'. In reaction to this, the Campaign for Nuclear Disarmament (CND) was formed. To an extent, the ISS was created to sustain a cogent dialectic with such rejectionism.

Nor did the priorities change a lot for some years. The pioneers of strategic studies remained concerned to help those active in the defence and diplomatic fields come to terms with the nuclear revolution. They were therefore preoccupied with the management of nuclear deterrence and of the Atlantic alliance.

Undoubtedly certain benefits accrued from so single-minded an approach. Acting in response to a widespread desire for curbs on the nuclear arms race, some analysts promoted what is nowadays the accepted axiom that (a) deterrence and defence, and (b) arms control and disarmament have to be treated as the twin aspects of the quest for world security – 'not contradictory but complementary', to quote the study completed for NATO in 1966 by Pierre Harmel, then the foreign minister of Belgium. Seminal in this regard was a book the ISS published in 1961 by the late Hedley Bull.[15] He was, in effect, the leader of a coterie of Australian academics who would soon be contributing significantly to successive strategic debates.

On balance, however, one has to regret that the international community of strategic theorists expanded its horizons so little. Most of them took little interest in military history, and less in sociology and psychology. They largely ignored strategic geography as well as classical military science. Many were too dismissive of the cumulative wisdom of professional military men.

At the same time, there was a neglect of economics as a structural factor in strategy that would have seemed juvenile to, let us say, the Western European statesmen and publicists of two or three centuries ago (see below). This neglect was evident in several directions. On the global plane, the macabre menace of nuclear war was very generally discussed as if it were quite independent of the Malthusian threat of war through overpopulation. Then at the European level, there was a disposition to ignore the financial crash that would surely have been an early result of any warlike crisis in the centre of the continent.

Take, for instance, the great debate that raged across NATO through the early 1980s about the relative merits of flexible nuclear response or 'no first use', a debate cast very largely in relation to central Europe. Each side of the argument seemed indifferent to the likelihood that even an imminent threat of hostilities in this crucial theatre would cause a panic in the money markets worldwide. For one thing, such bourses as Basle, Frankfurt, London, Paris and Zurich could never conduct business as usual so close to what could quickly become a nuclear front line. For another, scores of billions of dollars were owed to the West by the Soviet bloc. Their significance was that the international monetary system had become so bizarre and fragile that any creditors stood uncomfortably exposed to ruthless behaviour by big debtors not least if these were professing Leninists with *dirigiste* economies and with what they could present as ideological justifications for the renunciation of debt. After all, even one such act would almost certainly have triggered a succession of others around a debt-ridden world.[16]

The Subcontinent

Looking further afield, the Indian subcontinent has long stood out as a demonstration of how lopsided modern strategic thought has proved to be. In the 1960s and beyond, analysts often weighed the likely consequences of India's armed forces acquiring 'the Bomb'. Rarely did they reflect on the possibly far-reaching strategic reverberations of its experiencing one or more of these developmental setbacks: an acute economic crisis; the breaking away of one of more states or regions; an administrative collapse in Calcutta or some other urban centre.

Nor did strategists *qua* strategists look much at economic and social change in, say, Tibet, Nepal, Sikkim, Bhutan, Assam and Nagaland – change liable to make the Himalayas much less of a barrier line than they have been historically. Nor, indeed, did any contemplate in advance, or even much in retrospect, the geopolitical ramifications (in terms of internal and external stability) of the secession of the eastern wing of Pakistan.

A particularly striking example of this blinkered vision was furnished by the closure of the Suez canal (due to war and its aftermath) from 1967 to 1975. Although this state of affairs put extra strain on the always fragile economies of such countries as India and Pakistan, a disposition was abroad to discuss its wider significance exclusively in terms of how it inhibited the movement of Soviet naval vessels between the Mediterranean and the Indian Ocean. Yet India was threatened with break-up because of the way communal tensions had increased in the aftermath of the weak monsoons of 1965 and 1966. By 1970 Marxian insurgency in rural West Bengal was spreading into a Calcutta already sliding towards being ungovernable as its population mushroomed. It was no time to be hampered by obstacles to maritime trade.

In the event, Calcutta came under very good government during the early 1970s. Nor were the grimmer projections of its population growth (maybe to 50 million by the turn of the century[17]) borne out. Meanwhile, however, the interaction between economic and political instability grew more acute in East Pakistan. In November 1970, a late cyclone smote the ill-protected delta-lands of the Ganges-Brahmaputra confluence, killing several hundred thousand outright and ruining much precious land. As a direct consequence, the lack of confidence between East and West Pakistan worsened to crisis point.

Things did turn critical in 1971 as military rule overseen from a full 1,000 miles away in Islamabad became nerve-wracked and hence repressive, thereby obliging seven million East Pakistanis to take refuge across the Indian border. That December was to see full-scale hostilities between the Indian and Pakistani armed forces in that theatre, the upshot being the secession of East Pakistan to become Bangladesh. Yet, with its economy under mounting pressure of population, and further debilitated by the ravages of war and then by a drought that was to kill a further half a million, the new state quickly sank into a morass of corruption and political violence. The Malthusian spectre loomed larger than ever in 1974 as another 300,000 died of malnutrition caused by further severe flooding. The following August witnessed a take-over by exasperated though confused army officers. Soon, this new regime was quarrelling bitterly with New Delhi over the intricate yet crucial question of flood-control in the delta-lands.[18]

Small wonder then that the very name 'Bangladesh' had become a byword for destitution and hopelessness. Nor has it been able to shake off this image since. Things came once more to a near desperate head in 1988 when – against a background of endemic communal and political tension – the most severe monsoon floods on record were made all the worse by the way rapid deforestation in Nepal had undermined the natural modulation of floodwater drainage into tributaries of the Ganges. That September over 75 per cent of Bangladesh was under water. Furthermore, the threat thereby posed to regional stability was aggravated by renewed dissent and insurgency in Assam and the border territories of north-east India, a neglected segment of the country joined to the rest only by a corridor 20 miles wide between Nepal and Bangladesh. Then in April 1991 came another cyclone, again rather unseasonably. This disastrous event (which has probably killed upwards of a 100,000) may have been triggered off or aggravated by soot from the blazing oilwells of Kuwait (see Chapter 8).

The above is only an outline account of how economic deprivation has recurrently compromised the peace of the subcontinent. No attempt has here been made to explore the interaction between economics and the evolution of what has long been a social and cultural geography of extraordinary complexity. Nevertheless, enough has perhaps been said to make the point that development economics, together with adjacent realms of sociology and political science, ought always to be an integral part of strategic studies. There are also strong indications, especially since 1988, that climatic trends or fluctuations need to be embraced. So do other aspects of ecology. Only reformed thus may strategic studies proffer henceforward guidance that is at all adequate on such matters as warlike contingencies, nuclear proliferation or arrangements for collective security.

Moreover, such a broadening of approach would be agreeably in line with contemporary academic tendencies. In various sectors, defined subject areas are interacting more than was usually the case a generation or two back: for example, physics and chemistry; languages and sociology; politics and economics. Likewise, interdisciplinary schools are being formed to study either major regions or themes like crime or urban renewal, not to mention war itself.

The British connection

All this sounds so blindingly obvious as to make it a shade surprising that a broad front was not established years ago. Undeniably, however, nuclear deterrence was an intriguing challenge. The radiative effects of nuclear release were singularly nasty. In addition, explosive firepower was thus transformed from being a vital but strictly finite resource to being one that was almost too abundant to unleash at all. Comprehending 'the Bomb' therefore came to be seen as a task fit for intellectual heroes, best left free from more mundane tasks. The other side of that golden coin was that the brutal visibility of what was called the nuclear balance of terror made all other threats to Atlantic security seem non-immediate, trifling or implausible.

However, some of the roots of this circumscription go deeper. The people who forged strategic studies into a separate discipline largely came from an anglophone world still sustained by memories of the wartime alliance and, in particular, of that remarkable scholar-statesman, Winston Churchill. Correspondingly there were close links with an English historical disposition, going back some time past, to favour the treatment of war as a phenomenon apart, something waged beyond the home territory and outside the normal political process. Such an understanding would not lead one to think instinctually of the economics of development, let us say, as an integral part of strategy.

But we should not forget an earlier tradition. From the middle of the 17th Century through to the late 18th, the Mercantilists in England (like the Colbertians in France) were suffused by a sense of the importance of colonial trade as the lynchpin for both the industrial and the fiscal chariots of war: 'trade is the source of finance and finance is the vital nerve of war', as Jean Baptiste Colbert put it. In this way they evinced, according to the lights of their time, a full consciousness of the economic bases of strategy.

Moreover, as religious bigotry lessened and scientific enquiry progressed in the late 17th Century, an awareness spread that the new renaissance thus engendered in science (with astronomy and mathematics as its spearhead disciplines) could proffer the prospect of technological supremacy in war, not least via ballistics, cartography and navigation. Scientific academies sprang up across Western Europe to be followed by the still celebrated Academy of Sciences in Russia, this having been established by Peter the Great in 1725. In 1662, the Royal Society had been founded in London. In 1666, the *Académie Royale des Sciences* was founded in Paris, with sustained encouragement from Colbert.

In *The Wealth of Nations* (published in 1776), the great Scottish economist, Adam Smith, scorned mercantilist notions about building up through trade surpluses the bullion needed to fill the war chests.[19] Nevertheless, he was quite prepared to qualify his free trade principles in order to uphold war-related industries. Moreover, a more comprehensive protectionist and blockade strategy was endorsed by the government in London throughout the French Revolutionary and Napoleonic wars (see below). From then on, however, this philosophy waned. This was in part because the United Kingdom herself was assured of commercial paramountcy for a while ahead. It was also because the economic philosophy that soon became ascendant in Britain – international free trade – was seen more as an alternative to military confrontation than as a foundation for it. The Manchester School of Liberalism airily assumed that a world that was intercommunicating fully, commercially and in other respects, would soon lose the will and the ability to wage wars within itself.

True, the evolution of the British Empire continued to be guided in no small measure by a desire to protect trade and to secure access to such materials as cotton, gold and oil. True, also, that in neither of the world wars that dominated the first half of this century were the London governments of the day slow to perceive the counter-economic potentialities of maritime blockade and strategic bombing. One is bound to say, however, that if the British military and strategic theorists of the inter-war period (meaning, first and foremost, J.F.C. Fuller and Basil Liddell Hart) had paid close attention to the economic dimension in war, the bombing offensive against the Third Reich might have been targeted with a clearer sense of her industrial strengths and weaknesses. One has to say, too, that some relevant analysis in the right circles of the importance to Germany of iron ore imported from Sweden via Narvik might have persuaded Downing Street and Whitehall to hang on to that port like grim death from May 1940, instead of meekly abandoning it in the light of adverse developments in France.[20] Combined with a scorched-earth policy, implemented when necessary, in the iron mines of Lorraine, this might have brought the Nazi war machine to a grinding halt in very short order.

It was a tragedy that the prevailing paradigms did not allow of this. Liddell Hart showed remarkably little interest in industry, agriculture or commerce as sinews of war in what otherwise was a magisterial review of war in history, published in 1929. As regards the collapse of Germany in 1918, he insisted that German morale was cracked that October by 'the collapse of Bulgaria, reinforced by the first reports of the renewal of the frontal attack in France'.[21] All that he allowed for the hunger of the German populace in the face of economic blockade is that it was one of the factors that prevented morale from being revived. Three years later, Fuller contributed a work of comparable stature. In its pages, no little emphasis was eloquently laid on the controlling influence on war of economic and technical development. However, the presentation was too abstract on this score. It was rather like opining that only armed strength could save us, without ever suggesting how this strength might be configured. So it was not the kind of affirmation that might change the priorities of those in the corridors of power. Part of the problem was that Fuller was too consumed with the structural transformation being attempted in Soviet Russia and the material-cum-ideological challenge that could thus be presented: 'The supreme military problem is not the prevention of another European civil war but the consolidation of Europe to meet Asia'.[22]

In general, however, a basic weakness of the British quest for strategy has been a disinclination to consider how fragile the cohesion of a sovereign state may often be, yet how basic to its very survival. We consider it so little because our own experience has been so benign in this regard. The 'pacification' of the Scottish highlands (after 1745) and the miseries of Ireland apart, the British Isles have been exceptionally free – for centuries past – from internal unrest of an intensity such as to threaten governmental collapse. A key reason is, of course, that the Straits of Dover have historically done for England and Britain what the NATO nuclear umbrella has done for much of Europe since 1949. They have cut to a minimum the scope either for outright aggression or for polarising interference. So it was that, not even during the political-cum-religious civil war between Cavaliers and Roundheads during the 1640s, did England experience anything approaching the horror of the Thirty Years' War in Germany or the earlier religious strife in the Low Countries and France.

National schools of thought

Much of what has just been said about British strategic thinking applies, in general terms, to Australia, Canada and the United States. It does so partly because of an extensive sharing of memories and traditions. It does so also because what can be said, even in this day and age, about the offshore insularity of Britain similarly applies to the others. If there is a distinction to draw at this level, it is that the turbulence of nation-building is more readily recalled by them.

Alfred Thayer Mahan, the doyen of naval theory, is almost an archetypal example of an Anglo-American approach, by virtue of the way he blended his professional experience as an American naval officer with deep study of maritime history, above all the Royal Navy's. He was conscious of the need for naval strength to be underpinned by a suitable civil infrastructure, marine and otherwise. More importantly for our present purposes, he wrote insightfully about the economic warfare between Britain and post-revolutionary France that reached its climax around 1810. Napoleon's introduction of his

Continental System of embargoes in reply to the British naval blockade led him progressively to extend his realms, thereby dissipating both the military resources he could call on and his own mental energy, while turning much of Europe more fiercely against him. The upshot was the invasion of Russia, spoken of by Mahan as 'one of the most impressive and gigantic military catastrophes recorded by history'.[23]

The fact remains, however, that Mahan's focus was always on sea control, at times almost for its own sake. Convincing though he is when assessing the effect of the blockade on Napoleon's psychology and strategy, he rises little above the trivial when talking of its economic impact as such. William Pitt, the British Prime Minister from 1784 to 1801 and then 1804 to 1806, had been far more definitive on such matters.[24]

In the decade from 1958, there was a revival of the French tradition of strategic thought. At first sight, one could be surprised as well as disappointed at its failure to provide a broad alternative to the increasing preoccupation of 'les Anglo-Saxons' with nuclear deterrence. After all, the French are heirs not just to Colbert and Louis XIV but to a European continentalist tradition, established by Napoleon and preserved through the writings of Clausewitz, of war as a very comprehensive struggle between nations in arms. Furthermore, both the desolation of 1940 and the grim colonial struggles after 1945 in Indo-China and then Algeria should have brought home to them anew the need to see conflict in the round.

However, that was not how things worked. A desire to restore national pride, autonomy and resolve by means of nuclear deterrence became all the more dominant after de Gaulle's return to power in 1958. The President himself saw *la force de dissuasion* as the modern expression of the principle he had extolled in the 1930s, the discouragement of attack by the evident excellence of one's preparations for counter-attack. At the doctrinal level, the debate was led by two retired generals, André Beaufre and Pierre Gallois.[25] The former was not so solidly Gaullist as the latter; but they worked to much the same nuclear-driven agenda.

In terms of its military culture, the Soviet Union has long been understood to come within the Clausewitzian orbit of continental Europe. The thought of Karl von Clausewitz (1780–1831) was never cast quite in the Hegelian mode of dialectical transformation that, after much agonizing, the young Karl Marx was to adopt and adapt. All the same, he was director of the *Kriegsakademie* in Berlin

(1818–30) while G.W.F. Hegel reigned supreme at the university there. Later on, first Friedrich Engels then (in his Zurich days) Vladimir Lenin made detailed notes on the great Clausewitzian treatise, *On War*. Not least remarked was its dictum that 'war is politics continued by other means'. Also it was Engels who, in *Anti-Dühring*, sought to interpret the role of weapons development in the class struggle. The gist was that cannon had helped the bourgeois state to defeat the feudal baronies; and that, in due course, the musket would enable the proletarian *levée en masse* to defeat the bourgeoisie.

Much scope remained for fierce disputation as to what such notions actually connoted for the cherished hope of a distinctively socialist way of warfare. In terms of idiom and perspective, however, *On War* is clearly compatible with revolutionary precepts about perennial struggle carried on violently and by any other means – everything from social transformation to economic warfare to peace offensives.

Pragmatic responses

As Marxism has weakened as an ideology, those who would claim to subscribe to it have become more diverse than ever in their beliefs and practices. Nevertheless, the formulation just alluded to is a typical Marxian version of what students of war in the West call 'grand strategy';

> The highest type ...that which so integrates the policies and armaments of the nation that resort to war is either rendered unnecessary or is undertaken with the maximum chance of victory.[26]

During the Second World War, a massive totalitarian threat drove the democratic West to see its security problems more in global terms than ever before. After 1945, the same happened again. However, apart from an American endeavour during the short span of the Kennedy presidency (see below), there has never yet been any attempt to generate a countervailing strategy that is grand in the other sense of addressing all the roots of world conflict and the various remedies. Undoubtedly, one reason has been the belated emergence of strategic studies and its pristine devotion to matters nuclear. But another has been a dearth or more general thought, above all, general political thought. In the first two post-war decades, there was little of a seminal kind from any quarter.[27] Since then, more contributions have come forth but these largely from either the utopian Left or the *laissez-faire* Right. All of which is a curious commentary on the sustained expansion of university education, not least in social studies. One thing surely to admit is that the more political science has expanded, the more political philosophy has atrophied.

Nevertheless, one has only to look at the Gulf situation as from August 1990 to recognise that, in this post-war era, governments have often been prepared to take cognisance of the economic dimension as particular warlike crises have unfolded. This has been true since what has just been identified as the academic watershed of 1958; and it was no less true before. The rub is that their responses on this score have tended to be improvised and piecemeal, this in the absence of an apposite overview.

In fact, quite the most thoroughgoing application, since the Lend Lease arrangements of the Second World War, of economic leverage for strategic ends began in 1947 with the launching of the Marshall Plan. Its immediate origins lay in how slowly and uncertainly the post-war recovery of Western Europe was progressing, especially in the aftermath of a bitter winter (see Chapter 7). As late as October 1947, not even a basic ration scale as meagre as 1,550 calories per day could always be ensured in parts of the Anglo-American occupation zone in Germany.[28] The Marshall Plan was intended to block Communist exploitation of this crisis by (a) stimulating economic growth by all the European participants, (b) challenging the USSR to join in this reconstruction itself or at the least to allow East European states to participate and (c) laying the foundations for West European unity. The supreme architect of the plan, General George Marshall, had been Chairman of the Joint Chiefs of Staff during the Second World War.

Since those days, there have been various situations in which the pressure of population growth on the resource base has helped fuel armed conflict, not least insurgency war.[29] In addition, a wish to make mineral supplies secure has featured more often than may generally be appreciated. Gaining access to readily workable ores of uranium as well as certain other mineral deposits may have been a prime motive behind Soviet imperialism in Eastern Europe from 1944 onwards. Likewise, tin deposits and rubber plantations added to the importance, as seen from each side, of the campaign against Communist insurgency in Malaya in the decade or so from 1948. During those years, a good third of the world's natural rubber came regularly from that peninsula and over half the remainder from elsewhere in South-East Asia. Similarly, almost half the non-Communist world's tin was still coming from Malaya as late as 1963 and almost half the rest from elsewhere in South-East Asia.[30]

An oil import embargo was one of the economic levers used by the West to undermine the radical nationalist regime under Mohammed Mossadeq that held power in Iran, 1951–53. Needless to say, too, the ensuring of oil supplies long-term was a prime motive. Maintaining the flow of oil through a routeway encompassed about by the Arab-Israel conflict was a major Anglo-French concern during the Suez crisis of 1956. Five years later, British forces were deployed to Kuwait in moderate strength (roughly two brigades plus air and naval support) after Baghdad had publicly claimed that this oil-rich sheikhdom actually belonged to Iraq, a claim of which more later. Thrice between 1958 and 1976, the Royal Navy and the Icelandic coastguard service were locked in dour non-lethal confrontations. Attempts at secession by Katanga in the Congo in 1960–63 and by the Eastern Region, Biafra, in Nigeria in 1966 were encouraged by the proven existence of large deposits of non-ferrous metals and of oil within the respective territories. But those same assets also made secession even less acceptable to other interested parties than might otherwise have been the case.[31]

Yet all these episodes pall into insignificance in comparison with how sharply a deepening crisis in world trade was aggravated by the Yom Kippur war of October 1973. Soon there was talk of cartels of producers of other minerals (for example, copper) doing what OPEC had done. Responding to an initiative by Houari Boumédienne of Algeria, acting as President of the Non-Aligned Group, the United Nations held a special session of the General Assembly in April-May 1974 to review raw materials access in relation to economic development. In a keynote address, Boumédienne advised the primary producers to nationalise their various resources and band themselves together, hopefully to shift co-operation with the industrialised nations more onto a basis of autonomy, equality and mutual benefit.[32] Early that year, a more blatantly self-centred approach had been adopted by China as she wrested the Paracel Islands from the South Vietnamese, thereby extending her own claims to offshore drilling.

Duly, a few academic strategists took within their purview not only the energy crunch but also such related subjects as the ramifying role of multinational firms. Nevertheless the treatment of this subject area remained episodic, peripheral and unintegrated so far as strategic studies was concerned. The odd monograph, however rewarding in itself,[33] was no indication of a paradigm change. Had this taken place in such a manner as to link development issues to security issues within a grand strategy, a region like the Middle East might now be doing less to cause the world's problems and more to solve them. 'If you want peace', said the Romans, 'prepare for war'. Such advice is needful but not sufficient. If you want peace, prepare for war but also prepare for peace.

2

Indivisible Peace

AT THIS TIME, above all, no one can be sure which issues will loom largest in the quest for peace over the next decade or two. What questions will be taken as read and which will engender controversy? Early in 1990, the indications from the United States were that analysts had started to ask how apposite the globalism of the last half-century now was. While the Cold War was raging, it had seemed axiomatic that peace in the Caribbean, say, depended in the ultimate on peace in the Himalayas or wherever. But need the international order still be seen as that indivisible?

Perhaps Baghdad took notice, maybe too much notice, of this questioning. At all events, any further discussion of the matter is bound to be much influenced by whatever is the final outcome of the big contest of wills that began in the Gulf in August 1990. Is Saddam Hussein to be counted among the last of the long and ugly succession of charismatic dictators of the *blitzkrieg* era, a genre unlikely to survive in a more interdependent world? Alternatively, may he be the first of a new generation of psychopathic despots, well attuned to the electronic age in the way they combine an implacable hatred of the mores of our open society with a new style of televisual opportunism in confronting it? If the latter interpretation be the more correct, can we afford to take up every such challenge? Can we afford not to? Dare we do without a strategy that is grand not only in the sense of being global but also in that it addresses every aspect of world stability.

If such comprehension is sought, we do well to remember that it has been attempted only by one administration in the West these last 45 years, that which President Kennedy formed upon assuming office in 1961. Unfortunately, this attempt was badly flawed; and must now be studied in part to remind ourselves just how easily a grand strategy can unravel, how hard such an agenda is to implement even at the best of times.

The New Frontier

From the outset, the young President and his 'new frontiersmen' affirmed with a refreshing zest that the United States would give a positive lead in all things. As Secretary of Defense, Robert McNamara expanded every fact of military capability. But he also espoused as fervently as anybody higher levels of overseas development aid. A Peace Corps was established. So was an Arms Control and Disarmament Agency (ACDA). Even such domestic aims as civil rights and urban renewal were deemed to restore the world influence of the United States by bolstering her international image and national self-confidence.

The parameters the new frontier was to work within, particularly on the global plane, had mostly been outlined by Kennedy himself over the previous two or three years; and had been encapsulated in *The Strategy of Peace*, a collection of speeches and interviews he published early in 1960. Thus in April 1959, he averred that

> If Negro colleges and universities will assume leadership – in training students for their global responsibilities – they will contribute mightily to the strength of America ... and turn the battle for men's minds in favour of freedom.

Two months before, he had 'urged a convincing demonstration that we have ... an enduring long-term interest in the productive economic growth of the less developed nations'.[1] In opposition, and even more so in office, he and his political colleagues interacted extensively with the liberal intelligentsia, abroad as well as at home. Progressive economists, either drafted into the administration or freely given its ear, ensured that the White House adopted Keynesian paradigms for macro-economic planning more explicitly than ever before; and, against the background of increased federal expenditure, these secured good growth rates. Secretary McNamara encouraged the Pentagon to be similarly interactive. The administration and its strategic advisers drew especially close to the Institute for Strategic Studies.

What has again to be borne in mind, however, is how young a subject strategic studies was, still feeling its way towards what was in any case far too exclusively a nuclear concern. Obviously it is not possible to gauge how far this impoverished thinking within the new frontier about world affairs in the round. What is undeniable is that Washington missed or mishandled various specific opportunities in the international realm during the Kennedy years. A sense of hope unrequited is made the more acute by the fact that in 1962 the USA had become ascendant, if only transiently, in strategic nuclear terms. She had done so through the deployment of two systems initiated by the Eisenhower administration. The one was the Earth's first reconnaissance satellite. The other was Minuteman, the world's first solid-fuelled Intercontinental Ballistic Missile (ICBM). Using solid fuel, it could be cheap, compact and responsive.

Yet it was also in 1962 that overly forceful diplomacy by Washington in support of a British application to join the Common Market proved highly counterproductive, not only in Paris but in Bonn. Meanwhile, nothing of consequence was done to arrest the onward march of *apartheid* in South Africa. In the Middle East, there was an abject failure to address, during what may have been the most propitious years in the last 40, the conflict between Israel and her neighbours. The outcome of the Suez campaign of 1956 had left Israel slightly more relaxed and Egypt mildly gratified. The Lebanon crisis of 1958, the dissolution in 1961 of the Egypt-Syria union launched in 1958 and the Yemeni civil war from 1962 all set limits to radical pan-Arab nationalism, as led from Cairo. Meanwhile, Israel stayed firmly under the control of the social democratic mainstream of the Zionist movement. Menachem Begin and his fellow fanatics in the revisionist wing (*ie* those who adhered to the supremacist doctrines of Vladimir Jabotinsky, 1890–1940) remained very much on the sidelines.

In 1964, the year after John Kennedy's death, this particular window of opportunity was abruptly to close. On balance, the fall of Nikita Khrushchev from the Soviet leadership was unhelpful. At the same time, the continuing dispute over the allocation of the Jordan waters suddenly became fiercer. The Palestine Liberation Organisation was founded. The Soviet navy returned to the Mediterranean, after a six-year absence. Israel negotiated with France the supply of a nuclear reactor, with no controls against diversion to military ends. Thus was the scene set for the 1967 war, among the results of which were (a) an Arab world rendered more obdurate by stark humiliation on the battlefield, (b) a Palestinian movement pitched further towards the fascisto-Marxist Left, (c) the first participation by Begin in the government of Israel and (d) Israel saddling herself with what has increasingly come to look like a desperate demographic contradiction for the Jewish democracy – namely, her occupation of the West Bank and Gaza.

Likewise, the Kennedy administration failed to explore the opportunities created by Chairman Mao's revolt against Moscow's dominance of the Communist world, a revolt evident enough from the autumn of 1958.[2] What thus became the mirror image of a Gaullist reaction against Atlanticism had followed hard upon Charles de Gaulle's return to power in France in May. That seminal year may also have been the one in which Senator John Kennedy set his cap firmly at the White House.

Through 1959, relations between the two Communist giants grew ever more strained. Things were to reach a grim *démarche* in July 1960 when, at only a month's notice, Khrushchev withdrew every Soviet expert from the People's Republic, thereby reneging on all of 600 aid agreements. Yet John Kennedy had continued to view 'Red China' as merely a monolithic satellite of Moscow that had to be defeated in economic competition by a pluralist and democratic India, hopefully supported better than before by the West: 'If India fails and China succeeds, I would say that the decisive struggle in the Cold War in the next 10 years will have been lost'.[3] It was a struggle for the economic leadership of all Asia.[4] Granted, the notion of underpinning India's democracy with economic aid was progressive enough in itself. Even so, the pitch as regards China, and by extension, Japan was most unimaginative and was never modified in office. Awareness that divergence between Beijing and Moscow could be turned to the West's advantage was not to dawn on the White House until the Kissinger-cum-Nixon initiative of 1971.

How richly earlier overtures would have borne fruit is, of course, impossible to say. Perhaps, however, they would have done something to stave off a challenge that the new frontier did anticipate, but most inadequately. This was insurgency war, especially as presented in the jungles, plantations and paddy-fields of South-East Asia.

Unready, too, was the strategic community at large. As a result, a doctrine of counter-insurgency for application to South Vietnam was evolved from scratch by analysts imbued with the all-too-narrow rationalism of their culture-bound social science, applied to a skewed and patchy data base on a geography that was utterly unfamiliar, both in its natural and in its man-made dimensions. For anybody who stayed any time in Saigon during the 1960s, there will be a mortifying ring of truth in David Halberstam's thesis that Vietnam was lost

mainly by the 'best and the brightest', the youthful scholar-politicians
from Ivy League universities who coldly accepted the commitment as
just another containment 'mission'.[5] Likewise, anybody who passed
through Washington during the Kennedy years will hear his further
contention that what was intended to be a comprehensive *modus
operandi* for counter-insurgency was cobbled together breathlessly,
decision on such vexatious questions as the use of defoliants and
napalm being taken almost *ad hoc*.[6] Nor was there enough regard for
geographical specifics. Those concerned rarely reminded themselves
that Geography does not repeat itself; and that the jungle can never be
neutral.

Initially, too, the Outer Space dimension was neglected, *The
Strategy of Peace*, having just the one reference to the desirability of
placing Space exploration 'on an international footing as soon as
possible'.[7] But in the campaign for the White House, Kennedy
warmed to the theme that Soviet successes in Space were one factor
driving the world 'to the conclusion that the Soviet tide is rising and
ours is ebbing'.[8] Then within a few short weeks in the spring of 1961,
his administration thrashed out a 'national commitment' to go to the
Moon by 1970, hopefully ahead of the Soviets.[9] Still, such instancy
may have been more allowable in this domain then in counter-
insurgency. At any rate, the interaction with any adversary was less
intricate and immediate. The Moon, as they say, never fights back.

For many people in the United States and elsewhere, the most
spectacular and significant man-made event in Space thus far had
been the launch, in the autumn of 1957, of Sputnik I. To most,
however, its prime significance lay in that it betokened 'in a way that
stark and subdued reports of monitored ICBM tests could not'[10] a
readiness to deploy ICBMs, ahead of the Americans. The Democrats were quick to incorporate into their political platform USAF
apprehensions that, within a very few years, the Soviets would establish a yawning 'missile gap'. It was central to their thesis that an ailing
and lackadaisical Republican administration was out of its depth.

Yet, on assuming office, the New Frontier did not hesitate to accept
hard insider evidence that, since the parameters of the arms race did
not coincide with those of Space flight, the 'missile gap' that was
really emerging was one much to the detriment of the Soviets. Next,
those concerned moved fast to elaborate what it was hoped would be
viable and relevant nuclear doctrines, drawing a lot of inspiration
and guidance from the burgeoning of strategic studies within that
sphere. Among those who, between 1959 and 1963, brought out

books about or bearing on nuclear deterrence were Patrick Blackett, Bernard Brodie, Alastair Buchan, Hedley Bull, Pierre Gallois, Margaret Gowing, Samuel Huntington, Henry Kissinger, Klaus Knorr, Basil Liddell Hart, Robert Osgood, Anatol Rapaport, Thomas Schelling, John Strachey and Maxwell Taylor. For nuclear strategy, it was both sunrise and high noon.

In the middle of it all came 'Cuba'. It was another case of what today would be called a 'one-off'. The Cold War as such witnessed but one of the non-nuclear 'limited wars' (frontal campaigns confined to one theatre) that strategic theorists went on to write so much about. This was the conflict in Korea, 1950–53. By 1960, the theorists were starting also to write about confrontations that might still be constrained but which did involve strategic weapons. The Cuban missile crisis of October 1962 was and has remained the nearest thing to this.

Speaking at the Ann Arbor campus of the University of Michigan that June, Robert McNamara had extolled the 'total counterforce' option then opening up, thanks to Minuteman and Space reconnaissance. He said that the United States had concluded that 'principal military objectives, in the event of a nuclear war ... should be the destruction of the enemy's military forces, not his civilian population'.[11] The implication was that it was becoming feasible to launch a strike against a Soviet ICBM force that (being as yet entirely liquid-fuelled) remained small, clumsy and susceptible. Nor were the USSR's other strategic echelons, the heavy bombers and the submarines, able adequately to redress matters.[12]

McNamara's concern was to scotch Gaullist contentions, which owed more to Cartesian abstraction than to hard information, that a trend to strategic parity as between the superpowers was already eroding the US guarantee to Europe. He may have discounted too much the anxiety that would be aroused in Moscow by his indicating what the situation actually was and how doctrine had evolved to exploit it. On the other hand, the new frontier then responded admirably to a gauche Soviet attempt to reduce the imbalance by advancing missiles to Cuba. The measures adopted were well judged and were effected in a style most suitably in line with what was already renowned as the laconic idiom of strategic analysis.

Then, once matters had been resolved in the Caribbean, the President went on a peace offensive. In a trenchant speech at the American University in June 1963, he warned against the superpowers being 'caught up in a vicious and dangerous cycle in which suspicion on one side breeds suspicion on the other, and new weapons beget counter-weapons'. This admonition embraced two or three emergent themes. One was what it came to be known, from 1964, as Mutual Assured Destruction (MAD); a state of affairs in which either superpower could always ride out any attack from its opposite number, then inflict on it awesome retaliation. Another was the action-reaction phenomenon: the tendency for the hawks on each side of a divide to reinforce one another or, more rarely and tentatively, for the doves to do so. Related to which is the interplay between defence and arms control.

Quite the most tangible fruit of the post-Cuba peace offensive was the Partial Test Ban (PTB) Treaty, initialled by the USSR, the USA and Britain in July 1963 and ratified by them that October. Every state that has signed is committed not to conduct nuclear tests in Outer Space or the atmosphere or the oceans. Today this is widely read as an authentic measure of arms control because it precludes certain lines of development in strategic defence from Space. But in the years following its launch, it came to be discounted as an arms control provision since nuclear tests could still be conducted in underground chambers. Nobody ever denied, however, that it afforded a valuable measure of environmental protection, despite the non-adherence of China and – till now – France. A study was completed some 10 years ago for the Stockholm International Peace Research Institute (SIPRI) by Joseph Rotblat, Professor Emeritus at the University of London and a veteran of the atom bomb development, Project Manhattan. He concluded that the 300 megatons exploded in the air or at sea by 1975 (over 90 per cent before the PTB had come into force) would most probably have caused 150,000 early deaths worldwide through cancer or other genetic damage.[13]

The ecology renaissance

All the same, the PTB has to be seen as a singular departure, one related to how nuclear weapons have always been treated as menacing and nasty in a very special way. No one could say that in 1963 those in power in Washington or anywhere else felt under much public pressure to go environmental across the board. What would be fair to say instead is that the literati throughout the West were then expressing a deal less sense or sensibility in this regard that had the Romantic movement 150 years and more earlier.

Yet soon, attitudes began to shift. In 1962, Rachel Carson had published *The Silent Spring*, the book that was to prove the morning star of environmentalism. The resonant term, 'Spaceship Earth' was coined by Barbara Ward in 1966.[14] From then on, interest spread steadily, driven by the nuclear syndrome as well as by certain of the more dubious applications by the military in Vietnam of high technology and exotic chemistry. This theme became interwoven with the general youth revolt of the late 1960s.

What has long struck me as a most opportune and important commentary was made in 1972 by Zbigniew Brzezinski, later to be National Security Adviser to President Carter. He contrasted the time-honoured 'international' approach to world affairs with the more 'planetary' perspective lately adopted by radicalised youth. He argued that political leaders guided by new concepts were needed to blend the two.[15]

From the early 1970s, however, the progress of the ecological idea became less steady for a number of reasons, one being the failure of the environmental activists (and of the 'counter-culture' movement as a whole) to formulate a critique of the *status quo* that was comprehensive yet cogent. Nor did they ever proffer an alternative political agenda that was not stultified by utopian naivety or Marxian doublethink.

As much became only too obvious in 1968, the year in which youthful protest surged through so much of the world. Two examples may be cited, respectively from the 'hard' and the 'soft' wings of the protest movement. Acute industrial unrest, triggered by student revolt, suddenly gripped France that May. Duly, the young Cohn-Bendit brothers sought to set this turbulence against broader perspectives of history and geography. They rallied to an ultra-Left banner that the fiery Polish-Jewish Marxist, Rosa Luxemburg, had first raised in the wake of the Bolshevik revolution of 1917:

> No matter what Trotskyist historiographers may tell us one day, it was not in 1927 nor in 1923 nor even in 1920, but in 1918 and under the personal leadership of Trotsky and Lenin that the social revolution became perverted ...'[16]

From which one was surely entitled to infer that a Russian revolution that had careered off the straight-and-narrow at its very outset, yet ploughed on regardless for half a century, must have become enough of a menace to warrant some provision for collective defence on our part. Yet during that long, hot summer, some 25 admirers of the Cohn-Bendits on the New Left in Britain rushed into print with their interpretation of the world scene. A chapter on 'America and Europe' since 1945 made no reference to the over-hanging might of

Moscow as the reason why the New World had come yet again to redress the balance of the Old. Then so far as a chapter on 'New Imperialism' was concerned, the USSR might never have existed. Thus the Polaris missile was solemnly depicted simply as a means of retaining dominion over the developing states of Afro-Asia and Latin America.[17]

The example from the 'soft' of 'flower power' side of the 1968 upsurge is afforded by Theodore Roszak, a Californian academic who had become very much a prophet of the youth revolt. He condemned comprehensively our highly technological civilisation. He cared not that for very many people, not least those who dwell in the academic groves of the American Pacific, it has ushered in a lifestyle more comfortable yet expansive than any in recorded history. He declaimed how everything looked set for a 'final consolidation of a technocratic totalitarian ... wholly estranged from everything that has ever made the life of man an interesting adventure'.[18]

Expounding this thesis, he gave vent to many anti-scientific things. Among the more fatuous was the contention that 'the strange youngsters who don cowbells and primitive talismans and who take to the public parks or wilderness to improvise outlandish communal ceremonies are in reality seeking to ground democracy safely beyond the culture of expertise'.[19] What they were actually doing, of course, was either larking about or else keeping the voice of protest so callow as to leave it wide open to a hijack by some political mountebank purporting to personify the 'general will' (see Chapter 10).

Three years later, Roszak was suggesting that the 'decline and fall of scientific orthodoxy' ought not to be feared as some 'betrayal of reason that threatens a new dark age'. After all, 'the barbarian may be at the gate because the empire has decayed from within. He may even come to voice well-founded grievances which for the good of our soul we dare not ignore'.[20] What this might read like to some is a heavy allusion to one of the greatest intellectual catastrophes in all history; namely, the sacking of Alexandria and its fabled library in AD 389, at the hands of marauding Christian zealots. Roszak seemed thus to engage in the unabashed celebration of the triumph of single-minded ignorance over effete enlightenment, of the closed mind over the open. Many a despot from Attila the Hun to Saddam Hussein would have made good cheer at that.

Come 1979, however, Theodore Roszak was writing a lot more sympathetically about 'this vast monolithic adventure we call Science'[21], a conversion that may have been influenced by the

end of the Vietnam involvement but which seems to have owed a lot
to a new-found awareness of the philosophical connotations of
astronomical research.[22] Moreover, this shift on his part well betokened a general maturing of the environmental movement as a
whole. It had been shedding a good deal of the intellectual lumber it
had acquired in the New Left/counter-culture heyday of the 1960s,
the cramped logic of the Marxian dialectic and the wilful disdain of
fact and reason that characterised the 'flower people' at their worst.
The foundation of Friends of the Earth in 1970 and of Greenpeace in
1971 were important steps in this evolution, not least because of the
willingness of these bodies to debate on their scientific merits many of
the issues arising.

Yet, there is no guarantee that this progress can be maintained
indefinitely. On the contrary, if the world situation goes really sour,
for ecological or whatever other reasons, it is more than likely that a
hard core of environmentalism will turn closed-minded and destructive, perhaps as part of a decline in democratic values across the
political spectrum. As of now, however, things continue to evolve
more positively, with the result that 'green' issues command more
and more public attention throughout the West and also further afield.

Commercial nuclear power is a good measure of the current influence of the ecological radicals. Their almost absolute opposition to it
may actually be very misguided, given that fossil fuels are liable to
become less available and far less acceptable well before renewable
forms of energy (solar power and so on) can be adequately deployed.
There is no denying, however, that this is a front on which they have
made political advances. By the end of 1987, rather over 400 reactors
were providing but 16 per cent of the world's electricity or three per
cent of its total energy output. Only five or six countries had programmes that were a major source of electrical power and which still
enjoyed very solid government support. These were Belgium,
France, Japan, South Korea, Taiwan and the USSR. In the United
States, a series of cancellations from 1973 onwards had slowed the
US nuclear industry virtually to a halt. Countries that seemed firmly
committed either to the outright rejection of nuclear power or else to
its being phased out included Austria, Denmark, Greece, Ireland,
Italy, the Philippines and Sweden.[23]

An even clearer indication of the balance of advantage had been
afforded in the immediate aftermath of the Chernobyl catastrophe of
1986. According to the Worldwatch Institute in Washington, the
percentage of the public declaring themselves opposed to the building

of any more reactors rose from 67 to 78 in the USA, 65 to 83 in Britain, 46 to 49 in West Germany, and so on.[24] What this meant was that blame for this disaster was being attributed to nuclear power as such, not to the backwardness of the Soviet nuclear industry and its lack of accountability.

Then dawned 1988, the year in which hundreds of millions of people around the world came to feel that ecological instability throughout their planet posed a most fundamental threat to the international order – a feeling to which governments were vocally to respond. The floods in Bangladesh together with drought in the American Middle West engendered a widespread fear of climatic instability as the atmosphere was warmed by the accelerating accumulation within it of carbon dioxide (CO_2), methane (CH_4) and other man-produced 'greenhouse' gases. The point was being reinforced by the sharp acceleration of a global warming trend. The five warmest years between 1860 and 1990 (as judged in terms of the air temperature averages at sea level) were, in ascending order and on the best estimates, 1984, 1987, 1983, 1988 and 1990 itself.

Influential, too, was the revealed depletion of stratospheric ozone: the thin spread of tri-atomic oxygen, predominantly between 20 and 30 kilometres up, that has well protected life on Earth from the malign effects of the shorter-wave radiation (X-rays and gamma rays) from the Sun and Outer Space. Initially, a remarkably wide assortment of people confused this tendency with the greenhouse effect. In fact, of course, ozone depletion most crucially alters the quality of the solar radiation received at the Earth's surface, whereas greenhouse warming is due to shifts in the quantitative balance between the total amount of heat flowing into the Earth and the total radiating from it.

Whatever misunderstandings there may lately have been, however, there is no doubt that ozone depletion is a major problem in itself. It is mainly brought about through the catalytic action of the man-made chlorofluorocarbons (CFCs). An international study released in Washington in March 1988 confirmed that depletion in South polar latitudes (where the effect had first been discerned by the British Antarctic Survey in 1982) was being replicated in the North polar, albeit not yet so intensively. Quite possibly, too, some thinning was starting in latitudes in between. In 1990, nearly one hundred countries committed themselves to phase out CFC production within the decade. But even on that basis, this stratospheric menace will persist throughout the next century.

By definition, as one might say, the wavelength spectrum of what we know as visible light (800 to 400 nanometres) penetrates the ozone layer very readily. On the life forms used to receiving it below, it inflicts little damage and confers immeasurable benefit. Surveying then the wavelengths that are shorter and so of higher energy, one comes first to Ultra-Violet B (UV-B), that part of the electromagnetic spectrum which lies between 320 and 290 nanometres.[25] As things stand, this is partially absorbed by high altitude ozone. Such evidence as is available to date suggests that every one per cent reduction in high-altitude ozone is likely to cause, on account of UV-B alone, a five per cent increase in non-malignant skin lesions and a broadly proportional increase in the incidence of eye cataracts. Rises in the incidence of malignant skin growths will probably be less but not negligible.

Mankind itself may soon have the benefit of quite good vaccines against skin cancer and more natural lotions against suntan. To that extent its unique virtuosity will stand our species in good stead yet again.[26] However, many other forms of animal life are also susceptible. Also most of the several hundred plants so far tested exhibit at least some sensitivity to UV-B. Yields of soya beans, indeed, are said to drop by a quarter when this radiation gets a quarter more intensive.[27] In the oceans, phytoplankton appear sensitive to UV-B as well; and these minute beings are basic both to the marine food chain and to the sea-air carbon cycle (see Chapter 6).

Furthermore, any very acute diminution of the ozone would admit to the Earth's surface what is termed the Ultra-Violet C (UV-C) part of the spectrum, that from 290 nanometres to 240. Since UV-C is not usually observed at ground level, the effects on life forms are uncertain. Therefore, we tend to fall back on *a priori* arguments which go either way. On the one hand, the Sun emits rather less intensively in the UV-C waveband than in the UV-B, the peak solar emission being at 485 nanometres. On the other, shorter-wave radiation tends to be more penetrative of organic matter. In any case, none of our terrestrial life forms would have any prior experience of adapting to UV-C.

So what we could be facing is a danger that embraces many of the radiative effects of nuclear war. Nor is this surprising. The Sun is, after all, a big fusion reactor. The only basic difference here is that it does not conduct nuclear fission as well.

A variety of other events and tendencies in 1988 were disconcerting in ecological terms. Among them were several marine epidemics that did not really lend themselves to easy explanation. Thousands of dolphins died off the US east coast. Thousands of common seals died within the North Sea and Baltic.

In the light of such evidence, the global impact of ecological stress begins to resemble that which might be engendered by a world war, nuclear of otherwise. For this reason alone, it seems but plain common sense for strategic studies to draw unto itself the contemporary concerns of international economists and of planetary ecologists. Only thus may it create structural paradigms appropriate to the 21st Century. However, any such integration will also have to accommodate a social and cultural scene that is in constant flux.

3

A Globe Distracted

AN OPINION expressed in Chapter 1 was that Mikhail Gorbachev had recast the map of Europe, geopolitically and philosophically, more profoundly than any individual since Martin Luther. What was suggested was that this transformation has taken place within the context of an information explosion as dramatic in its impact as any since the introduction in Europe of printing by movable type. So the Renaissance as well as the Reformation is, in a sense, recapitulated.

Now, as then, the spread of knowledge is accelerating so fast as to cause drastic changes in life style and outlook, the full import of which as yet remains obscure. The impact on the prospects for world peace will be indirect but could be profound.

Many factors contribute to the current transformation. The number of international tourist arrivals doubles every 12–15 years. The number of telephones installed around the world, having quadrupled to 160 million in the 20 years to 1965, quadrupled again the next 20. By now there may be one for every eight persons worldwide. Meanwhile, the real cost of a phone call from Europe to the South Pacific, say, has fallen by well over nine-tenths since 1962, the year of entry into service of Telstar, the first satellite able to relay data (on either 60 telephone channels or one television) in 'real time', that is to say, as it is being obtained.

Undoubtedly, however, it is the big expansion now under way in Direct Broadcasting by Satellite (DBS) that at present attracts most comment. What DBS involves is the projection of signals via the satellite to be picked up (if in line of sight and 20 degrees or more above the horizon) by ground receivers, each using a disc antenna perhaps only a metre across and costing a very few hundred pounds. Already the relay power of such satellites has risen to several hundred watts as against the two watts registered with Telstar. Within a very few years, in many countries around the world, viewers will go from receiving one or several television channels to having several dozen trained towards them. Granted, individual discs may not be of the right size of alignment to pick up many of these. Even so, this constitutes a mammoth extension of access, one that will present a challenge to all regimes and to all cultures.[1]

Nor will it be at all feasible to exclude these transmissions by jamming. Before the advent of Gorbachev, the USSR used to expend several billion dollars a year running a network of radio jammers said to have been several times as numerous as their own broadcasting stations. Yet even so expensive a screen was nothing like dense enough except around the big cities.[2] Besides, television would be much harder to jam than High Frequency radio because the shorter wavelengths on which it operates tend to make its beams something like a 1,000 times less divergent.[3]

All of which seems a far cry from the fabled anti-Utopia we reverentially recalled a mere seven years ago. In *Nineteen Eighty-Four*,[4] George Orwell depicted a totalitarian hell that had been rendered savagely stable, largely by dint of television and other electronic means of indoctrination, instruction and surveillance. So why has a prevision that nearly all of us had treated with such earnest respect throughout the first 40 years of its currency come so suddenly to be seen as mercifully remote from any world we shall ever know? The collapse of fascist imperialism in 1945 and of Communism in 1989 were most welcome watersheds. But can euphoria be justified?

On the Orwellian front, in particular, one answer could be that, although Orwell in his prime wrote much more directly than do most authors from the heart and from his own experience, in this terminal phase of his life his insights were, alas, too narrow, morbid and banal. Surely, nobody would chase political power as blindly as all those party members did if that power was always so empty. Nor would even the most bamboozled legion of zombies switch the identity of the hated external foe in the middle of an orchestrated sentence.

The collapse of Marxism

More to the point for today, however, is that George Orwell never understood that, because the spread of information would be increasingly global, it posed a particular threat to closed minds in closed societies. No matter that *Nineteen Eighty-Four* was written several years after Arthur C. Clarke had first anticipated the development of communications satellites and, of course, nearly half a century after Guglielmo Marconi had first spanned the Atlantic by wireless. To which one might add that, until the 1960s at least, more or less all Leftist intellectuals everywhere gave far too little analytical attention to the progress of information technology, directing themselves instead to the travails of heavy industry, agriculture and international trade. It is at one with a long-standing disposition on the part of Marxist historians to see the High Renaissance more in terms of the cloth trade than of printing.[5]

Correspondingly, a prime reason for the collapse of Marxism in practice has to be the failure of its practitioners to assimilate the electronic revolution except as a driving force in such realms as weapons development and Space research. The wider connotations for cultural change left them cold. Witness the inability of the Soviet leaders to accept as in any way genuine the international youth revolt in 1968,[6] one difficulty for them being that this 'global village' phenomenon did not fit at all well classical Marxist-Leninist notions about economic cause and ideological effect. Another source of confusion was that its mores were discordant with the ethos of martial puritanism that Communist regimes still felt obliged to extol, not least as regards the life style of party members and youth cadres.

Meanwhile, as the gaps widened between what Communists said and how they themselves lived, their credibility and, indeed, their legitimacy were seriously eroded. Still more fundamentally, this Communist legitimacy and, of course, self-esteem were undermined by the way the promised land of 'socialist abundance' all round was receding into an ever-more distant future. What has become evident this last year or two, as well, is that degradation of the natural and urban environments has also played a major part in the disillusionment. In theory, a command economy should do far better in this respect than a perfectly free market driven just by a myriad of individual decisions about sale and purchase, because these fail properly to recognise what growth may mean in terms of 'external diseconomies' within individual countries and across the world at large. In practice, however, a pure market mechanism can be modulated by straight regulation or by financial inducements or penalties. In practice, again, the Marxist command economies have failed almost comprehensively in this regard. The great push to freedom in 1989 revealed European Communism as still having an atrocious record on ecology even though 'Stalin's pathological determination to achieve impossible victories over Nature, regardless of cost, had given way to a more rational analysis of the environmental consequences of development'.[7] A simple comparison will suffice. In East Germany, one single power station due to come into service in 1989 threatened to cause more acid rain than all the facilities in Sweden combined.[8]

Likewise, the data that came more freely out of China after Mao's death in 1976 served to shatter the officially-projected legend of a Maoist transformation of the landscape 'with green hills and massive afforestation ... assorted industrial wastes thoroughly recycled, and much advanced planning devoted to the prevention of pollution. And, of course, no flies and a broad smile on everybody's face'.[9] Through the early 1980s, for sure, the situation was comprehensively bad and getting worse. Nor will it have been redeemed since. Severe unemployment and under-employment will have militated against this. So will have persisting corruption. So will the fact that less notice is now being taken of official exhortations to plan families.

The relative prowess of the West, even in those spheres of public policy in which Communism might have been expected to come good, constitutes grounds for modest satisfaction. As Western leaders have thus far recognised, however, to wax more triumphal might be to ensure that we slide, as too often before, from winning a war into losing a peace. All else apart, it is not entirely to our advantage that the erstwhile Communist world is in such a mess in virtually every respect. Our own way of life could still benefit from some vigorous competition from a different philosophic standpoint. It could do so as regards the triteness and vulgarity of so much of our popular culture in general and of media features in particular. It could do so most obviously as regards preservation of the environment; urban, rural and natural. Besides which, a slide into utter chaos behind the old Iron and Bamboo Curtains could be a serious distraction from the formulation of an adequate strategy for survival and stability at planetary level.

The new Renaissance

Yet, there is every indication that such a formulation will be a task big enough to demand our more or less undivided attention. All else apart, History affords much evidence that times of rapid cultural and philosophical change are liable to experience a lot of intolerance and strife. A huge amount of violent conflict emanated from the

Renaissance and Reformation, both between the nation-states then emergent and within them. Much of it has to be described as wildly irrational, violence and persecution for their own sake.

Witch burning was perhaps the ugliest manifestation. As Hugh Trevor-Roper (now Lord Dacre) has warned us, this maniacal craze which was to besmirch Europe for a good two centuries as from the death at the stake of Joan of Arc in 1431 (and which leaves us with little to choose regarding culpability as between Catholics and Protestants) cannot really be seen, as 19th Century liberal historians preferred to see it, as a mere 'delusion', detached from 'the social and intellectual structure of the time'.[10] And the wider contradiction thus betokened was epitomised by Eric Fromm in the seminal essay he wrote during the Second World War to launch himself on the exploration of the interaction between individual psychology and cultural change: an interaction that he felt, rightly or wrongly,[11] Sigmund Freud had ignored. Fromm, himself a refugee from Hitler, was concerned to recognise and interpret the sado-masochistical appeal of fascism. He spoke of an inner insecurity in modern man that could be traced back to the cavorting of an archetypal Renaissance personality with his ill-judged sanguineness, unsettling learning and restless enterprise. Harried and manipulated by him, the masses may have felt less calm inwardly than ever before.[12] Simone Weil, the French cultural patriot and Christian Jewish humanist, said much the same when she traced modern 'uprootedness' largely back to how the 'Renaissance everywhere brought about a break between people of culture and the mass of the population'.[13]

Alas, the era of multi-channel satellite television may witness the rise of mass communicators that match such stereotypes disconcertingly well. Not least will they add to the impetus towards a global mass society, far removed from the tiny tribal communities our hominoid ancestors evolved during their several million formative years – those during which they emerged from the long, long Pliocene drought in their ancestral East Africa and then battled their way through the innumerable vagaries of the Pleistocene Ice Age.

Undeniably, the electronic transmission of an ever-wider spread of images and information is the prime driving force behind this colossal melding. But among the other contributory factors are the sheer physical mobility of humankind today coupled with the diminishing diversity of landscape, be it urban or rural or blended. Undoubtedly, too, the universities – archetypal institutions of the European Renaissance and, no less so, of the current global one –

have contributed mightily to the modern intermingling. With but few exceptions their performance has thus far been mediocre as regards the creative interaction of trained academics from different disciplines, the Renaissance ideal. What they have done *par excellence*, however, is generate ever more partnerships and friendships between young people from diverse backgrounds, often far apart. In other words, they have been, for good and ill, a cultural melting pot. In varying measure, the same is true of the tourist trade, worker migration and the many other forms of global interdependence.

One indicator of the resultant spread of cultural uniformity is the burgeoning of consumerism, Western-style: a burgeoning likely itself to be a cause of major political strains. Another is the ever wider use of the English language. Of the 5,750 million people in the world today, 350 million speak it as a mother tongue. That is less than half those who speak Guoyo, Mandarin Chinese. But to that figure for speakers of English as a birthright can be added the same number using it as a second language and roughly the same again speaking it with some facility: all in all, some 18 per cent of humanity. At one time, some people thought that English would fractionate into various regional forms quite distinct one from another, very much as Latin fractionated into French, Galician, Italian, Spanish and so on, after the collapse of the Roman Empire. Instead the trend is firmly much the other way.

The value of English as an official language in a multicommunal democracy is well illustrated by the case of India. At the time of independence the intention was to abandon English in this role by 1965, leaving Hindi as the sole official language. For some good solid reasons, that intention has receded almost to vanishing point: 'Professional advancement and social prestige among middle class urban Indians still depend upon skill in English. In the southern states, where the indigenous languages are unrelated to Hindi, many people are reluctant to learn the northerners' tongue when it is more social and no harder to learn English.[14] Now the assassination of Rajiv Gandhi has reminded all concerned how unwise it would be to do anything gratuitously to stoke up communal resentment. Hence the comparative success of the Congress Party in the election of June 1991.

Communal tendencies

Yet it was as all the tendencies towards cultural integration were gathering pace across the turbulent world of the 1960s that it became fashionable – not least on the campuses – to deny that the mass society really was gaining ground overall. The antithesis advanced was that, while certain of the bigger nationalisms were thankfully being eroded, more localised ethnic affinities were enjoying a revival.

However, reaffirmation fed by insecurity was not the same thing as a firmly-based revival. On the latter score, the hard evidence has consistently been that the local nationalisms ostensibly being re-discovered – Basque or Catalan or Scottish for example – are alto-gether too riven with inconsistencies, in the terms the modern world is bound to dictate, to stay stable long. Either they have to dissolve or else they have to retreat deep into what Pierre Trudeau, as Prime Minister of Canada, characterised as 'the wigwams of the past'. By this he meant a regime of communal exclusiveness and antagonism coupled with the repression of individualism, a regime that sought to turn its back on the outside world and, of course, the Renaissance ideal. Although the communalist agenda at any given time and place is going to be conditioned by particular circumstances, there is in the final analysis no way in which you can be a modernising commu-nalist, given that modernisation has fundamentally to involve the ever-more-global exchange of ever more information.

In fact, of course, few of those who extolled ethnicity in the 1960s really wanted to retrogress very far towards what could only be the fascistic restoration of a phantasy past. Inevitably, however, there were significant exceptions. Among them were those who resumed IRA insurgency in Ulster in 1969, a Celtic fascist and fascisto-Marxist reaction that sought a coercive reunification of Ireland on the basis of the rejection not just of England but of Europe. Another such was the *Euskadi 'ta Askatasuna* (ETA) among the Basque people of northern Spain. Though subject to inward migration from the 12th Century, the Basques had historically felt themselves to be well delineated by a language stretching back perhaps thousands of years and by a singularly puritanical branch of the Catholic Church. They were always a target for suppression by the Franco regime, a strategy foreshadowed by the Nazi bombing of their holy city of Guernica in 1937. Yet even before the demise of Franco in 1975, two of the four Basque provinces had virtually detached themselves from the cause whilst, thanks to heavy immigration, less than half the population of the other two actually spoke Basque. Meanwhile, in the three French *departements* normally regarded as Basque as well, assimilation was visibly under way, aided by a steady brain drain to Paris and Toulouse.[15]

In the light of this, one does have to ask whether the post-Franco democracy in Madrid has done the populations in question a good and lasting service by making three Basque provinces into an autonomous region with exceptionally wide-ranging local powers. Did not this initiative allow too much to romantic nostalgia? Had not the new Madrid and the democratic world at large been too willing to appease violence, too willing to accommodate too much of the political agenda of ETA – a narrow clique of gunmen and bombers always happy to terrorise their own people as well as others? Has not the result been to freeze Basque politics in a communalist mould which is dangerously irrelevant to the economic and social problems that region faces, especially as regards the conversion of its industry from the 'smokestack' to the electronic age? What is striking about the history of the Basque question these last several years is the resolve with which politicians in Madrid, Paris and also Bilbão have collaborated to curtail sharply the gunpower of ETA. You could say this is because a fair measure of autonomy has been conceded but it owes a lot also to deepening disgust in the Basque country itself at the inner wells of hate and prejudice that inform ETA and its 'Carlist-Leninist' ethos.[16] It is closely equivalent to the way the Roman Catholic church in Ulster, notably in the person of Archbishop Daly, is increasingly condemning the IRA as 'satanic'. Yet even now the Basque Nationalist-Socialist coalition in office in Bilbão is pressing, however vainly, for separate representation alongside the Madrid government before the European Commission in Brussels. The contradictions within this so-called revival are as blatant as ever.

Similar doubts have to be raised, and more poignantly, where communal identities are not shored up by banditry. Thus 1969 was a time of exceptionally high confidence and hope on the Zionist side of Jewish experience, with Israel on top militarily and sure of herself politically. Yet that same year, a most scholarly and empathetic observer from the inside of Jewish life in Anglo-America wrote:

> American Jewry, wholly caught up in the turmoil that today envelops the great cities of that country, does not expect to survive the end of the century in its present form.[17]

Today, that particular prognosis looks considerably premature. Even so, such trends as secularisation and 'marrying out' surely mean that its basic thrust is correct. No doubt much the same applies to many other religious groupings in the West. So must it to, let us say, such English provincialisms as Wessex, where the cultural environment is even harder to defend than is the natural.[18] It is amazing that Marshall McLuhan, customarily hailed as 'the oracle' of the electronic age, should have persuaded himself that one of 'the most extraordinary developments since TV in England has been the upsurge of regional dialects'.[19] The truth of the matter is that the era of radio and television has witnessed a comprehensive dissolution of the rich mosaic of local dialects that still existed all across Britain as late as the turn of the century. Now provincial dialects are going the same way, this notwithstanding valiant early efforts by BBC radio to uphold our provincial cultures and our Celtic nationalisms.

It is, of course, fair to say that, ever since the Renaissance at least, Europe has repeatedly experienced fresh affirmations of nationalism. But to quite an extent, this tendency has been the product of the progressive undermining of more local loyalties. Obversely, it has from time to time, and not least during the fascist era of the 1930s, generated a repressive and unstable backlash against a further widening of horizons, the instability expressing itself in a gratuitous lust for warfare.

Unfortunately, however, many in academe and among the literati have remained disposed to treat this whole phenomenon as grounded more solidly than it has been or ever could have been under modern conditions. As late as 1980, a British student of such matters wrote:

> far from creating a single world culture, the mass media have been ready instruments of state authorities who have used them to mould or instil a national culture in every citizen and every household ... Travel and education can just as easily bring home to men and women their cultural differences and reinforce their national loyalties as erase them ... So that, far from being merely a transitional phenomenon, the nation state and nationalism have become more firmly entrenched within the world over, even in the most advanced industrial societies.[20]

But now – as 1992 approaches – nobody in Europe, at any rate, would write as firmly in that vein. Among young people, in particular, travel around the continent is strongly conducive to a pan-European consciousness, not to say a planetary one.

Meanwhile, in those parts of the developing world where traditional tribalism is still a reality, its erosion gathers pace. The liberation often implied for individuals, especially the young and the female, as their backgrounds dissolve around them ought to brook no denial. As Prime Minister in New Delhi, Indira Gandhi used to express the hope that television would strengthen regional cultures and consciousness within India. She was always well aware that this would be at the expense of more localised affiliations but came to accept this as progressive. Once she recalled how on the North-East frontier the 'vociferous demands of elder tribal chiefs that their customs should be left undisturbed, found support from some noted anthropologists'. But against this had to be set 'the protest of the younger elements that while the rest of India was on its way to modernisation, they were being preserved as museum pieces'.[21]

Mass society

Even so, changes that may be ameliorative in regard to the particulars of each local situation may still be alarming as regards the total prospect. In terms of human contentment and security, the whole may be less than the sum of the parts. For very many people around the world, 1989 was much further from 1939, say, than that year would have been from 1789. With this social flux has come rootlessness and also the loss, by long-standing communities, of cultural mores and practices that might have been of great value not only to themselves but to all of us.

Correspondingly, there has been among political scientists and political sociologists a disposition (stretching back from William Kornhauser at least to Alexis de Tocqueville) to regard multi-differentiated mass society as peculiarly susceptible to irrational and extremist mass movements. However, some of the most insightful observations about this and related aspects of our societal evolution have come from thinkers less tied to one particular subject area. George Orwell is a striking example. Some eminent practitioners of pure and applied science, such as Jacob Bronowski, Freeman Dyson, Peter Medawar and E.F. Schumacher have also been contributive within this sphere. Nevertheless, H.G. Wells probably remains the doyen of thinkers in this tradition, not least because he stands out as 'the last literary figure' to exemplify 'the profound effect that scientific developments had on the literature of the nineteenth century' in contrast with a 'lamentable lack of cross-fertilisation in the twentieth'.[22]

In fact, Wells' achievement was more as a prophet of social change than as what he is celebrated as, a forecaster of scientific advance. True, he did display an uncanny prevision of one dread possibility when in *The World Set Free*, published in 1913, he envisaged how, six years after the advent of the 'atomic bomb' in 1953, hundreds of cities experienced 'the unquenchable crimson conflagrations' as the great powers respectively sought security through pre-emption. That could serve as a fair summation of the worst-case scenario conjectured by those pioneering nuclear strategists of the early 1960s. More generally, however, his approach to military science was episodic. He oscillated between a blimpish insensitivity to change and a skittish indifference to continuity.[23]

Then again, he was never the herald of the Space Age he is often cracked up to have been. Though he was imbued with a strong sense of historic influence of astronomy, his insights into future Space travel are either simplistic or downright silly. His novel *The First Man on the Moon*, published in 1901, proffers less technical or psychological sophistication than do most episodes in Hergé's *Adventures of Tin Tin*.[24]

In the realm of social and political thought, too, the restless Wells chopped and changed. But he did so here in a more controlled fashion. The alternation was between pessimism and optimism and was symptomatic of his awareness of how narrow is the divide between triumph and tragedy for mankind in this century. A very similar alternation is evident in Winston Churchill; and ensured, in fact, that his leadership in 1940 was an invaluable blend of hope and realism. As near contemporaries, Churchill and Wells came to full maturity amidst that Kiplingesque mix of pride and apprehension so characteristic of the English literary scene in the last quarter of the 19th Century; and very characteristic once again, one may add, of the Western world in 1990. The saddest thing was how in both men the pessimism got much more dominant and personalised as they grew old.[25,26]

A remarkable manifestation of the Wellsian social vision is to be found in *Anticipations*[27], a prediction of how things would be towards the end of the century then beginning. Writing interchangeably of Britain and of the world, Wells foresaw a great 'confluence' (p. 61 in the fifth edition) of town and countryside; and the continued erosion of the vocabulary, idiom and inflections of local dialects (pp. 223–5) coupled with 'the reconstruction and the vast proliferation of what constituted the middle class of the old order' (p. 82) and the breaking down of its sub-divisions. All these insights have proved well-founded though it is not clear how Wells might have reconciled them with further expectations of 'a quite unprecedented diversity in the various suburban townships' (p. 56) or that there 'is no reason why the essential charm of the country should disappear . . . the lanes and hedges, the field paths and wild flowers' (p. 63).

He is surely at his most prescient when he foretells how, once

German aggressiveness has been shattered or weakened in a series of wars, the destiny of Western Europe will lie in a federalism based on the six states of the Rhine valley that cannot but become a single economic entity in the course of the next 50 years (p. 241). Unfortunately, however, this 'splendid' grouping is bound to retain 'her Irelands of unforgettable wrongs' (p. 260): pseudo-revivals of petty nationalisms affording great opportunities for 'literary quacks, in national movements, language leagues, picturesque plotting and the invention of such national costumes as the world has never seen' (p. 260).

Of most immediate concern to us, however, is the way he apprehended that 'the development of democracy also is, after all, not the opening phase of a worldwide movement going on unbendingly in its present direction, but the first impulse of forces that will finally sweep round into quite a different path' (p. 146). Moreover, this foreboding was part of a none too oblique condemnation of the way political philosophers have left the very term 'Democracy' as 'a large empty object in thought, of the most vague and faded associations and the most attenuated content' (p. 145); and have failed to make any 'case for the elective democratic government of modern states that cannot be knocked to pieces in five minutes' (p. 146). No less relevant, however, is the 'confusion of moral standards' (p. 132) liable to result from the intermingling of cultures through increased communications. In their confusion, governments might be driven more towards demagoguery and belligerency, drawing 'the voter to the poll by alarms, seeking ever to taint the possible nucleus of any competing organisation with the scandal of external influence' (p. 167). Periodically, this could bring all concerned to the brink of war.

No doubt it came naturally to Wells, writing in 1901, to warn how the inner insecurity of democracies could lead them into hostilities because they might seek to compensate by reasserting their respective nationalisms. It was, after all, the time of the Boer War and the international expedition to Peking. In fact, however, the interaction between internal tensions and external peace is always complicated. In the 1930s, for instance, internal political divisions tended to weaken the resolve of the democracies in the face of fascist dictators that themselves had mostly arisen in the face of economic collapse. Maybe, too, the reluctance of countries like Britain, Sweden and the United States to face up to their world responsibilities during those years (and, in Sweden's case, beyond) should be seen as a rather narrow form of national self-expression.

Yet however one defines the causal linkages, there can be little doubt that for many polities, democratic or otherwise, to be under acute inner stress would be bound to augur ill for global stability. It is therefore all the more worrisome that various of the measures of rootlessness or alienation or anomie (the nuances may be different but the essence the same) have generally confirmed negative tendencies of late, not least as far as the mass democracies are concerned. Take crime. Inchoate though any overview is bound to be, there does seem to have been a more or less continual rise in crime (not least violent crime) more or less worldwide and throughout the post-1945 era. Furthermore this trend has gone hand-in-hand as a rule (and certainly within the advanced industrial democracies) with a widespread amelioration of what have classically been regarded as the underlying causes of crime: primary poverty, social inequality, inadequate public services, and so on. Having fallen by a gratifying 16 per cent in the period 1951–55, recorded crime levels in England and Wales rose so insistently during the next two decades as to become a good five times what they had been in the depths of the inter-war slump. Nor did an apparently steep rise in reporting rates in some districts do so very much to distort the overall picture.[28]

Since when, the world crime scene had got a lot worse, aggravated further by drug trafficking and political terrorism. Intensifying urban congestion may, in fact, be one of the underlying factors. At all events, the preliminary indications are that 1990 was quite the worst year yet for recorded crime in Britain. In the United States, the 1989 returns to the FBI indicated a 3.9 per cent increase in the overall crime rate with a 5.5 per cent rise in crimes of violence, thus continuing trends under way ever since these returns began in 1960. In the USSR and South Africa, the last year or two have seen much more crime on the streets against the background of a more open political milieu. Meanwhile, the International Foundation for Art Research listed more than 30,000 works stolen in 1989 as against 1,300 in 1979. Violence associated with 'the burgeoning trade in illicit drugs from Latin American countries to North America and Europe reached new levels of ferocity'. This 'narco-terrorism' apart, the extent of internationally-related terrorist activity remained essentially unchanged in 1989 'following a record 856 incidents in 1988'. At the same time, several Western democracies witnessed proceedings arising out of allegations of financial corruption by people prominent in public life.[29]

If a planetary mass society promises to be so mixed a blessing, we ought not to be too surprised if the roads that lead us towards it are rocky throughout. Perhaps the most widespread and negative characteristic of the contemporary world scene is rising tension between two or more adjacent communities, usually within the same state boundary. Conspicuous among the current or very recent locales are Burma, the Soviet Caucasus, Croatia and Slovenia, the Holy Land, the Kurdish heartland, Kuwait, the Lebanon, the Punjab, the South African townships, Sri Lanka, the Sudan, Tibet, Ulster and Uzbekistan. At the most basic psychological level, this tendency has been ominously interpreted by E.P. Thompson, the British historian and nuclear neutralist: 'There appears to be a universal need for *the Other* as a means of defining the identity of any group and the individuals within it ...'[30] Evidently, this is bound up as well with the territorial inclination in the outlook of our species. Nor is there any denying that groups that are delineated more clearly may often prove the more productive and creative in various fields; and also the more able to stand solid in the face of threats to their security and general well-being. One implication would seem to be that we will never make the mass society truly stable at planetary level until we can develop a strong conceptual awareness of a close-knit 'Spaceship Earth' surrounded by an awesome and remorseless Cosmos. It is a matter that sociologists, not to mention cosmologists, moral philosophers and theologians, need to address determinedly.

But to dwell for the moment on the near-term world order, one can note that the global revolution in communications now under way is liable to effect, within a generation or two, considerable melding of communal identifies through common education at one level or another, intermarriage, occupational mobility and (as and when suitably promoted) the stronger emergence of planetary perspectives. Already, the 20th Century is rich in manifestations of this process. In the interim, however, ethnic groups living in close proximity may become more antagonistic as contacts increase (not least in expanding urban areas) and as each comes to feel more threatened by an ever-more-dynamic cosmopolitan culture: the 'all-devouring world Satan', as Ayatollah Khomeini was pleased to call the West in general and the United States in particular. Indeed, a backlash effect may develop at global level. Thus an eminent British historian, of sceptically conservative persuasion himself, has come to this view concerning the origins of the First World War: 'A major part in the initial processes which led to the unleashing of the

armed forces was played by a kind of desperate and irrational con-
servatism seizing what it felt to be its only chance of avoiding social
and political revolution'.[31] Shades of Eric Fromm?

In some of the particular situations here alluded to, the malign
spirit of communal antagonism could stay alive for several decades
yet, even assuming that mankind as a whole does keep moving
towards multi-racial, scientific and ecumenical enlightenment.[32]
Should this be the case, certain persisting tensions may then be re-
charged by contrasting experiences in respect of the impact of global
warming: a redefinition, if you like, of the customary antagonism
between 'haves and have-nots'.

All of which seems to confirm that the battle for democracy has not
yet been won irreversibly. Nor should we discount too finally the
Orwellian argument that modern information-driven techniques of
social control may make authoritarian regimes more adept than
before at seizing and consolidating control. As one scans the scene
from, let us say, Havana through Tripoli to Damascus and Pyon-
gyang, one sees still some revolutionary dictatorships that have
achieved surprising longevity by allowing of nothing in the way of
liberty, openness and pluralism. Likewise, the last Communist
'domino' to fall in the erstwhile Soviet bloc in 1989 was the
Romanian, the most desolating and also the most 'Big Brother'-like
of them all. Much the same has applied to nearby Albania. Likewise,
again, when the authorities reimposed a clamp-down across China,
after what had seemed the irresistible flower power of the student-led
'democracy movement' had been broken in Tiananmen Square in
June 1989, they were able to ensure that that clamp-down was very
comprehensive.

It may be that the electronic revolution favours at one and the
same time the two approaches to government that stand in most
diametric contrast. It may be able to lay the foundations for more
participatory democracy, with much emphasis on referenda,
opinion sampling and local initiatives. Yet at the same time it may
afford more scope to those regimes (including armies of occupation) that are prepared to buck the trend by becoming more repressive than ever before. As in *Nineteen Eighty-Four*, xenophobia (one
of the more obvious threats to general peace and harmony) may be
a key element in the requisite rationale: a wilful rejection, if you
like, of the vision of 'a world without borders' or 'a global village'.[33]
Under conditions of economic and environmental stress worse than
those we have lately experienced, such a system might have a

greater capacity to survive than one would wish, so long as it remained prepared to make no concessions whatsoever. To do otherwise, would be to release the flood-gates, much as happened in Eastern Europe in 1989.

4

The Soviet Heartland

SINCE CLASSICAL TIMES, the European world has recurrently felt a morbid fascination with what it has dimly seen as the looming strength of inner Asia. By the 19th Century, this perception had assumed a sharper and more spatial definition, influenced by the geometric distinction drawn by the Swiss soldier and scholar, Antoine Jomini (1779–1869) between 'interior and exterior lines' of military movement. The former run inside the curve of a boundary between protagonists, the latter outside. Jomini's inference that operation on interior lines conferred a big advantage had been encouraged by Napoleon's reflections on the battle of Austerlitz.

The concept in question surfaced on the continental scale in the years following the defeat of Napoleonic France. The British in London and in Calcutta became obsessed with the vision of a mighty Russian army, strategically mobile along lines interior to all Eurasia; and presumptively available as an instrument of aggrandisement wherever opportunity beckoned but especially towards the 'warm water' ports of the Persian Gulf and Eastern Mediterranean. A Muscovite preoccupation with that particular direction was seen as confirmed by Peter the Great's seizing the Black Sea fortress of Azov from the Turks in 1696 and establishing a naval squadron there.

The Eastern Question

So it was that, for most of Queen Victoria's reign, a prime concern of British external policy was the resolution of what was called the 'Eastern Question'. How do you encourage the emancipation of emergent nationalisms in the Balkans and elsewhere without opening the way to Muscovite expansionism. Save that we did not then talk much about 'the Balkans', that sentence also encapsulates the West's debate on foreign policy between 1944 and 1989.

As so often, the intellectual rationale was forthcoming well after the paradigm of thought and practice had become more broadly established. In this case, it was afforded by Sir Halford Mackinder (1861–1947), doyen of British geographers and man of public affairs. The gist of his thesis, as presented to the Royal Geographical Society in January 1904, was as follows.[1] The interior of Eurasia, the 'heartland', was a vast natural fortress delimited by the watersheds of rivers draining either into the Arctic or else into stretches of water with no outlet to the open sea. Solid protection against incursions by sea power was provided by the Arctic ice and the Himalayas. Once the heartland had harnessed its huge resources under unified political control and exploited its advantages in terms of mobility, it would hold the key to world supremacy.

In 1919, Mackinder published *Democratic Ideals and Reality*, a book generally seen as the zenith of his geopolitical thought.[2] Oddly, he saw the main exit from the heartland as being via 'the sea-way through the Straits of Constantinople' (p. 174). No less oddly, he suggested that Persia be counted a heartland territory. More plausibly, he argued that, since the Baltic and the Black Sea are virtually enclosed, their basin areas must be within its compass (p. 141). He next averred that whoever 'rules East Europe commands the Heartland' (p. 194). Therefore, they command the world.

Mackinder saw the First World War as having started as 'a German effort to subdue the Slavs who were in revolt against Berlin' (p. 193). He went on to warn that the post-war settlement then being thrashed out would have to 'provide for a balance between German and Slav, and true independence for the new East European states' (p. 194). Elaborating the argument, though little refining it, he insisted that now was the time to 'focus our thoughts on the stable resettlement of the affairs of East Europe and the heartland. If we accept anything less than a complete solution of the Eastern Question in its largest sense we shall merely have gained a respite and our descendants will find themselves under the necessity of marshalling their power afresh for the siege of the Heartland' (p. 200). He warned his readers not to 'trust the future peace of the world' (p. 200) to a simple assumption that the 'German mentality will be altered by the German defeat' (p. 200). In reality, the 'end of the present disorder' (p. 201) in Germany 'may only be a new organisation, and ruthless organisers do not stop when they have attained the objects which they have first set before them' (p. 201).

A stable peace between German and Slav, vital to the avoidance of another world war, would rest on the division of Eastern Europe 'into self-contained nations' (p. 203). Unfortunately, however, such a settlement could be undermined by 'the growth of the peoples' (p. 200) there or in the heartland itself. A long-term programme of economic development was needed to cope with this Malthusian threat. Nor is there any doubt that Mackinder was right about this, certainly as regards the pressure of agrarian society on cultivable land in Eastern Europe. It is a rare but welcome example of a geopolitical theorist addressing so 'planetary' a factor.

When they respectively were launched, neither of these studies attracted much attention anywhere. Eventually, that situation changed. The essence of the heartland thesis was imbibed by Karl Haushofer, the German geopolitician who was a background influence on Nazi thought by dint of his Chair in Geography at Munich and his friendship with Rudolph Hess. Then by 1942, 'Haushofer and Mackinder had become household names in the United States where geopolitics had become all the rage'.[3] The vogue of Mackinderism or variants thereof was furthered at the academic level by the writings of Nicholas Spykman and William R. T. Fox. Inclinations in a similar direction could also be traced in the thought of George Kennan and, later on, of Henry Kissinger.[4] Still, the only hard evidence of direct political impact seems to be Isaiah Bowman's advising President Roosevelt of the close correspondence between 'Mackinder's theory about the heartland and the geopolitical aims of Hitler'.[5]

Perhaps, however, the enduring impact of the heartland concept was not via the thought patterns of certain individuals (a kind of linkage that is always hard to confirm) but in an acceptance all round that the Soviet Union was set against the United States: the former was seen as the adversary superpower apparently well ahead in the most tangible military terms and more or less on par otherwise. From 1950–75, there was a tendency to exaggerate Soviet economic growth.[6] More recently, there has almost certainly been a disposition to overrate Soviet progress towards the development of beam weapons for strategic defence, a disposition that has been reinforced by a propensity to (a) take Soviet technological optimism too much at face value,[7] (b) disregard a growing tendency for Soviet military researchers to work on non-military projects[8] and (c) forget the difficulties inherent in beam warfare. Shades can here be seen of Sputnik and the 'missile gap'.

All the same, the belief (which Mackinder had done his bit to sustain a while) in Moscow's endless yearning for 'warm water' ports was on the wane well before the emergence of Mikhail Gorbachev. Witness the West's reaction to the invasion of Afghanistan from 1979. Earlier that year, Dr. Harold Brown, then US Secretary of Defense, had spoken of 'the combination of traditional Russian interest in the area of the Persian Gulf and the growing costs of Soviet domestic energy supplies which, under deteriorating regional conditions, could propel the Soviet Union towards various forms of intervention in the Middle East'. Likewise, early in 1980, André Fontaine, a distinguished French commentator, was to remark that the USSR 'has always been aspiring to reach warm seas'. Nevertheless, each of these observations was made within a commentary that was measured and perspicacious. Throughout the West, in fact, the pitch in relation to the incursion into Afghanistan was one of recognition that, however illicit and brutal, it was probably a defensive move by a Moscow anxious to stabilise the Muslim republics of Soviet Central Asia. As much was heavily hinted at by the Soviets themselves.[9]

Now their military presence is reduced to a small advisory team in Kabul. Nor does any re-entry seem at all likely, given the precept that history rarely repeats itself because the actors in the present drama have seen the dénouement of the previous one. In September 1990, President Bush flew to Helsinki to engage President Gorbachev in dialogue about the Gulf crisis, a quest on both sides for regional concordance. The understanding reached was every bit as solid as could have been hoped for, given all the circumstances.

At an earlier stage in the Cold War, the 'warm water' hypothesis had been clearly evident. In February 1947 the British government suddenly declared itself unable to continue as chief backer of the Royalists in Greece in their civil war against Communist insurgents (see Chapter 7). Within days, President Truman had gone to Congress to secure special aid for Greece and also Turkey on the grounds that 'totalitarian regimes imposed on free peoples by direct and indirect aggression' posed a threat to world peace and hence the security of the United States.

He had included Turkey because, from early 1945 until the summer of 1946, that country had been subject to a diplomatic offensive by Moscow, the declared aim being so to revise the Montreux

Convention of 1936 as to secure Soviet participation in the protection of the Turkish Straits. In spite of the discordance in timing, the President linked that offensive with the Communist insurrection that had resumed in Greece that same summer, presuming them to be the twin spearheads of a Muscovite drive to the Mediterranean.

Yet Stalin was utterly unenthusiastic about the Greek Communists' uprising in 1946 just as he had been about the previous one, late in 1944. Two other Communist leaders, Josif Tito in Yugoslavia and George Dimitrov in Bulgaria, were giving the rebels moral and material support. However, this was because they sought to enlist Greek (and, above all, Macedonian) Communism in an endeavour to create a South Slav Federation, hoping that this would be able to stand on its own against Stalin as well as against the West.

All the same, the simple perception of a monolithic threat may have helped sell the new Truman doctrine of containment in Europe, against what still proved to be a significant measure of Congressional resistance. One has also to say that without that doctrine Europe would soon have collapsed, economically and politically. Undoubtedly, too, it was good to draw Turkey into the alliance so early on, given the national and democratic resolve inherent in the Atatürk legacy. However, a tendency then to lose sight of how far Moscow defined its strategy in terms of its own perceived interests without regard to those of other Communist movements may have left the West less astute in its management of the Cold War, not least as regards China. Visiting Athens during the civil war in December 1944, Winston Churchill had well observed the divergence between the local Communists and the Kremlin, the former being for revolution and the latter for retrenchment.[10] But then, Churchill was never much sold on the geopolitical theorists and their two-dimensional worlds.

A vivid illustration of how understanding could be confounded by treating the Middle East as a sector of extra special import for Moscow is furnished by the Yom Kippur or Ramadan war of October 1973. At that time, the Kennedy wing of the Democrats in the United States was seeking to square two conflicting tenets within what was then its world view. One was that the situation was ripe to consolidate *détente* in Europe; and that the best way to further this might be a unilateral reduction of US forces in Germany. The other was that Israel was virtually blameless in its quarrel with the Arabs. So by providing the latter with the wherewithal to wage war against her, the Soviet Union had connived in – not to say instigated – an act of entirely unprovoked aggression. Towards the end of the month, Senator Edward Kennedy sent a personal message to the Ankara meeting of the North Atlantic Assembly urging an early cut in US force levels in the European theatre and cheerily averring that 'what the Russians are doing in the Middle East should not destroy our confidence that we can move beyond the Cold War in Europe'.[11] In reality, of course, to have pulled troops back from Europe at that juncture would have been badly to undermine US credibility everywhere.

Flawed interpretation

Besides which, the notion of an incurable yearning for warm water is implausible psychologically and lacks historical support. A synoptic review even of Peter the Great's progress by no means reveals a preoccupation with what we currently know as the Middle East. He it also was who annexed the large Kamchatka peninsular and the northern part of the Kuriles island chain, all territories within the Pacific Ocean basin. Furthermore he remained so fired by the idea of a north-east passage from Archangel to the Indies that he determined to solve the debated problem of whether Asia and America were joined together. At long last, almost on his deathbed, he sent his Admiral Behring out on the first of his expeditions to the straits that have since borne his name.

What is more, this same monarch was the founder of St Petersburg on the Baltic, the city which was to remain the capital of Russia from 1712 until 1918. Likewise, 1699 – the very year in which that Black Sea squadron became operational – was spent by Tsar Peter welding together a Baltic coalition against Sweden, a coalition that precipitated a Great Northern War which was to last over 20 years. So what we see is a personality far too restless and opportunistic to lend itself to the pursuit of a single-sector strategy. Besides which, the sector on which he mostly focused was Northern Europe, including Britain. There 'towered the mighty monuments to his reign: a European-type army and navy; an industry newly established on European models; a new secular culture, an integral part of the culture of Europe'.[12]

Well before that, however, a countercurrent had built up among the populace. If one allows that the Renaissance came to Russia at all, one has to say that it did so slowly and belatedly. Printing came only in the second half of the 16th Century. Moreover, the nearest

Russian equivalent of the Reformation, the Great Schism, was triggered off by a Russian Orthodox Council decision, taken in 1667, to accept steering from the Greek Orthodox and even the Catholic persuasions in corrections to the Bible and reforms of the liturgy. In this the council had Tsarist backing but was fiercely opposed by a broad stratum of middle-ranking priests, peasants, cossacks and merchants – the 'old believers'. Instinctually they were gripped by an overwhelming sense of 'the Other' and so were opposed to any foreign importation, theological or material. They were sure always to react against any whiff of spiritual pollution from Europe. They split into various sects but long continued as a force to be reckoned with: fearless, resourceful and obdurate. Some ended up as colonisers on the southern steppes, thereby escaping the savagery of Tsarist persecution.

No review of the two centuries left to Tsarist Russia after Peter's death in 1725 will show a concern with warm water to be at all insistent unless every Kremlin initiative in the entire arc from Turkestan to Hungary is treated as consequent upon it. Yet to see things thus would be to encompass in a supposedly grand design a diverse assortment of more particular motives. Among them were advance into central Asia because God was understood to abhor a vacuum; reforging the nexus with the Ukrainians that the Poles had managed to sunder; and, later on, securing the export routes for Ukrainian grain. Even on this interpretation, however, the record is interspersed by developments apropos Europe or maybe the Pacific; and in 1907, indeed, Russia was to strike an historic compromise with the British in Persia in order to combine with them against Germany on the wider plane.[13]

If there was an underlying theme in terms of geographical orientation, it was that Russia must seek acceptance as part of Europe potentially and culturally, while making ready to fend off any security threats from that fractious peninsula. Much the same thrust was to be sustained by the Communists, never mind the vacuous yet cross-grained dialogue between Molotov and Ribbentrop in Berlin in November 1940 about the extension southwards of their respective spheres of influence. That exchange has been quoted too often though rarely within the full context of the Nazi-Soviet pact, a contrivance by Berlin and Moscow to buy time against each other on the basis of an agreed carve-up of Eastern Europe. Then, as the USSR moved into the novel sphere of strategic nuclear deterrence, her development and deployment of strategic offensive weapons bespoke a preoccupation with the European theatre that was nothing less than obsessive. Witness the exposure to an American first strike, between 1962 and 1967, of the USSR's Intercontinental Ballistic Missile (ICBM) force. American virtuosity was certainly one reason for this (see Chapter 2). But another was the priority the Kremlin always accorded the option of nuclear strikes against Western Europe. Hence the installation within the western borders of the USSR (between 1961 and 1963) of no fewer than 700 medium-range and intermediate-range strategic missiles, nearly 10 times as many such weapons as the number of ICBMs the Soviets had emplaced by then. Then in 1977 the replacement of the former with the formidable SS-20s commenced.

Now both the SS-20s and what is left of the 1961–63 generation are being totally eliminated under the Intermediate Nuclear Forces agreement of 1987. Meanwhile, Soviet tactical formations are being withdrawn from elsewhere in Eastern Europe, just as from Afghanistan and Mongolia. So does this mean that Europe no longer has a special place in the Muscovite psyche? What of the 'common European home', a term coined by Leonid Brezhnev in 1981 and revived by Mikhail Gorbachev in 1985? Has it served as nothing more than a smokescreen to cover Soviet disengagement? Has it been seen as a way through for Western economic aid? Was it envisaged as a home with two doors, designed to ensure that each superpower continued to be involved in the management of Europe and, above all, the two Germanies – entities that could thus remain stably and agreeably divided? Well into 1989, the European issue about which Soviet opinion remained stolidly monolithic was this one. The received wisdom in Moscow was that the 'German question' (ie reunification) will be answered 'by History', not the present generation.[14]

So what price now the 'European home'? The strategic frontier of the USSR no longer dissects central Europe. Instead, it virtually coincides with the 1941 boundary of the Soviet state. In so far as its internal ruptions will allow, Moscow has been looking more to other horizons: to a more special relationship with the United States, to a much more positive role in the United Nations, and towards the Pacific. Speaking in Vladivostok in July 1986, Mikhail Gorbachev portrayed his country as 'an Asian-Pacific' power eager to contribute to the 'Pacific Renaissance' through good relations with China and Japan. As an individual, he has come across as fascinated by the Japanese economic miracle, and entirely free of the paranoia about the Far East that was among Stalin's less savoury hallmarks.[15]

Yet what also is clear is that, in at least one cardinal respect, Eastern Europe is still of the singular importance to the Muscovite polity that Mackinder said it had to be. This is that political and cultural change in countries like Poland and Romania stimulates further the aspirant nationalisms of the Baltic states, the Ukraine and other peripheral republics of the USSR. That is to say, Moscow is faced with a threat of 'falling dominoes' that is potentially far wider than anything she faced, on account of Islamic revivalism, as the Afghanistan crisis broke in 1979. In the Soviet Far East, however, no such dominoes are immediately poised to fall in line with political changes in Mongolia or the larger Communist neighbours.

Glasnost in crisis

Viewed from another standpoint, the situation the Kremlin is confronted with (regardless of the outcome of the August coup) arises out of how *glasnost*, the new openness that Mikhail Gorbachev has so swiftly engendered in Soviet life, has moved much too far ahead of *perestroika*, the institutional restructuring he has been striving for. This has especially applied in the economic sphere.

No doubt the impetus behind *glasnost* has owed a lot to notions about reasonableness in public affairs that simply derive from innate human feelings about common decency. Yet no less obviously, it has also owed much to Western models of toleration, pluralism and democracy. At the same time, however, it has drawn on certain deep reserves of ethnic or national prejudice. These may be directed against the Kremlin but may also act against local minorities or neighbouring nationalities. The USSR is reckoned to embrace 200 ethnic groups. Within the basic political framework of 15 republics, there are 20 autonomous republics, eight autonomous regions and ten autonomous areas.

The Jewish community has not yet been subject to ethnic violence in the new situation. Nevertheless, it has felt under Gorbachev that a menacing divergence was opening up. On the one hand, there was much more individual and cultural toleration at the official All-Union level (*eg* the teaching of Jewish history or the Hebrew or Yiddish languages is no longer taboo; and Moscow now has its first rabbinical school in half-a-century). Yet on the other hand, expressions at grass roots level of an atavistic anti-semitism did appear more common among the Russians and also certain other nationalities. Besides which, their history makes the Russian Jews apprehensive of the connotations for themselves as scapegoats of any economic collapse. Correspondingly, Jewish emigration from the USSR rose to 70,000 in 1989 as compared with the previous post-1945 high of 52,000 in 1979.[16] Quite possibly, one million will leave over the next several years, should relevant doors remain open.

What cannot be denied the while is that the chief result of *glasnost* to date, in many aspects of Soviet life, has been to highlight and sometimes exacerbate discontent and malaise. The full extent of corruption has been revealed. So has that of ecological misman-agement, an aberrant tendency that in the Kremlin's case has had overtones of discrimination against some of the nationalities on the territorial periphery.

Twice in the last five years alone, there has been a serious accident at a nuclear installation. Tens of thousands may be doomed to die early as a result of Chernobyl, a fair proportion in the near vicinity. There will, of course, be genetic abnormalities as well, though these are hard to quantify. So backed by Kakimbek Salykov, Supreme Soviet Chairman for Energy and National Resources, the Ukrainian regional government has been pressing for a final shutdown of the whole Chernobyl site.[17] Less dreadful but still bad enough was the way that, in September 1990, perhaps 100,000 people in Kazakhstan were placed at some risk by a toxic gas vent from the military facility for nuclear reprocessing at Ulba. This event underscored only too well the Kazakh sense of grievance about how much and how carelessly their land has been used for nuclear weapons de-velopment.

Frustration and low morale throughout the Soviet population have been reflected in the usual indicators of malaise. Take alcohol. Between 1955 and 1984 consumption nearly trebled. In 1985, an estimated one in 60 of the entire population was an advanced ineb-riate while one in 12 (one in seven of males) was unduly dependent. Health, family life, lawfulness and productivity were visibly affected. That year, Mikhail Gorbachev launched an anti-drink campaign. By 1988 it was being drastically run down as a virtual failure.[18]

Meanwhile, crime has seemed to be rapidly on the increase. Also, hundreds of strikes occurred in 1989 and again in 1990, with ethnic resentments often interwoven with the material grievances. Inflation accelerating to 20 per cent or more added to a sense of things sliding out of control. So did falling output. So, too, have grotesque econ-omic disjunctions, not least on the wholesale side. A Yugoslav academic has spoken of the 'dramatic character of the contemporary

Soviet situation caused by mounting problems, bitter disputes, growing and open discontent, and ever more open polarisation on the socio-political scene . . . .'[19]

At the heart of it all was the fact that the moral authority of the Communist Party had collapsed because of its being so blatantly a vehicle for corruption and privilege and because 'socialist abundance' had become a lost horizon. Nor had President Gorbachev, for all his charm and courage and energy, worked out how to make an inspirational appeal on a new philosophical basis, thus breaking decisively with his own Marxist-Leninist upbringing. Nor did he seem able to revive the debates that were waged so vigorously within Russian Communism before Lenin made it a Bolshevik monolith. Nor has he broken the KGB.

Shortly after his election as General Secretary, in March 1985, Gorbachev squashed the concept of 'developed socialism' expounded by his predecessor, Konstantin Chernenko. What it had ostensibly meant was that the Soviet Union was poised to enter a phase in which 'a reorientation of social consciousness' could be achieved by 'the wider flow of information through society'.[20] Yet having jettisoned this dubious mumbo-jumbo, Gorbachev enunciated no alternative paradigm. In the book on *Perestroika* he published in 1987, he even chose to invoke Lenin as 'an ideological source of *perestroika*'. Indeed he was adamant that Lenin's works and

> his ideals of socialism remained for us an inexhaustible source of dialectical creative thought, theoretical wealth, and political sagacity. His very image is an undying example of lofty moral strength, all-round spiritual culture and selfless devotion to the cause of the people and to socialism ... Gravely ill, Lenin was deeply concerned for the future of socialism ... Hence the utilisation of methods which did not seem to be intrinsic to socialism itself or at least diverged in some respects from generally accepted classical notions of socialist development.[21]

Gorbachev was alluding to the New Economic Policy, a programme for recovery through heavy reliance on market incentives and quite a wide sector of private enterprise, principally in agriculture. It was started in 1921, as the modified version of a plan Leon Trotsky had been working on to save Communism from economic collapse by allowing some short-term accommodation to capitalist principles. The long-term vision was unaltered; and the primacy of the Party preserved.

Early on, Mikhail Gorbachev did commit himself to a degree of economic liberalisation that would go much further than the NEP and be long-lasting. He also accepted that political liberalisation was a necessary concomitant. But right up to the time of the August coup he remained loth to step outside the Communist Party in order to achieve these aims, and simply engaged in equivocal talk about advance 'within a framework of socialist choice'. The de-collectivisation of agriculture (long since undertaken by Communist regimes in Yugoslavia and Poland) had been eschewed.

What made procrastination all the more disturbing was the absolute criticality of this very question: how close the USSR should move to the moderated capitalism of the modern Western world. On the one hand, we were advised that 'there is no Russian national understanding which would permit the early establishment in Russia of anything resembling the private enterprise system as we know it'; and that 'many features of the Soviet system will stick, if only for the reason that everything has been destroyed which might seem to have constituted an alternative to them'.[22] Yet on the other hand, popular pressure in favour of a market economy visibly built up. A public opinion poll carried out in November 1989 favoured capitalism against socialism by 51 to 32 per cent. Correspondingly, the Institute for the Study of the USA and Canada (actually an academic window on the Western world in general) had come to be seen as 'the centre of know-how'.[23] It was, of course, this mood that impelled Boris Yeltsin into the presidency of the Russian Republic.

What then of the twin-track strategy for *perestroika* that the more radical of Mikhail Gorbachev's colleagues have been concerned to promote? Perhaps the most authentic encapsulation of their thought is to be seen in a programme advanced for a while in 1990 by Stanislav Shatalin, a progressive economist. The hope must still be that some broad approximation to it will be carried through, with the forceful encouragement of the West.

According to Shatalin, the most basic of the twin tracks had to be a dash to reshape the economy along market lines within 500 days. The other had to provide for the transformation of the Soviet Union into a confederation. A lot of decision-taking would devolve as of right to the constituent republics, including much that is concerned with economic change. In return, the All-Union central government would retain or regain control over a number of spheres of common interest: defence and foreign policy; money supply; environmental standards; anti-trust laws, and certain more mundane services.

Lately, President Gorbachev had been warning that if the interaction between *glasnost* and *perestroika* failed to achieve the required political and economic alchemy, the USSR could disintegrate into a 'Lebanon' on the grandest of scales. A year ago, Eduard Shevardnadze was warning that failure would mean a return to dictatorship.[24] These admonitions were different sides of the same coin. Evidently, too, a fascisto-Marxist regime reimposed to crush *glasnost* and block both *perestroika* and secession would perforce be more thoroughly repressive than a straight continuation of the Brezhnev era might have been. By the same token, it might seek its ultimate rationale in an aggressive foreign policy, perhaps using the pretext that the planetary management crisis was bringing about the convulsive death of capitalism. Early in 1991, Valentin Pavlov, the new Soviet Prime Minister, was trying to blame Western banks for a Soviet inflation crisis obviously fuelled by domestic overprinting. This 'old believer' helped stage the August coup but dropped out on the second day.

Mackinder revisited

But has heartland decay gone too far to allow of an active resurgence of threat? Should we accept as a verdict definitive and final, the observation of Sir Michael Howard, R. C. Lovett Professor of Naval and Military History at Yale, that 'Far from the geopolitical fantasies of Halford Mackinder and his disciples being proved valid, with the Heartland and the World Island pressing out to control the Rimlands, we are seeing instead the communities of the Rimland increasingly penetrating and transforming the stagnant Heartland.'[25]

Howard is here applying the test of contemporary evidence. But other tests that Mackinder frequently failed as well are those of definitional accuracy and conceptual rigour. Take the thesis, adumbrated above, about the pressure of German on Slav. Enunciating it in 1919, he made a string of observations, some of which do appear intuitively prophetic in relation to the world of 1939 or of 1989, or both. The fact remains, however, that he treated the problem of Eastern Europe as coincident with the Eastern Question and Austria as synonymous with Germany. Both these equivalencies were gross oversimplifications. Nor ought Germany to exist at all in relation to Mackinder's notions about the geographical basis of history. It is not enough of a geographical expression.

Nor were Mackinder's arguments ever sufficiently watertight at global level. However much he may have apprehended the looming shadow of heartland power, another part of him subscribed to the maritime imperialist hope that the links that bind the British Empire will survive more or less indefinitely:

> The whole course of future history depends on whether the Old Britain . . . withstand(s) all challenge to her naval supremacy, until such time as the daughter nations shall have grown to maturity and the British Navy shall have expanded into the Navy of the Britains.[26]

Most crucially for our current purposes, he was at his least convincing when suggesting that Russia might launch 'centrifugal raids' from her 'central strategical position' much as the Mongols had done in their day.[27] The fact of the matter is that Muscovite armies have long been peculiarly deficient in strategic mobility. In the Crimean War (1854–56) an Anglo-French expedition only 60,000-strong and with far from adequate logistic support, captured the key naval base of Sevastopol although the Tsar had a million men somewhere in the field. Meanwhile, it was the British who had geared themselves up to what today would be called 'horizontal escalation', in this case extending the war to the Baltic.[28] During the next crisis, the Russo-Turkish war of 1877–78, apprehension waxed strong in Calcutta about the way Tsarist armies were drawing ever closer to the Khyber Pass, the invasion route to the subcontinent for Alexander the Great, Tamerlane, Babur, Mahmud of Ghazi and Nadir Shah. One event in sight was their annexation of the ancient city of Merv. It took place in 1884. But 'Mervousness', Foreign Secretary Lord Salisbury had quipped in 1878, 'would not stand the test of large-scale maps'.[29] In other words, rough terrain and poor communications ruled out a Russian thrust straight through the Khyber.

Mackinder and his admirers would, of course, protest that he did stress that the potentialities of the heartland would not be fully realised until the railway age and, indeed, the air age had well and truly dawned. But with the signal exception of the reinforcement of the Moscow front from the Far East in the autumn of 1941, even those dimensions have never yet been well exploited. All that the Trans-Siberian railway did for Russia in the 1904–5 war with Japan was encourage a theatre build-up that made defeat all the more comprehensive. A situation no less bathetic next developed in the First World War. In the preceding years, St Petersburg had sought to constrain road and railway development opposite Germany, the aim being to limit the offensive threat. Yet in 1914, she launched an offensive in that direction herself, the upshot being the disaster at Tannenburg.[30] Then again, Mackinder predicted that the advent of air power would enable the heartland to take 'easy possession of Suez via Arabia'.[31] Never has there been any sign of this.

From 1944, the take-over of Eastern Europe gave the USSR much readier strategic access to all the European theatre. From about 1960, she began steadily to develop a global naval presence. The treaty of friendship signed with the Mongolian People's Republic in 1966 gave added leverage to the military build-up then under way against a China alarmingly in the throes of the 'cultural revolution'. Consolidation of the presence in Afghanistan from 1979 would likewise have threatened Pakistan via the Khyber. A century late, some 'Mervousness' would have been excusable.

Under Gorbachev, not only have these territorial extensions of influence been all but abandoned; there has also been some contraction of the naval spread. Furthermore, there have been various indications (not least the 1991 war with Iraq) that the West's lead in military technology has grown formidably. Besides which, even a restored dictatorship might find that the difficulty of binding all-Union armed forces properly together was aggravated by a tendency for soldierly disaffection to be legitimated by the secessionist aspirations of constituent republics. Military conscription is central to the renewed crisis in the Baltic States. In October 1990, the government of the Ukraine felt obliged to endorse a vote by its parliament against Ukrainian conscripts being obliged to serve outside their home territory. Very similar moves had already been made in Armenia and Azerbaijan. Such stipulations could pose a challenge to the authority of any All-Union government, were it authoritarian or democratic. The state militias in Yugoslavia illustrate the point.

On current showing, however, a Muscovite dictatorship would retain some significant military options, despite the new political geography and in spite of the intrinsic weaknesses just identified. The risk of nuclear blackmail in Europe still exists. So does the possibility of a Soviet air offensive, sectoral or general. Likewise, contention for the High Seas must remain of concern as long as any risk of a showdown with Moscow remains; and this means, in its turn, that the defence of Scandinavia must continue to be a key requirement. Maybe, too, pressure could still be exerted on China. All through the period 1965–85, the Soviet threat to China was much more substantive than the much-vaunted Chinese threat to the Soviet Union.[32] Scope for further action in the Middle East might also present itself.

What a belligerent Moscow might be most tempted to do, however, is lurch heavily towards a nationwide deployment of ballistic missile defence. That would be consonant with a long tradition of all-round protection of the homeland. One manifestation of this, ever since the 18th Century, has been the maintenance of a large navy, albeit one divided between several constricted seaboards. Likewise, in 1914, the Tsarist army had no fewer artillery guns overall than had its adversaries on the Eastern Front. The trouble was that too much of this ordnance was tied down in fortresses[33], mostly close by a frontier or coastline.

The roots of this quest for comprehensive defence can be traced back to feelings of inferiority and exclusion resulting from the Muscovite polity's having stood so much apart from the diversifying influences of 16th Century Europe, the individualism cherished by the Renaissance and the pluralism engendered by the Reformation. Meanwhile, Moscow remained only the fifth city in patriarchal precedence within the Orthodox realm, after Constantinople, Alexandria, Antioch and Jerusalem. Under the Bolsheviks this action-reaction, this sense of 'the other', was intensified, as witness the shift of the seat of government back to Moscow from Petrograd (alias St Petersburg to 1914; and Leningrad from 1924). For a long time, too, 'old believers' within the Communist Party quietly welcomed the massive expenditure that all-round defence involved. The alternative might have been to release resources into something of a Western-style consumer boom which might, in its turn, have encouraged Western-style political aspirations. Better to preserve the martial ethos of the pristine revolutionary days.

So it is that the USSR retains in service even today as many as 350 minesweepers, many of them designed for coastal or inshore service against a minelaying threat hardly worth presenting in waters so landlocked and ice-locked. Furthermore, the Soviet fleet as a whole has (especially since 1961) prepared assiduously for active maritime defence in considerable depth, the declared aim being to protect its own missile-firing submarines in Arctic waters and to inhibit naval nuclear strikes against the motherland. The latter purpose is, of course, a form of strategic defence with strongly pre-emptive connotations.

Still, nowhere has the defensive rationale been more manifest than in the huge effort so long devoted to home air defence, this largely under the rubric of *Protivo-Vozdushnaya Strany*, an élite force dedicated to the vain task of ensuring that the heavy bomber would never get through. Early in 1941, PVO-Strany was accorded direct representation on the high command; and in 1948, it became an independent service.[34] A decade later the Soviets were reckoned to be spending three times as much on continental air defence as were the Americans.[35] Then in 1966, they led the way into the era of limited ballistic missile defence.

Competition between the superpowers in the field of strategic defence might in itself induce a return to something of a Cold War atmosphere. Avoiding it is a strong argument in favour of the call made in October 1990 by James Baker, US Secretary of State, for a close dialogue between Washington and Moscow over defence policies as well as about arms control and the management of regional crises. That in its turn argues for the West doing whatever it can to preserve and sustain its once implacable Soviet adversary during the unfolding of *perestroika* and as long as the Kremlin does remain committed to the process of needful change.

Obviously that is a strategy with risk attached. But in principle it is no different from the policy of political rebuilding, in furtherance of wider geopolitical aims, pursued so positively in regard to West Germany from September 1946 and to Japan from January 1948. In practice, however, such a remedy could become that much harder to proceed with if Boris Yeltsin and his allies end up as the chief power brokers in the aftermath of the August coup. For these people profess themselves to be relaxed about the prospect of the non-Russian republics now under Soviet sovereignty moving to complete independence. Yet even they admit how uncertain it is, especially in the South, that the post-independence regimes would be stable democracies. Herein can perhaps be seen the first dim twilight of a dawning awareness that the ultimate alternative to a confederal all-Union democracy may be communalist anarchy leading back to Muscovite dictatorship, perhaps as imposed by Great Russian 'old believers'. This danger is not diminished by the reality that, whatever else happens, the Soviet heartland faces many years of painful economic adjustment. Under these circumstances, the best hope for the heartland and so for the world may lie in an alliance between a Yeltsin suitably chastened and a Gorbachev outside the Communist Party.

5

Far Beyond Dunkirk

THE BURTHEN of the strategic revolution is that, for the next decade or two, the armed forces of the West are likely to assume roles that are much reduced and less defined, especially in Central Europe. Later on, however, a readiness to deploy further afield may be more needful as warlike crises erupt more often around a world wracked by environmental tension. But exact requirements will be hard to conjecture.

So the big danger is that public attitudes towards the profession of arms will gyrate between extremes. For most of the Cold War, we focused too narrowly on the military dimension in stability. With that conflict now apparently won, we may all too easily slide into a mood of discounting not only this dimension but even the notion that any external threats to our security remain. Moreover that slide could gain added impetus from the failure of the August coup to consolidate itself. Nor may strategic studies, as customarily defined, impose an adequate intellectual check on such a progression.

Yet too euphoric a reaction could itself give way eventually, and perhaps suddenly, to a lurch back to military remedies for discords that will have their roots in ecological, economic and cultural stress. Not only would such lurching represent the rejection of any planetary perspectives; it would likely give rise to military stances that were in themselves inappropriate. As much proved largely to be the case in 1914 and again in 1939.

Perhaps the most graphic demonstration ever of how to win a war laboriously and then lose a peace immediately was afforded in 1919. It was a collapse of various aspects of policy, one of them being a sudden lack of any strategic perspective. This even applied to military affairs as such. In Britain, for instance, the three services all went

65

their separate ways. The Royal Navy sought equivalence with its American counterpart, this for reasons that remain obscure. The Royal Air Force fancifully prepared for a showdown with the French. The Army turned again to India. When at long last rearmament against the fascist dictators got under way, it was breathless and ill-considered, too uneven and desperately late.

So those in serious pursuit of a stable peace should be concerned to dampen down all swings of the pendulum of opinion. Limit the decline lately under way in public concern with defence. Uphold through what is bound to be a time of substantial contraction both the public status and the self-esteem of the profession of arms. Look towards a programme of positive restructuring.

The formal cancellation of the Cold War, in the CSCE agreement of November 1990, has underlined the crisis of purpose the military now face. So, indeed, has the brusque devastation of Iraq's mighty panoply. But an underlying reality is that various strands in our modern culture militate against a martial ethos, almost regardless of external circumstances. Let us start with the vexed question of gender balance. During the 1960s, Western society accelerated its transition from the traditional stereotypes of womanhood. Yet in their place has come a virulent dogmatism, its gist being that there are no innate differences of temperament between the sexes. A corollary could be that young men should be under no stronger an obligation than are young women to perform military service.

Indeed, this theme might well figure in the debate about the desirability or otherwise of conscript service that is very likely to break out across Europe these next few years. At the same time, some will argue (as a point of ideological principle) that all occupations within such armed forces as may still be required must *ipso facto* be open to both sexes. Thus will they undermine the macho appeal of the profession of arms.

Of course, a welter of historical evidence can be adduced to show that, the stereotypes notwithstanding, women in a war situation come rapidly on terms with men in terms of courage, resourcefulness and resilience. Moreover, there are not a few examples of individual women shining as the leaders of their people in war. Yet this does not mean that the female of our species can involve herself in the killing of other people's children as instinctually as her male counterpart may. If she could, the armies of Napoleon, Wellington, Grant or Lee might have had female regiments marching into the thick of battle. What has to be avoided, in the present media and intellectual climate, is armed forces falling foul of what may be termed the 'Private Benjamin' syndrome. First, the critics insist that girl recruits are trained and otherwise treated exactly the same as the lads. Then these same critics turn round and suggest that this denies their femininity.

This whole matter warrants a more thorough debate than it has anywhere been the subject of yet. It is something that could usefully draw a good deal on anthropology, history, psychology and sociology. So could it, too, on comparative studies-in-depth of contemporary armed services and also police forces.

Nor is anti-sexist over-reaction the only strand in our modern culture that saps the martial ethos, especially in the absence of an immediate external threat. Hostility to authority in general, and big government in particular, is another. So is a widespread rejection of customary ritual and etiquette and, indeed, uniform dress. So is the continuing decline of the balanced nuclear family within an institutionalised marriage, a social norm often seen as basic to the moral support and general well-being of troops in battle and in cantonment. Added to which are the negative connotations for social cohesion in the wider sense. Then again, access to exotic gadgetry and travel to exotic places are ever less exclusively the military preserve they have appeared to be in the past.

Above all, the culture of dissent that remains endemic within Western youth (see Chapter 2) challenges the martial values not only through its celebration of egoism and, all too often, of non-licit violence but also through its gentler and more caring manifestations. For instance, the counter-culture tendency within the Green movement calls for tenderness towards all sentient beings as the way through to a more comprehensive environmental respect. Attractive though many of us may find this, however, it is hardly a preparation for the brutal dynamic of 21st Century war. The notion that one must not distract colonies of toads as one trains to mow down echelons of human beings may not be a complete contradiction within the context of a free society committed to a lasting peace underpinned by environmental stability as well as by a sufficiency of military strength. But not every young recruit will easily take the point.

Turning again to the less savoury side, one observes how strong a tide of hedonistic materialism is running throughout all the generations in modern mass society. Arguably, too, this craving for glitter and gratification is related to an altogether too neurotic fear of death or even ageing. Granted, such tendencies are hard to compare, one time and place as against another. How typical were the literary hypochondriacs of 18th Century England, say, of the society in which they lived and moved? How did their attitude relate to such British feats of arms as Blenheim and Gibraltar, Plassey and Quebec ...? Any answer would have to be intricate. None the less, there is something disturbing about the fact that, at the very time when Britain was recalling the first year of the Second World War from half a century on, she was smitten by successive waves of panic about food contamination: listeria, salmonella, mad cow disease, verminous plagues. In 1940, public calm scorned a palpably mortal threat in the aftermath of Dunkirk. Yet this time round, public anxiety allowed casualties to mount not in hard reality but in a media world of lurid imaginings. Good humoured stoicism had been replaced by hysteric self-concern.

Thankfully, this irrational nonsense died away when Saddam Hussein emerged as a more substantial menace. But still the question remains of where all the trends towards a mass society are leading us. Earlier, it was argued that we must strive towards enlightened globalism rather than narrow nationalism or communalism if we are to cope with our planetary crisis of survival. By the same token, we must allow all sectoral loyalties (religious, political, ethnic) to dissolve into a sense of obligation to all mankind and to the planet itself. There is no denying, however, that men have always fought and died for some exclusive group affinity far more readily than they have for a universal ideal. In 1943, in Tunisia, the Irish Guards of the British army fought a seize-and-hold action which, it has been said 'must rank as one of the finest feats against odds achieved by the British infantry.' Afterwards, a guardsman (*ie* private soldier) attributed their cohesion in the face of terrible casualties to the fact that 'We're all Micks, we're all Catholics, and we're all guardsmen'.[1] Edward Thompson's notion about the importance of 'the Other' in defining ourselves (see Chapter 3) has tangible relevance here.

Yet already the cultural transformation typified above as a new Renaissance has gone too deep in many respects, good no less than bad, to be overturned except through an upheaval so convulsive as to put at risk the whole fabric of a free society. Even so, there are no grounds here for giving up on the profession of arms. History shows that societies in which the classic martial virtues are lauded uncritically, even in peacetime, tend not to be ones well at ease within themselves and may not always achieve an effective military posture either. Their armies may be grandiloquent and ponderous, not lean and reactive. Illicit and maladroit interference in politics may be an attendant risk. Open societies in which any wars are continually the subject of stringent televisual critique may eventually discover a deeper resilience.

Indeed, the imperatives of environment protection in general, and energy efficiency in particular, may before too long be impelling us towards a society that is rather less self-indulgent, more disciplined in certain ways. Nor do the military have to mirror, in any case, all the characteristics of the society they serve. Every calling from university professor to village postman has something of an *émigration intérieure* about it. What is important is that the profession of arms reflects society at large sufficiently to retain its trust and regard; and that it does so without impairing too much its own ethos and operational efficiency. Ensuring this in what we look forward to as a post-Cold War era will never be easy, even with extensive restructuring. But it need not prove impossible.

Military electronics

Keeping sufficiently in step with unprecedented changes in the civilian world around it has, in a sense, to be one side of the military's adaptation to the information explosion, the electronic revolution. Dealing with the changing modalities of insurgency has to be another. But a third has to be a coming to terms with the quantum gains in the performance in pitched battle of advanced weapons systems and related equipment. Hopefully, such operational considerations will be rendered less urgent by the emergence in Europe and maybe even the Middle East of new regimens based on arms control pacts and confidence-building measures. But they will not lose all relevance, even in Europe.

To an extent, of course, the weapons improvements in question lie outside the sphere of electronics as such. They relate instead to better structural materials, the more efficient use of fuel and so on. By any historical standards the consequent gains in ruggedness and mobility can appear impressive. None the less, they are a minor theme in comparison with the advances in firepower now being registered, very largely through an extending exploitation of the electromagnetic spectrum coupled with the accelerating growth of computer science.

As early as the Yom Kippur war of 1973, the indications were that the weight-for-weight effectiveness of air-delivered ordnance, in particular, was improving by one or two orders of magnitude. With precision attacks on hard-point targets, a key criterion is Circular Error Probability (C.E.P.): the radius of a circle drawn round the aiming point of such a size that a warhead being delivered across a given distance stands a 50 per cent chance of landing inside it. When a bomb is dropped from two or three thousand metres up, the CEP may still be as much as 50 metres if it is free-fall (*ie* unguided) after release but can be well below 10 metres if instead it is steered (via its fins) along laser beams. Admittedly, the CEPs registered by the élite Stuka squadrons of Goering's Luftwaffe could be as low as 30 metres but that was only because the aircraft themselves were aimed at the target in sustained dives to very low altitude to release a single modest-size bomb. Even half-a-century ago, this was a perilous business against a well-found air defence.

In one alternative to beam guidance, the sensor in the bomb's nose is 'electro-optical'. The descent to target is televisually controlled, with a switch to automatic once the crew of the parent aircraft are satisfied it is exactly locked on. As used in the Maverick air-to-ground rocket rushed to the Israelis by the Americans during the 1973 war, the electro-optical principle reportedly ensured a 95 per cent success rate against Egyptian tanks deployed on flat open landscapes near the Suez Canal.[2] True, this guidance mode is sensitive to mist and haze and has to limit missile speed to perhaps 20 metres a second. Even so, the CEP proffered is, in principle and often in practice, close to 10 metres.

Nor is it only in the exotic world of air war that such developments have been taking place. They figure, too, in what have usually been seen as more prosaic or stable facets of military applied science. Take tank gunnery. In 1945, a stationary US battle tank had to fire its main gun a dozen times to stand a 50:50 chance of hitting an adversary tank positioned side-on 2,000 yards down a test range. By 1975, a single round could offer an even better probability.[3] What is more, the relationship between performance on the range and performance in action would have been closer in the latter case.

Evidently, too, certain of the new Precision-Guided Munitions (PGMs) pose a particular threat to prepared fortifications, minefields excepted. Between even the most solid of forts and the battlefield around, there have to be points of contact (embrasures, casements, periscopes and antennae) which must be susceptible to the kind of accuracies described above.

Among other developments worth a special mention are two which are able to turn mobility into a source of vulnerability rather than a means of evasion. The discrimination of moving targets by doppler radar (the kind that registers the apparent changes of frequency as an object either approaches or recedes) is by no means new but continues to be refined. Meanwhile, miniature mines ('minelets'), are coming into service, and are so compact yet lethal that they may readily be broadcast across an operational runway, say, in order to render it useless for a brief yet maybe critical period or sown across or around a moving column of tanks so that it proceeds further at its peril.

Then again, the development is well under way of sub-munitions that autonomously react to suitable targets and home on them individually. Clearly, the progress in the first generation of weaponry so novel and exotic is bound to be rather unsure. Even so, there is every likelihood that, by early next century, this concept will have been implemented in Western armed forces. Perhaps its notable application will be when a descending artillery shell separates into several capsules, each able to steer onto a tank or some other 'hardpoint' target. Here then is the prospect that, provided its general location is known beforehand, even a moving vehicle can be individually engaged without the artillerist or whoever is observing for him being on a 'line of sight' to the target: veritably the gunners' equivalent of the philosophers' stone.[4] Some of us believe this triumph for artillery has to be at the expense of two other modes of combat: Close Air Support and the advance in close formation of armour.

All the same, even the most exotic weapons will heavily rely on comprehensive surveillance of the enemy and co-ordination of one's own measures. Yet the continuous flows of data in all directions needed to meet these requirements will not always be easy to sustain. Accidental interference is bound to occur. Furthermore, much scope remains for deception. The active forms of Electronic Warfare (EW), jamming and attrition, may often compromise both communications and surveillance.

Even so, EW is unlikely to undermine the other's surveillance and control capabilities completely, unless facilitated by a large technology gap. Otherwise, the pattern will be patchy and erratic. Though at certain times the data flow will lapse, at others it may be voluminous and definitive. Meanwhile, the most basic electronic contribution to the increasing lethality of war will be through the more accurate delivery of weapons. Most of the techniques employed are not too susceptible to interference; accidental, natural or deliberate.

Defence ascendant?

However, what has lately been the fashionable view that the Defence has become dominant in European-style land war did not stem from an examination of the electronic trends as such. Rather its origins were to be found in a thesis propounded in 1960 by the late Sir Basil Liddell Hart.[5] This was that, these last two centuries at least, 'the Defence has been gaining a growing material ascendancy over the Offence' because of a steady reduction in the number of troops needed to hold a mile of front in a pitched battle.[6] That reduction was said to be due largely to successive improvements in firepower as well as in mobility and communications. It was deemed to bode especially well for the non-nuclear defence of the inter-German border.

However, there were complications. Among them was an implicit assumption of qualitative parity between the opposing sides. Yet almost always in war there are significant contrasts in technology, not to mention such other factors as logistics, combat training, morale, leadership and command structure. The tendency today is for electronic 'technology gaps', in particular, to become wider (see Chapter 11).

Then, even if one works to his terms of reference, Liddell Hart has to be challenged on a variety of grounds, either logical or empirical. Not least among them is that the only particular trend identified by him was the growing feasibility of night warfare; and even in this regard, he conspicuously omits to mention the adverse connotations for the weaker side inherent in anything approaching round-the-clock combat, and this at unprecedented levels of intensity. As a rule, of course, the weaker side will be the one resting on the defensive.

What also works against the weaker side in war, and probably to an increasing extent, is the axiom famously formulated in 1916 by F. W. Lanchester, a British engineer already outstanding in the field of aerodynamics. This was that 'the fighting strength of a force may be broadly defined as proportional to the square of its numerical strength, multiplied by the fighting value of its individual units'.[7] No matter for the moment that comparison of 'fighting value' is nowadays far harder than it was in 1916, though it would have been damnably difficult even then. No matter either that it continues to get harder all the time. Nor that the consequences of physical attrition are often aggravated by an associated loss of morale and cohesion. The fact still remains that what this 'Lanchester square law' does *par excellence* is keep firmly in our minds how important even a marginal difference in numbers can sometimes be. Suppose one unit is engaging three. Then, on average and other things being equal, shot and shell will rain down on the former nine times as intensively as it does on the latter.

What can also be said is that, in the ultimate, this logical validation of the principle of mass holds good for all forms of military force. Historically speaking, however, it has tended to be most readily applicable to combat in the air and on the High Seas. Though his prime concern was to address contests between rival air fleets, Lanchester felt best able to validate his deduction through an interpretation of the Royal Navy's battle plans at Trafalgar.

In land campaigns, geography has often imposed severe constraints on effective fire and movement. Therefore, the relationship between numbers and effective strength has tended to be more nearly linear in that dimension of war.[8] However, that tendency may be weakening as improved surveillance and target acquisition makes it easier to override obstacles, be these natural or man-made. If so, this must help the stronger side to press its advantage. Above all, it may often be better placed to exploit decisively a surprise attack, whether overland or by air or both. For to the infliction of terrible damage must be added the sheer shock that a modern onslaught may cause to armies and societies ill-prepared for the hardships of war, let alone its dangers. To make things worse, the modalities of contemporary conflict leave little scope for the stratagems of trading space for time, resorted to so freely in two world wars. Conflicts tend to be localised; and a high premium is attached to allowing adventurism no rewards at all.

In the hypothesis here being tested, Liddell Hart also ignored the air dimension to an extent all too typical of the land-oriented military historian. Nor did he address what is surely a crucial distinction in the realm of land combat: that between the heavier and the lighter kinds of weapons. The former genre are crew-manned, use explosive shells, and fire plunging shot versus targets not usually in view to the gunners. As a rule, the latter genre are carried and fired by individuals, loaded with solid shot, fired at a high rate in quite prolonged bursts, and (almost invariably, to date) aimed over 'open sights'. By engagement over 'open sights' is meant that the targets are visible to the gunners. It is customarily spoken of as 'direct fire' in contrast with the 'indirect' or plunging fire against targets beyond the horizon.

Both common sense and a deal of historical evidence seem firmly to indicate that, while more lethal light weapons do favour men holding prepared positions, at any rate against a frontal assault by infantry, improvements in the heavier systems usually work the other way. On balance, this may well be true still. Inevitably, however, the sheer diversity of modern technology will create exceptions. A broadcasting amidst it of miniature mines might cripple an armoured advance. So, too, might the projection of self-homing sub-munitions. Meanwhile, the Anti-Tank Guided Missile (ATGM) has emerged as an important hybrid on the definitions just given. It may be man-portable, and has always been fired over open sights; but it packs a high-explosive warhead.

Yet regardless of these more particular considerations, the pace of an all-out war these days may not leave the Defence time to develop its countervailing strategy: reserve mobilisation, outside involvement, nuclear dissuasion or whatever. Anticipating the Allied invasion of France in 1944, Field Marshal Rommel warned that D-Day itself would be 'the longest day'; that was to say, the most agonising and momentous one. Against an offensive *à l'outrance* in the year 2020, say, it might be more a question of that 'longest' first hour. So much for the rising power of the Defence.

Geography does not repeat itself

Besides, even if one could demonstrate that, in whatever might be deemed the average case, the progress of firepower did favour the Defence, this could hardly guarantee its doing so in the context of more open warfare. A salient characteristic of the confrontation so long maintained across a divided Germany was that unless heavily reinforced beforehand, the brigades and divisions on the NATO side would have had to cover sectors of front which were abnormally wide, compared with Second World War experience. Accordingly, they would have had to adopt a mobile pattern of defence, relying on counter-attacks or fighting from unprepared positions.

Moreover, in theatres of possible conflict characterised by such extended fronts (*eg* parts of Europe and the Middle East; the Indo-Pakistan border; and the Sino-Soviet border), it may become harder than before to distinguish between a defensive adversary posture and an offensive one. This will be because concentrated assaults across open ground are liable to become as costly as they were between the advent of the machine gun and the invention of the tank. Accordingly, the principle of mass is liable to be applied not via the classic *blitzkrieg* format (narrow concentration to effect one or two deep breakthroughs) but through the early commitment of all available forces to a contest of attrition virtually all along whatever lines of contact geography allows. Such a pattern may, under certain circumstances, increase the risk of war through a precipitate misreading of adversary intentions. In October 1973, the Egyptians deployed to attack along more or less the entire length of the Suez Canal. Observing something of their preparations, the Israelis considered a pre-emptive strike but lacked evidence sufficiently unambiguous to justify this to themselves and, most important, the Americans.

In more particular ways, too, Geography never repeats itself, not over the land. Richly instructive again is the Middle East in 1973. Much as the American Civil War looked back to 1815 yet forward to 1914, so the struggle of Ramadan or Yom Kippur evolved from what may be characterised as an essentially mechanical past to a more electronic future – 1940 and 1991. None the less this 1973 campaign hinged throughout on the intricate geography of where it was enacted.

Take the Golan. On casual inspection, this short-grassed plateau looks almost formless, topographically speaking. Yet the variations within it of geology and thence landscape proved to be of great tactical importance. Thus the Israeli forward defence rested on 14 *telal*: or small hills of volcanic origin, each of which had been capped by a complex of barbed wire, concrete metal sheeting and sandbags with bunkers below.[9] Though subject to the full weight of the Syrian onslaught by land and air, a number of these strongpoints survived the entire war.

Likewise, the Israelis turned subtle contouring to good advantage in Close Air Support (CAS). On the first afternoon, they suffered mortifying losses from Surface-to-Air Missiles (SAMs) as well as from mobile anti-aircraft guns. As dusk approached, however, pairs of their Skyhawks 'skimmed in a low northward curve over Jordanian territory, hugging the contours until they rocketed up and over the Golan plateau to take the Syrian armour in the flank, then curve away west of Mount Hermon – hopefully without passing over the deadly SAM sites'.[10] In due course, that stratagem was to turn the tables, especially after the Syrian armoured vehicles had crossed onto ground sloping more towards Galilee.

Warplanes ascendant?

In the Lebanon War of 1982, the Israeli air arm disposed of a Syrian air umbrella, both surface-based and airborne, much more conclusively than in 1973.[11] This was partly because Israel had the initiative in preparation. It was also because the tortuous geopolitics of the South Lebanon meant the SAM screen could only be thin and feebly structured. In the coalition air offensive against the Iraqis from January 1991, different considerations obtained. Yet the result was even more one-sided.

Nevertheless, the future of the manned warplane (especially as an intruder into hostile and well-defended air space over land) remains among the more problematic issues in the whole defence arena. The problem breaks itself down into six distinct questions. How relevant are the roles air power has customarily performed? Is the ability of air power (as represented by the manned warplane) to perform them compromised by the vulnerability of its airfields? How does the destructive potential of the warplane now relate to the full cost of its procurement and retention in peacetime service? How does it compare with its susceptibility to destruction in the air if not on the ground? How far does technical evolution favour the displacement of the manned aircraft by other means of performing the same tasks – pilotless vehicles, helicopters, artillery or satellites in orbit? How much may such judgements be affected by technology gaps between one adversary and the other?

Throughout the Cold War decades, an ancillary but important role for strategic bombers has been the swift projection of military power across great distances, either to deter aggression or to counter it.[12] Barely three days after the outbreak of the Korean War in 1950, B-29 Superfortresses of the USAF were attacking North Korean columns on the roads to Seoul. Then early in 1951, when the United Nations field army was in danger of bring overwhelmed by the Chinese intervention, President Truman ordered to Guam some B-29s bearing 'complete atom bombs, and training was begun for their tactical use'. Similarly, 60 B-29s had been deployed to Britain on 17 July 1948, during the Berlin blockade. These machines were not then nuclear-capable but this was not the message sent to the Soviets at the time.[13] Such reactive demonstrations of ultimate intent may have their place in the 21st Century as grand strategy becomes global once more and especially if threats of nuclear blackmail proliferate.

What then of the recognised roles of tactical aviation; Close Air Support, interdiction strikes against targets (especially lines of re-supply and reinforcement) in the enemy's deep rear, attacks on air-fields and other nodal targets to rearward, deep reconnaissance, and active air defence? Arguably, the swift concentrations of firepower that characterise Close Air Support will count for less whenever a land attack is launched across an extended front. But perhaps the safest generalisation to make is that, under conditions of highly dynamic land war, there may not be time to profit from attacks on the enemy's routes for resupply and reinforcement. Airfields, on the other hand, will remain quite critical targets even if warplanes do lose some of their influence. Certain nodes in the command and control network should still be worth going for, too, even though devolution, mobility and compaction may make the network as a whole less susceptible. Meanwhile, land-based aerial cover could assume more prominence at sea (see below).

All the same, the argument about the future of air power hinges not so much on the tasks still to be done as on the merits of warplanes as a means of doing them. Undeniably, a serious weakness of the large strike monoplane, in particular, is its dependence on extensive and elaborate base facilities. When over 60 years ago, Major General J. F. C. Fuller yearned sardonically for a 'portable landing ground', he characterised the manned aircraft as 'a kind of animated rocket fired ... from an aerodrome, a weapon ... as immobile as a fortress ... in brief, the future of air power is not to be sought in the air but on the ground ...'[14] The Second World War was to afford dramatic examples of pre-emptive attacks on air bases. Such a stratagem was likewise crucial in the 1956, 1967, and 1991 wars in the Middle East. Both PGMs and scatter weapons aggravate this threat.

Since the Arab debacle of 1967, priority has widely been given not just to the active defence of airfields but to their 'hardening', notably the shielding of aircraft in individual revetments. Work has also been done on off-field dispersion, with short or vertical take-off and land-ing from roads etc. But even when such remedies do limit the im-mobilisation of planes on the ground, they add to the logistic and psychological burden of operations and inevitably interfere with sortie generation. Nor should we forget that the more comprehensive applications of this philosophy of survival on the ground have been confined largely to Europe, the chief exceptions having been Iraq and North Korea. As the coalition build-up proceeded in the Gulf last year, there were many media pictures of aircraft on Saudi airfields parked line abreast with no sheltering at all.

As regards the effectiveness of warplanes once they have been committed to offensive operations, the trends are in contrary directions. A strike fighter of today may routinely carry a warload equivalent to the maximum a four-engined bomber could manage half-a-century ago; and this improvement multiplies several times when account is taken of much higher sortie rates, much greater accuracy of delivery, better weapons efficiency and variety, and so on. Meanwhile weather is a facet of geography that is becoming less constrictive in war, not least for air arms (see Chapter 7) and at night.

However, anti-aircraft defences are also becoming more robust in the face of adverse weather. More generally, one has still to ask whether aircraft are not bound to become a lot more susceptible to destruction in flight, assuming an arms race does go on. Not that there is much evidence yet from actual hostilities. Towards the end of the Second World War, the average attrition endured by aircraft during particular campaigns almost all ranged between a minimum of one per hundred sorties and a maximum of 35. Within these limits, placings were determined by tactics, topography, weather, the Lanchester square law, electronic technology gaps, the element of surprise, and so on.

Much the same has applied in the more recent past. One per hundred sorties was the mean in the Indo-Pakistani war of 1971. The average percentage loss suffered by the Israeli air arm was 1.4 in the 1967 war and 1.0 in the 1973, the overall level having been driven up in the former conflict by too free an application to Close Air Support of Magister light strike-trainers and in the latter by the high initial losses. Obversely, the Egyptian rate of loss in the many hundreds of close support sorties launched in desperation in the closing stages of the 1973 conflict is believed to have risen to over 20 per cent. At the climax of the Falklands campaign (21–25 May 1982), one can probably reckon on an attrition rate of 10 to 20 per cent for those Argentinian strike planes that actually entered the British air defence zone.[15] Coalition losses in the Gulf air offensive in 1991 seem to have been below 0.1 per cent. Flat landscapes, the electronic technology gap and superb training will all have contributed, as will the bathetic character of the opposition.

Within this range of experience, the distribution of particular results will have a 'left-handed' skew. In other words, the peak rate of loss will be well towards the lower end of the total spread – maybe 4–8 per cent on the above showing. It is this peak that could rise significantly over the next 20 years or so, the trend potentially being as steep in that time frame as the corresponding ones for weapons platforms deployed on the surface on land or at sea. A rise in loss rates could be especially pronounced with aircraft intruding very fast and low, the only tactic that these days is generally seen as holding sufficient promise of survival over well-defended target areas. Basically, this rise will be because low-flying manned aircraft have little scope left for reducing their time or altitude of transit, assuming those on board are to remain actively involved in the management of attack and evasion. If they are not, why bother with aircrew at all?

In any case, the responsiveness of surface-to-air weapons looks set to improve considerably. Among the factors in this progression will be the entry into service, around the turn of the century, of Self-Initiating Anti-Aircraft Missiles (SIAM). Clearly, the term 'Self-Initiating' is a bit of a misnomer. Nevertheless, a SIAM can proceed independently of all surface-based equipment from the moment of launch; and so may be able to sustain pursuit beyond the original 'line of sight'. With this autonomy also comes reduced susceptibility to certain Electronic Counter-Measures (ECM) In addition, it is possible to use vertical launch tubes. These relatively simple structures may be borne on smallish vehicles and may also be used by missile variants designed to attack surface targets. One overall result will be an anti-aircraft screen too proliferated to be susceptible to adversary suppression.

At the same time, improved computer analysis in tactical radar will make target registration by all surface-to-air weapons (guns as well as SAMs) faster and more assured. Such electronic advance is also allowing interceptor aircraft to engage low-flying aircraft from above with rather more assurance. A further possibility is that the progressive development of lasers will eventually extend to their use as a means of short-range destruction as opposed to mere range-finding and target designation, their prime roles in warfare at present. In 1987, a Pentagon report opined that Soviet 'efforts to develop high-energy air defence laser weapons are likely to lead to ground-based deployments in the early 1990s and to naval developments in the mid-1990s'.[16] By that time, too, the West Germans were working to have in service by 1998 an anti-aircraft tank that could make interceptions (across slant ranges of up to four kilometres) by means of an infra-red beam of several megawatts. Hopefully, the twin problems of target-hold and rapid retargeting, which some of us had assumed would be impossibly acute in such tactical applications, would be resolved by using 'the high-energy beam itself as a sensor element in a closed control loop'.[17] No doubt the first of these prognoses was too alarmist and, by the same token, the second too sanguine. Even so, it is likely that close-range interception by surface-based lasers will be feasible within 20 years.

The impression that comes over is that warplanes engaged in offensive operations will be then be much more vulnerable to well-found defences, except as and where they fire 'stand-off' missiles from outside the defensive screen. In other words, the air dimension will experience the mortifying increase in losses faced for some time by, let us say, tanks coming under direct fire or ships similarly exposed in narrow waters. Contrary to what is widely assumed, however, the economics of construction and peacetime operation may now be trending less adversely for the manned aircraft relative to other weapons genre. For a good 30 years after the Second World War, the progress of the warplane as an arbiter of war was bought at a high price: that is to say, the costs associated with high-performance fighters and the like rose much faster than did those of other major types of weapon. This applied, above all, to the basic cost of procurement; and it is in this same sphere that the divergence is most visibly straightening out at last.

As usual, it is from American sources that the most solid evidence comes. The P-47 Thunderbolt, a long-range air superiority fighter, was mass-produced for a 'flyaway cost' of $100,000 apiece in 1944; the equivalent of $300,000 in 1975. The flyaway cost of an F-14 Tomcat (a machine of similar specification, in Navy service since 1975) was originally $17,000,000, a good 50 times as much. On the basis of such comparisons, a study sponsored by the Brookings Institution in 1974 concluded that it could 'become entirely plausible' that 'the replacement for the F-15 and F-14 that can be anticipated *in the mid-1980s* . . .will cost $100 million or more apiece (plus the cost of research and development and accessories, and an inflationary mark up)'. (Author's italics.)[18]

Had anything of the sort ever some to pass, the debate on tactical aviation would surely have been foreclosed. It would have been absurd to invest in flying machines, a single exotic one of which might cost as much as a thousand light tanks. In fact, however, the phasing out of the F-15 and F-14 is still years away. Meanwhile, the next American tactical fighters to enter service have given a more moderate impression of cost-escalation. This has been especially the case with the F-18 Hornet, an air superiority/strike fighter that began to replace Corsairs and Phantoms in the United States Navy from 1982. Thanks in part to a freer use of low-weight structural materials, the all-up weight was to be but 70 per cent of the F-14's. Likewise, the flyaway unit cost (on a production run of nearly 1,400) was kept down to $16 million at 1975 prices.[19]

There are several reasons for believing that one may here be observing a more generalised trend. Prominent among them are the maximum speeds of manned interceptors. Between 1945 and 1965, these rose from 0.6 to 2.2 on the Mach scale, 1.0 being the speed of sound in air at a given altitude. Yet there they have effectively stayed, thus reining back cost escalation. This is because, if one does exceed Mach 2.2 one soon approaches a threshold of increased heat resistance negotiable only through heavy extra expenditure on development and construction. Besides which, this kind of speed is no longer the most critical in air combat. The acceleration, forwards and sideways, of air-to-air missiles counts for more. So does the alacrity of airborne computers.

To all of which may be added the way other trends are facilitating reductions in overall weights and hence flyaway costs, performance for performance or task for task. Among them are fuel economy, electronic miniaturisation and better structural materials. Nor should one forget how much, in the field of aviation, this multiple revolution can benefit from a 'knock-on' effect. The designs of tactical warplanes are so finely honed that, if the designers do directly save a pound in weight through one of the routes available, they end up saving another five or six pounds derivatively.

No doubt some will argue that, contrary to what has just been said, costs are now being driven upwards again by Stealth technology: the quest for image diminution through a combination of absorbent paints, absorbent structural materials, and rounded surfaces. Certainly, Stealth can be expensive. The F-117A Stealth fighter, in service with the USAF since 1983, has been costing $106 million apiece (c. $50 million at 1975 prices), albeit on a production run limited to 59 machines.

Very likely, however, Stealth has been celebrated altogether too naively, not least in regard to how far it enhances the operational survival of manned aircraft. Shortly before he retired as US Secretary of Defense in 1981, Dr Harold Brown reiterated his view that this innovation might prove the most significant development of the decade.[20] Not long afterwards came a Pentagon claim that, with its 'flying-wing' configuration, the Advanced Technology Bomber will be 'all but impossible' to track, even when at high altitude.[21] What ought to have been borne more firmly in mind throughout is that advances in the computer resolution of radar and infra-red images are bound easily to outstrip any tendencies for those images to diminish through Stealth. Nor should one forget that the extending application of millimetric radar is going to make concealment through Stealth all the harder. Nor that the 'flying-wing', regularly commended as the ideal Stealth configuration for aircraft, must present a very sizeable image when viewed, whether from below or above, at oblique angles, its only being 'stealthy' when seen head-on. Nor that to configure an aeroplane with image reduction too exclusively in mind may be to leave it deficient in other respects. Reportedly, the single-seat F-117A can only reach 600 mph (Mach 0.9), has a limited range, and can carry but one 2,000 pound laser-guided bomb.[22]

In short, the nub of the argument about complete dedication to Stealth in aircraft design is akin to that about hypersonic speed: the penalties can become so high in relation to the prospective benefit that it may be best to forego it. To infer as much in either respect is to strengthen the expectation that cost escalation may be levelling off. Yet it may also confirm the view that an aggregation of several trends may soon lead to a sharp deterioration in the survival prospects for warplanes inside well-defended hostile air space. Stealth and ECM may moderate this tendency but not negate it.

None the less, a major caveat has to be entered. As long as human beings are involved in the operation of air defence, this will be subject to a learning process during the first few hours or even days of actual combat. Nor is there any sign of such an involvement being renounced. All else apart, the thought of critical decisions about war being left entirely to 'robots' is ethically unappealing, throughout the West and beyond. Yet, taken in conjunction with the exposure of manned aircraft to pre-emptive immobilisation on base, the near-inevitability of an initial 'learning curve' lapse in the otherwise increasing potential of anti-aircraft defence has a disturbing implication. This is that warplanes ought now to be characterised more categorically than ever, in the context of theatre war, as the instruments of the massive 'first strike'.

The instability inherent in this attribute in certain situations further argues for more reliance on other genre to help cover the tasks customarily given to warplanes. What has been said already about revolutionary types of artillery shell is one pointer in that direction. Another is a revived thrust towards longer range on the part of tubed artillery. Surface-launched missiles, pilotless aircraft, rotorcraft and satellites in orbit make big contributions already. Nor should one forget that several of these alternatives stand to benefit more than warplanes both from Stealth and from the trend towards weight reduction. This is precisely because they do not raise aloft crew members plus their life-support systems.

Even so, it would be utopian to expect the switch away from warplanes to be rapid. Nor may it be desirable that it be so very complete. Most of what has just been said about air operations hardly applies to the Long Range Combat Aircraft, a future counterpart of those B-29s high above the road to Seoul (see Chapter 11). Besides, tactical warplanes may retain a key defence role, including against tactical missiles. More generally, they may come more into their own on land once a lot of attrition and dislocation has taken place all round: that is to say, towards the end of a main battle. Likewise, they may fare well where terrain is flat and fronts are wide or flanks open, as in much of the Middle East. Certainly, they will when comparative levels of technology and training are well in their favour.

The maritime scene

As was well anticipated by Sir Halford Mackinder over 70 years ago,[23] warplanes are also likely to retain good prospects for surviving and being effective when they are over the open sea.[24,25] Sheer space is one factor. Freedom from topography is probably another. So is the singular value of a monoplane's speed in the hunt for nuclear-driven submarines.

Overall, both the submarine and the aircraft are making headway as against the surface warship. For one thing, a ship is a very discrete target for missiles dispatched through the air from shore batteries, aircraft, other ships or submarines: a state of affairs that can be eased but not negated by electronic jamming and deception. For another, the forward speed of a surface vessel of conventional profile is too constrained, even under calm conditions, by the way the fraction of its propulsive energy that is elegantly but uselessly absorbed causing bow waves, rises ever more steeply as speed through the water is increased. Thus the total drag at 27 knots may be 20 times what it is at 16 knots.[26] Another adverse consequence has been that all sonar is progressively degraded at speeds above 15 knots; and, at the present state of the acoustic art, has become almost useless by the time 28 knots has been reached.[27] Yet some nuclear-propelled submarines may exceed 40 knots when fully submerged. None of this precludes the surface ship's being one element in an anti-submarine task force but it does limit its contribution, at least against nuclear-driven craft.

In every respect, the progress of the underwater detection of submarines (and, one must add, of mines) remains decidedly modest, despite huge research efforts. A very basic constraint is the geometry of beam projection and reflection. Suppose you are operating an active sonar, one that emits pulses of sound energy and times their return after reflection off some object. Then if you double the range to contact, the intensity of the received echo is reduced by 15 parts in 16, regardless of absorption or diffraction en route. In practice, too, sea water absorbs or diffracts sound very readily. Biological noise must also be reckoned with. So, increasingly, must that from other shipping.[28]

True, the interpretation of sound transmissions is benefiting more and more from computer analysis. Even so, the mean range of acoustic detection (either active or passive) has not risen at all dramatically since 1945. Nor do any other approaches promise to transform the surveillance situation. Electromagnetic waves penetrate sea water hardly at all, except at wavelengths far too long (10,000 metres or more) to scan objects as small as submarines.

In Anti-Submarine Warfare (ASW) there is always a dialectic between dispersion and concentration that may be resolved only by ASW platforms that may proceed to an assignment far more swiftly, over extended distances, than even a nuclear-driven submarine. Hovercraft pose problems in regard to all-weather sea-keeping. Nor can the helicopter that a frigate or destroyer will nowadays bear always add enough of an extra dimension. What may have to be considered is a much more determined development of echelons of Long-Range Maritime Patrol (LRMP) four-engined monoplanes, shore-based of necessity. Only such machines have the speed, range and duration required for, say, mid-Atlantic coverage. Moreover, they have considerable individual autonomy in the ASW role, this by dint of their ability to (a) use their radar to search for obtruding periscopes or boats on the surface, (b) drop patterns of sonobuoys to locate fully submerged vessels and (c) use Magnetic Anomaly Detectors, across slant ranges of one or two thousand feet, to pinpoint very precisely boats that are submerged and more or less motionless, perhaps on the seabed. Evidently, there is some correspondence, technically and doctrinally, between this and the notion of the Long-Range Combat Aircraft as an instrument of power projection.

Another challenge for ocean-going navies is the survivability of aircraft carriers, when faced with heavy and sophisticated opposition. In the Second World War, no fewer that 25 were sunk outright, considerably because less attention was given to such damage-limitation features as watertight bulkheads or armoured decks than was the case with other capital ships. In the interim, that omission has been repaired. Now a fleet carrier may be hard to annihilate but still all too easy to cripple. In other words, one missile homing onto a key radar, say, might turn so magnificent a vessel into more of an obligation than an asset.

Nor is it adequate to suggest, as some American analysts are prone to, that the large fleet carrier can still, with a little bit of luck and as the kingpin in a well-balanced task force, be all-conquering: 'a *Nimitz*-class aircraft carrier, its accompanying warships and a US Marine amphibious assault force could have swallowed the Falklands in an afternoon'.[29] A task force optimised, in both composition and density, to ward off aircraft or missiles may be less adapted to the exclusion of submarines or fast patrol boats. In any case, the density of air defence is bound to be low compared with what would be regarded as normal – nay, imperative – by many commanders on land. Nor can concealment and deception within a task force two or three hundred miles across be guaranteed to preserve indefinitely its carriers or anything else. For one thing, the whole integrity of the task force may steadily be broken down, starting with attacks on the early warning ships and aircraft. Besides which, such a spread is not feasible in certain sea areas, including the Gulf.

Nor is any very satisfactory answer to be found by going for more but smaller carriers. The diseconomies of small scale become too apparent. A *Nimitz* is of 91,000 tons displacement and nuclear-driven. It normally bears 80 standard warplanes (mostly F-14s and F-18s) plus six helicopters. But in the Royal Navy, the *Invincible*, at a fifth that displacement, normally bears but five Vertical Take-Off and Landing (VTOL) monoplanes and nine helicopters. Accordingly, preliminary studies within Whitehall have favoured Britain's next generation of carriers being of 30,000 tons, able to carry up to 35 such aircraft.[30] Yet even *Invincible* is a most tempting missile or torpedo target, twice the size of British heavy cruisers of the Second World War.

What a satisfactory response might have to involve then is more recourse to land-basing in the provision of maritime air cover, this for strike-fighters as well as for larger machines. Another thing it might involve is the carrier with its aircraft giving way to smaller vessels armed with cruise missiles, weapons that require little in the way of servicing or launch facilities. Other technical changes now in train are placing the small ship at less of a disadvantage in various ways. Novel hull designs are easier to apply to it. In other respects, too, sea-keeping is less of a problem these days. Then again, electronic miniaturisation counts for a lot at sea, just as it does in the air. Meanwhile, the cruise missile will tend also to displace the traditional turret-mounted gun.

It may, in fact, be very important for the West that, as strategic arms control broadens out (see Chapter 12), sea-launched cruise missiles are a line of development that is still kept open. More generally, indeed, technological change should be allowed to shape arms control as well as *vice versa*. A current instance is the Anti-Tectical Ballistic Missile (ATBM). Over the last 30 years a fair amount of progress towards this capability has been made by upgrading Surface-to-Air Missiles (SAMs) designed to combat aircraft. Now, however, the emphasis is shifting towards the development of ATBMs in their own right. A direct challenge is thus presented to the Anti-Ballistic Missile (ABM) treaty of 1972 in anything like its present rendering.

Rightly or wrongly, everyone has thus far informally accepted that very short-range ATBMs are just as free from the treaty's constraints as anti-missile gunnery.[31] But for bigger ATBMs, awkward questions are seen to be raised by Articles V, VI and IX of the Treaty. The fifth Article rules out both ABM launcher mobility and preparations to fire 'more than one ABM interceptor at a time from each launcher'. The sixth forbids the upgrading to ABM status of other missiles, launchers or radars, while confining the deployment of ABM radars to the peripheries of the respective national territories. Under Article IX, 'each party undertakes not to transfer to other States, and not to deploy outside its national territory, ABM systems or their components limited by this treaty'. Agreed Statement G (one of the several initialled the same day as the main text) explains that Article IX blocks the provision 'to other States of technical descriptions or blueprints specially worked out for the construction of ABM systems and their components limited by the Treaty'. True, the Preamble stressed that the Treaty's prime aim was to help curb the strategic arms race. Ever since then, however, technical dexterity has blurred more and more the distinction between 'strategic' and 'tactical', just as it has with manned warplanes.[32]

In the American public debate these last few years, many have rallied round the existing ABM Treaty as being, in their view, a singular arms control achievement and a vital bulwark against the Strategic Defense Initiative. Their concern has been to preserve the regime of Mutual Assured Destruction (MAD) established in the strategic nuclear relationship between the two superpowers during the late 1960s. Graceless though MAD may be, it has come to be seen by many liberals as preferable to an indefinite continuation of the arms race at that level. What must now be a subject for urgent discussion, however, is whether a modification of the ABM Treaty might not be a precondition for the preservation of MAD (see Chapter 12).

6

Crisis through Climate

The Greenhouse mechanism

THE 'COLD WAR' is over, or at any rate much constrained. It is being replaced by a 'warm war' in which general pressure on the environment is led by the 'greenhouse effect'. A strategy for planetary response may be easier to formulate if all concerned address the geophysics. After all, any policy choice is likely to rest on physical and political predictions that completely interweave.

Essentially, 'greenhouse' is caused by the interaction between two well-established principles. One of them concerns the relationship between the surface temperature of a body (heavenly or otherwise) and the wavelength at which its profile of radiation peaks. The ultimate measure of temperature is afforded by the Kelvin scale, which is calibrated in degrees equivalent to those of Centigrade but which takes as 'zero' what would be rated as minus 273 on the Centigrade scale. That value is almost exactly what is calculated to be the point of absolute cold, the point at which all heat energy has been drained from a substance.

Obviously, surfaces vary in their intrinsic coloration. That apart, however, the peak wavelength of the heat and light radiating from a surface is inversely proportional to its temperature in degrees Kelvin. So, since the mean temperature of the Earth's surface is just under 290K and that of the Sun's 6,000K, the former has a peak wavelength some 20 to 21 times that of the latter – close to 10,000 nanometres(nm) or billionths of a metre – as opposed to 485.

The second tenet derives from the truism that the molecular structure of any particular gas is unique to it. For what this further means is that every gas has characteristic wavelengths at which it will absorb electromagnetic radiation. Take three atmospheric gases, each of them acknowledged to have 'greenhouse' properties. Water vapour has absorption peaks in or near the millimetric range and again in several places between 6,300 and 940nm. Ozone at low altitude absorbs most strongly at 9,600nm, while carbon dioxide does so at 15,000nm. In other words, they are all liable to block the relatively long-wave radiation out from the Earth more than they do the much shorter waves coming in from the Sun. In order to preserve equilibrium, in the presence of extra greenhouse gases, the Earth's temperature is bound to rise. A rise of two degrees, say, would shorten by about 65nm the peak wavelength at which the surface of the Earth radiates; and would boost the volume of heat emitted from that surface by about 1.3 per cent.

Water vapour has tended not to be included in standard projections of the concentration of greenhouse gases. This is apparently because (a) alterations in its incidence will be a consequence of greenhouse warming as well as a cause of it, and (b) these alterations are hard to predict. At present about 60 per cent of the greenhouse effect, other than from water vapour, is being caused by extra carbon dioxide (from fuel combustion and deforestation). However, this proportion is slowly declining. Already methane, largely from herds of cattle and fields of rice, contributes 30 per cent. The other tenth comes mainly from the chlorofluorocarbons (CFCs), nitrous oxide (N_2O) and low-altitude ozone (O_3), to place them in descending order of current importance. The CFCs, in particular, are highly greenhouse efficient, molecule for molecule.

The average level of carbon dioxide in the atmosphere has risen from perhaps 280 parts per million (ppm) in 1850 to 315 in 1958 (the year that systematic globe-related monitoring began) and 350 in 1988. The incidence of methane has risen from 0.85ppm in 1850 to 1.32 in 1958 and 1.70 in 1988.[1] Lately, the convention has been to ask what a doubling of the amount of greenhouse gas in the atmosphere would mean, the calculation of doubling being effected through the conversion to their effective equivalent in carbon dioxide of the quantities of the other gases involved. Clearly, this focusing on a two-fold increase has been altogether too narrow and exclusive, seeing that it can hardly constitute any kind of threshold. The greenhouse effect would be evident before it was reached and progressively more so afterwards.

But to proceed on this basis for the moment, one can observe how, as regards the overall temperature rise, computer modelling has led to the emergence in recent years of a fair measure of consensus along the following lines. In the absence of corrective action, a two-fold increase in the 'carbon dioxide equivalent' will be registered sometime around 2030 or 2040. The result is likely to be a concurrent rise in global mean air temperature at the Earth's surface of perhaps two or three degrees Kelvin. This will inevitably be followed by a further one degree over the ensuing half century or so, even without any more additions of greenhouse gas,

Nor will such rises take place evenly, one latitude as against another. This is chiefly because polar ice acts as its own coolant. It does so by reflecting perhaps as much as 85 to 90 per cent of the incident sunlight. This reflectivity (alias 'albedo') compares with an average of 15 per cent for the whole planetary surface. Therefore, when an ice field is extending, this factor will tend to accelerate the extension and thus encourage still more cooling. If, on the other hand, the ice field has begun to shrink, the progressive removal of so reflective a surface will speed the warming up. Either way, it is the 'ice-albedo' positive feedback. Some further warming or cooling, albeit local and transitory, will come from the 'latent heat' released by ice as it melts or absorbed as it freezes.

The effect on the south polar zone is hard to predict but may be delayed, given that Antarctica itself is virtually one great plateau of rock and ice several kilometres high[2], the repository of close to 90 per cent of all the ice currently to be found on this planet. The ambience of the North Pole, on the other hand, is mainly maritime pack ice a very few metres thick, and so is bound to be highly responsive in the manner just described. Accordingly, a mean global warming of two or three degrees, say, would be likely to involve a rise of five or six degrees in high northern latitudes as against less than one near the Equator.

The consequences of this differential may be serious, and not just for the Arctic. A key determinant of climate alteration in the northern hemisphere or, indeed, the southern is any change in the temperature contrast between the Equator and the Pole. At present, the North Pole is an average of 68° cooler than the Equator in deep midwinter and 32° in high summer. The global circulation of the atmosphere and, of course, the oceans ultimately depends on the thermal drive provided by these temperature gradients. Any reduction of the differences will eventually diminish this drive and hence circulatory vigour, especially in the atmosphere. Continental drought in temperate latitudes will be one serious consequence, not least in parts of the Eurasian heartland. Another may be more erraticism in the weather, season by season, of the temperate zone as a whole, as a weaker circulation exercises less overriding control.

Another general result of differential warming may be the gradual and irregular migration towards the respective poles of the boundaries of the main climatic zones. One thinks in particular of those which define the latitude limits of the sub-tropical belts of air pressure: the zones that are characterised by anticyclonic winds, descending air, blue skies, and dry (often desert) landscapes. The impression one gets is that so long as the decrease of gradient remains small this mechanism may count for more than the weakening of circulation just referred to. As the decrease gets greater, the reverse may apply. One complication is that circulatory patterns, air and sea, that have come under stress may at some point realign abruptly. For one thing, the continents will warm more readily than the oceans.

The most comprehensive and up-to-date assessment of the climate prospect to date is that afforded in June 1990 with the submission to the UN Intergovernmental Panel on Climatic Change (IPCC) of the report of its Working Group 1. This stresses that atmospheric concentrations of certain of the greenhouse gases (carbon dioxide, nitrous oxide and the CFCs) adjust only slowly to changes in emission rates. This is because individual molecules tend to dwell a long time in the atmosphere before being reabsorbed in one way or another. So to stabilise their concentrations even at today's levels within the next few decades would mean early reductions of over 60 per cent in the emissions due to human enterprise. For methane, the corresponding decrease need only be 15 to 20 per cent.

If all current trends were allowed to continue, says IPCC, the rate of increase of global mean temperature into the next century would most likely be 0.3°C per decade, meaning a one degree rise by 2025 and three degrees by the year 2100. Only with the most radical intervention in various spheres of economic activity might this trend be reduced to something close to 0.1°C per decade.

What makes the advice received yet more disturbing, however, is the acknowledged range of uncertainty. The mean change of temperature could, in fact, be anything from 0.2 to 0.5° per decade.[3] Were the latter sustained, the rise in high northern latitudes by 2100 could be 10 degrees. That would be a change in the upwards direction about as great, at regional level, as sufficed the other way to produce the Ice Age glaciation that reached its maximum extent 18,000 years ago.

A subject for debate is whether the projection of a relatively steady rise in temperature over the next century can ring at all true. Unless improvements in energy efficiency were very marked and sustained, one might expect the concentration of greenhouse gases to rise ever faster for a while, much as they have of late; and also temperature rise to accelerate correspondingly. On the other hand, certain of the contributory factors will eventually count for less, even in the absence of a deliberate 'anti-greenhouse' strategy. The explosion of the world's population should level out through the middle of the next century, thus slowing the growth in energy demand. The release of carbon dioxide through the destruction of the rain forests will also ease off if, come roughly the same time, there is little left to destroy. By that time, in any case, absorption on the waveband in question will be so complete that extra carbon dioxide will make little difference.

In the meantime, however, certain ramifications of global warming could further accelerate it, a positive feedback effect. The sea ice of the West Antarctic might quite suddenly calve away and melt. Another possibility much discussed is the gradual escape of the large reserves of methane at present entrapped in the Arctic tundra. This would come about through the melting of the permafrost (*ie* peaty soil, permanently frozen at depth) that has kept them locked in so securely since the last glaciation.

Curiously absent from the recent debate has been the possibility that the sheer volume of energy pumped out by mankind's economic activities will in itself be enough to cause appreciable warming at global level, irrespective of any changes in the chemical composition of the atmosphere. Over the least 20 to 30 years, various analysts, with Professor Budyko of the Soviet Union well to the fore, have done projections of this 'direct thermal pollution'.[4] As a first approximation, one can say something like this. As of today, the heat flux from mankind's thermal activities is one part in 5,000 of that from the Sun. Let us assume, not unreasonably on present showing, that the former output will grow at an average of two per cent per annum which means a doubling every 35 years. Then after a century the fraction would be about one part in 600. The effect could be to increase the temperature of the Earth's lower atmosphere by something approaching that proportion on the Kelvin scale: that is to say, by close to half a degree. That could prove a most unwelcome increment to the change being wrought by the greenhouse effect.

A cardinal reason why all climatic change has to be viewed with unease is that the biggest disturbance is liable to be that to rainfall patterns. One explanation lies in the diminished thermal drive anticipated above; and another in the likelihood that successive climatic belts will migrate towards their respective Poles as warming proceeds. At all events, no one ought to be surprised. After all, if you take the usual variations in weather, day to day or year to year, in any part of the world, the fluctuations in precipitation are much greater proportionally than are those of temperature, almost irrespective of how the latter is expressed.

To all of which must also be added the derivative threat of a rise in Mean Sea Level (MSL) as ice melts and as ocean water thermally expands. A complication here is that the thermal expansion of water rises ever more dramatically with temperature. It is only 0.53 parts in 10,000 per degree between 5 and 10°C (278 and 283 Kelvin) but no less than 3.02 between 20 and 40. Therefore the expansive effect of any oceanic warming may be the greater the less evenly that warming is distributed at depth. To uncertainties on this score must be added those about ice cap melt under given greenhouse conditions. Nevertheless, a mean rise in MSL globally of somewhere between 25 and 40 centimetres is the current prospect between 1985 and 2025, to be followed by as much again by 2060.

In many coastal locations, of course, the trend will be either constrained or reinforced by shifts, upwards or downwards respectively, of the land mass in question. Thus the south-east coast of England has been sinking isostatically at a rate of 20 centimetres every 40 years. Now Bangkok may be sinking at nearly 10cm a decade due to overuse of groundwater. A net MSL rise of half a metre or more would usually place a troublesome extra strain on the systems of embankments installed to protect low-lying and well-populated coastal areas. A rise of two metres, say, would require drastic reconstruction. Tendencies towards more freakish weather would aggravate the dangers.[5]

A slow awakening

How slowly the great majority of atmospheric physicists awoke to the challenge posed by 'greenhouse' affords a sobering example of the inertia professional communities all too frequently display in the face of changing circumstances. Intimations that there might be a problem can actually be traced back into the very infancy of meteorology and climatology as synoptic disciplines. Thus it was not until 1806 that Admiral Sir Francis Beaufort of the Royal Navy devised his famous scale for estimating wind velocity on the basis of its visible effects. But it was in 1802 that a British astronomer, W. H. Wollaston, found that the Sun's spectrum has dark absorption lines at certain wavelengths, lines that proved also to be distinctly characteristic of hydrogen and helium. From which the inference could be safely drawn that these were the elements of which the Sun and its gaseous envelope are composed. This discovery was followed up and made more familiar by Joseph von Fraunhofer (1787–1826), a Munich optician and amateur astronomer. In 1815, he produced a map of the solar spectrum with no fewer than 324 lines on it.

If the gases in this solar ambience could be known by their Fraunhofer lines, the presumption was that all other gases have absorption patterns that are similarly characteristic at a given intensity of radiation. In 1827, the celebrated French mathematician, Jean-Baptiste Fourier, pointed out that air seems to act like the glass cover of a box. Further experiments during the 19th Century identified carbon dioxide and water vapour as the two gases largely responsible for this phenomenon, and prompted episodic speculation that variations in their atmospheric concentration might account for ice ages and other phases of climate alteration. In 1896, a Swedish chemist, Svante Arrhenius, surmised that industrial pollution might, in the course of a century or two, double the amount of carbon dioxide in the atmosphere and so raise the global temperature by, he reckoned, 5°C.[6] His contribution was part of a brief flurry of interest, much in line with the perception of frontiers closing everywhere, that was so evident in literature and politics towards the turn of the century.

Then interest waned again. Indeed, the received wisdom eventually became that progressive changes in the Earth's own orbit would ensure the continuation of a natural cooling trend. Nigel Calder, a distinguished scientific journalist, suggested in 1974 that there is 'a virtual certainty of the next ice age starting sometime in the next 2,000 years. Then the odds are only 20–1 against its beginning in the next 100 years'.[7] Much the same was generally said at a conference held in July 1979 at the University of East Anglia, a campus from which much of the apprehension about cooling had lately stemmed. Likewise, in 1977, the then Director of the UK's Meteorological Office (himself a cloud physicist of considerable distinction) insisted that much more research was needed to predict 'the marginal effects of man's intervention in climate', effects that 'may well be masked by natural variation'. He also anticipated that the threat to stratospheric ozone from CFC and other chemicals would prove to 'have been greatly exaggerated'.[8]

But over the previous decade or so the weight of informed opinion worldwide had gradually swung towards the greenhouse thesis. One influence was the evidence coming in from the station for the monitoring of atmospheric carbon dioxide established at Mauna Loa in Hawaii at the time of the International Geophysical Year in 1957–58, this largely thanks to the active concern of two American geophysicists, Roger Revelle and David Keeling. Another such station set up at the South Pole was yielding similar results. A more general influence may have been the analogy with Venus. Probes to that planet (and especially the Venera soft landings by the USSR from 1967) had indicated that carbon dioxide, observed in 1932 to be abundant in the Venusian sky, comprised no less than 94 per cent of what was a very dense planetary atmosphere. Moreover, surface temperatures reached as high as 800K due to a 'runaway greenhouse effect'. As temperatures rose, the rocks lost their ability to take up atmospheric carbon dioxide and form solid deposits of carbonate. This particular mechanism is not now at work on Earth. Nevertheless the moral that climatic instabilities may be self-reinforcing instead of self-limiting is still worth our taking on board.

The reasons why

It is instructive to ponder how it was that the climatological-cum-meteorological fraternity was quite so slow, in the great majority of cases, to recognise the import of something as axiomatic as greenhouse warming now appears to be. It may caution other professional communities – from economists to hydrologists to military strategists to political philosophers – against being insufficiently responsive to the threat posed by environmental disturbance to our peace and general well-being. It may also act as a corrective to modish insinuations that the said fraternity of climatologists and meteorologists grabbed the greenhouse hypothesis quite uncritically because it was apocalyptic enough to attract research funding; and that this fraternal consensus is now resorting to 'McCarthyism' to crush alternative viewpoints.[9] After the Wall Street crash of 1929, the great Cambridge economist, John Maynard Keynes, was asked if a 'bankers' ramp' had been at work. He replied that we would all have been better off if it had. So today we might all be better of if 'greenhouse' had been endorsed more firmly a lot earlier.

In broad terms, the development of a sufficient sense of urgency about greenhouse was retarded by the three reactions natural scientists so often display in such circumstances. They see things too deductively, too much in isolation. They are almost obsessively reluctant to rush to professional judgements. They are naive about the ability of politicians to adjust.

More specific inclinations also played a part. Thanks to the exigencies of two world wars and to the explosive growth of civil aviation since, the world of workaday atmospheric science came to be heavily dominated by aviation meteorologists. But there preference was to treat climate as if it were an immutable norm against which weather could be judged: a predilection closely akin, in fact, to the one that most historians still have. Something very similar is also to be discerned among corporate planners in general and hydrologists in particular. With them, it takes the form of a disinclination to have their own decisions swayed by greenhouse predictions until such time as the latter have total assurance attaching to them.

To which one is tempted to add that, at the academic level in meteorology, there has traditionally been less of a focus than might reasonably have been hoped for on the study of prediction over whatever time scale: on the identification of aims and the improvement of methods. It may sound a harsh and even bizarre judgement but can be well confirmed by a scan of the professional journals. Still, this blind spot may be dissolving now that computer-driven modelling is bringing a more dynamic analysis to bear on the past and the present as well as on the near and distant future. A global programme devised to analyse this month's weather may serve as an entrée to prognoses of long-term climatic change. All you have to do, in principle at least, is change the variables.

Undoubtedly, a further distraction was that the first result of the upsurge of interest in climatic change in the 1960s was to make those concerned more conscious not of warming through human intervention but of a natural trend towards cooling. The latter seemed the more in line with contemporary experience, not to mention ancestral memories of the Ice Age. Moreover, it was already the subject of a rich body of research material.

Natural variability

Well understood to be of basic importance were the variations in the Earth's inclination and orbit that extend in overlapping cycles across tens of thousands of years. A correlation between these cycles and climate change was first explored over a hundred years ago. Then during the first four decades of this century, a painstaking review of the evidence across 600,000 years was carried out by a Serbian scientist, Milutin Milankovitch. A crucial phase in his labours was the time he spent at the Hungarian Academy of Sciences, on parole as a prisoner of war of Austria-Hungary.

Milankovitch died convinced that he had unravelled the whole truth of the matter. None the less, his findings have had to be modified, particularly to feed into the equations collateral fluctuations in the level of atmospheric carbon dioxide that are associated with variations in the amount of biomass (*ie* living material) distributed across the surface of the Earth. All the same, there remains little doubt that for centuries ahead (as for centuries past) the main natural trend must continue to be towards cooling. This is because the Milankovitch cycles favour icefield expansion (especially in northern high latitudes) as the summer-winter contrast diminishes. The connection discerned is that cooler summers mean less melting of the ice while warmer winters, being moister, yield more snowfall.

Not that these convolutions are the only natural influences on our terrestrial climate. Among the others can be the blasting to high altitudes by volcanic eruption of a fine and chilling dust. Not very long ago, climatologists in China were expressly reluctant to accept that warming had become the dominant problem. Some of them suggested that increased volcanic activity, since 1960 or thereabouts, has kept cooling at the top of the global agenda.[10] However, individual eruptions rarely leave much dust in suspension for more than two or three years. Furthermore, the presumption that we have now entered an era of vulcanism may be more like the reverse of the truth. Several major eruptions (*eg* El Chichun in Mexico in 1982) took place early in the 1980s. After such a spell, things usually go quiet for several decades. The best guess that one might make is that the first half of the next century may be volcanically more active than the first three-quarters of this, simply because the latter was exceptionally tranquil, subsequent to the great Caribbean explosions of May 1902 – La Soufrière, then Mount Pelée, each in the Lesser Antilles.

Then there is the reality that the 'solar constant' is rather inconstant. To be a little more explanatory, the amount of radiation emitted by the Sun fluctuates from Earth-day to Earth-day, year to year, and æon to æon, in accordance with a series of patterns, some or all of which will be more or less cyclical. A change over time of one per cent, say, in this radiation flux could probably alter by some two degrees the mean temperature on the Earth's surface.

For many centuries, of course, people have observed one such solar cycle, the sunspot one which peaks every eleven years, give or take a year or two. At present we are passing through or have just passed through an exceptionally pronounced peak, such as occurs every two to four cycles. However, the connotations of sunspot peaks for terrestrial weather are complex and problematic. This is essentially because, although sunspots are a collective manifestation of an increase in solar activity, the surface of each individual one is relatively cool and dark, a sunspot being essentially a vortex of plasma that is ascending, expanding and cooling. Thus within a few months of NASA's starting to orbit its *Solar Max* unmanned surveillance satellite in 1980, a solar radiation dip of 0.23 per cent was observed by it during sunspot transits. There may well be something in a Soviet contention that sunspots accentuate all weather systems, causing more searing droughts yet more drenching floods.

At all events, short-term solar irregularity may become part of the 'noise' that obscures any longer term trends in the Earth's climate. Cycles can also be observed in the behaviour of the Earth's atmosphere and oceans, these typically being of several years' duration. Unfortunately, however, such cycles are never regular enough to allow of prediction through extrapolation. Nor are they sufficiently understood to allow of prediction by more theoretical means. This makes it hard to abstract such influences from the record in order to assess better the greenhouse tendency.

The most noted among various long-distance interactions (the so-called 'teleconnections') is the Southern Oscillation, the tendency for air pressure fluctuations in a broad zone around Darwin to vary inversely with those in another such zone round Tahiti. It is a seasonal phenomenon which closely correlates with the El Niño surges of warm water along the equatorial Pacific and into the cold ocean current off Peru. These surges, averagely every several years, tend to be driven by rises in sea surface temperature in the West Central Pacific, an area in which a rise of even half a degree may trigger a significant increase in convective shower activity or typhoon genesis in the atmosphere above. That, in its turn may deny water to the Asian monsoon.[11] There may also be other El Niño linkages, including the prevalence of blocking anticyclones (belts of high pressure and dry weather) in high latitudes.[12]

In 1983, 1987 and 1988, the El Niño was strong and is seen, in fact, as a factor in the global warmth of each year. But nobody yet known the exact causal linkage nor, indeed, how long the whole EL Niño-Southern Oscillation (ENSO) mechanism would survive sustained greenhouse warming. There is still a lack of 'operational-coupled ocean-atmosphere models for prediction of phenomena such as El Niño and the Southern Oscillation'.[13]

Yet from all this one may draw an inference that is all the more alarming. A fairly steady natural trend towards global cooling may have retarded too long the onset of accelerating warming as the man-induced greenhouse effect takes command. Even now, indeed, this onset can still be masked somewhat by shorter-term natural fluctuations. We might therefore find that the shock that greenhouse eventually administers to the world economy may be all the more acute for having been delayed.

The need for refinement

While recognising this possibility, however, one has also to take account of legitimate doubts about whether greenhouse really is a looming menace. One of them is whether enough allowance has been made for urbanisation when comparing temperature records across a century or so. The point is that in areas like New Jersey or the Thames Valley, say, observatories that once were set in quiet countryside have now been encompassed by energy-rich suburbia, a change which may well connote an extra degree or two of local warming. Evidently, the sceptics see this as outweighing a trend whereby the recording thermometers have become better shielded and ventilated, thereby curbing tendencies to overheat. In fact though, they could well be mistaken here, seeing that it was only around the turn of this century that one got a tolerable measure of international accord about observational standards.[14]

Meanwhile, they scorn climatic models as allegedly inclined to 'predict' warming over, say, the last 150 years maybe several times greater than what we believe has actually occurred. They see the existing programmes as very arbitrary in their treatment of (a) the role of convection in reducing the differential as between surface warming and what may be stratospheric cooling or (b) cloud tops composed of water droplets which reflect the sun's rays efficiently as against those composed of ice crystals, which are strongly greenhouse. They always ask why there was global cooling between 1940 and 1965, a time when the level of greenhouse gases must have been rising almost every year.[15,16]

What is called for to resolve such doubts is a combination of a much richer data base and more elaborate computers. Not least do we need to know far more about the role of the oceans in all this. They bear in solution some 50 times as much carbon as the atmosphere does in gaseous form. They are possessed of hundreds of times more heat energy than is the air above. They interact globally and endlessly with the air. Yet still we plumb their depths in but a piecemeal fashion. Only recently was it realised, for instance, that on the floor of the Denmark Strait there is a continuous cascade of water plunging nearly four times as far as does any waterfall on land, with a throughput 400 times as great.[17]

The primary route to a comprehensive knowledge of the state of the sea surface and of the atmosphere lies in surveillance by orbital satellites. The first weather satellite – Tiros 1 – was placed in orbit by the USA in 1960, a year before the first one for military reconnaissance. In the ensuing decade, progress in data-handling kept pace with ever bigger and more varied inputs. By 1969, the World Weather Watch had begun, as had the systematic tracking by this means of Atlantic hurricanes. Synoptic and definitive coverage of temperatures in the lower atmosphere is deemed to have started with the launch of the Tiros N series in 1979. Lately an analysis of the data for the first decade (1979–88) has been published. Its findings highlight temporary fluctuations, not insistent trends:

> The Northern and Southern hemisphere trends follow each other for the slower international trends but often oppose each other on monthly to seasonal time scales. The warmest years, in decreasing order were 1987, 1988, 1983 and 1980. There is no obvious long-term trend, and anomalies during the first five years nearly balance those during the last five years ... During the 1983 El Niño Southern Oscillation, transfer of heat from record-setting sea-surface temperatures in the eastern Pacific to the atmosphere caused major changes that impacted weather conditions worldwide ... caused globally averaged temperatures to rise more in several months than what is expected within several decades if enhanced greenhouse warming is occurring.[18]

But these cautionary comments by no means invalidate the greenhouse hypothesis. All else apart, this analysis did not incorporate the data for 1990, now established as the warmest year on record. Besides, the said hypothesis ultimately rests four-square on the observable and increasing accumulation within the atmosphere of gases with radiative properties that are distinctive and germane. What nobody would deny, however, is the need for more information more evenly spread, handled by computers that are a lot more powerful and with much more sophisticated programmes.

Working Group 1 of the Intergovernmental Panel on Climatic Change (IPCC) drew attention to a number of other subject areas in which our state of knowledge was very deficient.[19] More understanding of 'the function of ecosystems in climate is important', starting with 'better global observations of the nature and extent of vegetation and soils' [11.2.5]. Knowledge of global precipitation and evaporation is imprecise; and up to a half of 'the water run-off from the continents to the oceans takes place as flow in small ungauged coastal rivers or underground' [11.6]. Yet 'experiments with many climate models have underlined the sensitivity of the climate to surface hydrology'.[20] Then again, at least ten more years of data are required in order to quantify the inter-annual variability of cloud systems, horizontally and vertically.

Meanwhile, an adequately precise 'assessment of the ocean's role in sequestering carbon dioxide from the atmosphere' [11.2] will have to wait upon the progress this decade of the international Joint Global Ocean Floor Study, a pilot scheme for which was launched in 1989. This sequestration has biological and physical dimensions; and there is the particular complication that warming of the ocean surface may actually depress the absorption of carbon dioxide, through its negative effect on plankton generation.

Not that insufficient information has been the only barrier to progress. The computers so far available are unable to cope without resort to gross over-simplification even when the actual data would allow of something more intricate and subtle. Data of one kind or another from an area the size of the British Isles, say, may be smoothed out to be recorded at a single point on a grid network. Likewise, assumptions that are too arbitrary and non-dynamic are regularly made about cloud formation and development. So far, too, the modelling has been very largely concerned with making a straight comparison between the situation today and that at some time in the future, most probably the time expected to witness a doubling of the carbon dioxide equivalent. It would be sounder to work through the sequence: a motion picture rather than a couple of stills.

Anticipating a combination of more information and more computing power, IPCC Working Party 1 anticipated the availability by the year 2000 of quite refined General Circulation Models (GCMs), incorporating the geophysics of the oceans as well as the atmosphere. Then by the year 2008 or thereabouts, the ecological dimension will hopefully be embraced satisfactorily.

Within a given set of parameters, achieving more sophistication in this way usually moderates the prediction of change, this by taking due account of negative (*ie* corrective) feedback mechanisms. On the other hand, fuller recognition of the threat of eventual 'non-linear' changes (the melting of the permafrost and so on) may work the other way long-term. Furthermore, the whole IPCC approach is to ignore other forms of pollution. Yet such influences as acid rain or acidified oceans may seriously vitiate the ability of many life forms, from plankton to pine trees, to take excess carbon dioxide out of the atmosphere.

Constructive response

What then of the formulation of a response to greenhouse within the context of a new grand strategy, planetary and geopolitical? We have to be talking about a 'twin-track' approach that (a) reduces and delays the onset of the climate crisis, and (b) suitably adjusts to it. The former thrust may require, among other things, new modes of influence upon nation-states by an international community in pursuance of such aims as energy economy. However, the sheer novelty of such a response may delay its implementation awhile. In the meantime, national governments are sure to be reluctant to push irksome adaptation to a threat that is still surrounded by uncertainties. Thus John Sununu, the present White House chief of staff, is brutally explicit in his opposition, at the present state of knowledge, to any restrictions on carbon emissions liable to cause economic pain.[21]

Often discussion of greenhouse seems geared to the assumption that, although now we see through a glass, darkly, come the turn of the century all will be revealed in true millennial fashion. My suspicion is that, through the year 2010, a debate will be continuing about the rate of global warming, the outer limits then being set between 0.15 and 0.35 degrees a decade. The chief imponderable may then be human behaviour, both generally in regard to population growth and living standards and more specifically in relation to anti-greenhouse measures.

Anybody concerned for international security might do well to work on the basis that the actuality will be near to the top of that spread, a rate of change several times faster than during any relevant historical comparison. The ultimate danger is that, if the impending era of greenhouse is not anticipated in a positive fashion, the eventual reaction to it will tend to be negative and even irrational, much as the great slump of 1929 led across much of the world (the United States and Scandinavia being the most creditable exceptions) to the rise of fascism rather than to some more constructive response. It is the risk that much the same could happen again that will make greenhouse a central part of the problem of peace or war.

7

Climate in History

As WE struggle to formulate a grand strategy appropriate to this new
Renaissance and Reformation, useful perspectives may be gleaned
from the impact of climate change historically. Not that assessment
can ever be easy. All else apart, it is hard to judge when what otherwise would be seen as the accustomed variability of the weather year
by year comes to represent an underlying alteration.

Weather and war

This point bears on particular battles or campaigning seasons.
Take the *kamikaze* 'divine wind' that in August 1281 struck the
Mongol expedition against Japan. This great storm came more or
less in the middle of what would still be seen as the normal typhoon
season there. All the same, the totality of the devastation (as confirmed by marine archaeology as well as contemporary records) was
extraordinary, seeing that the invasion fleet was by then marshalled
inside two anchorages, at least one of which, Imari, should have
afforded an exceptional measure of natural protection.[1] As is noted
below, the 13th Century was a stormy one in the North Sea as a
'climatic optimum' peaked out. Maybe it was a time, too, of more
vigorous typhoon activity in Japanese waters, thanks to the warmth
of the seas to the south.

The Armada launched by Spain against England in 1588 had to
contend with weather that all contemporaries seem agreed was abnormally severe. The mainly southerly gales disorganised the fleet in
the 'narrow seas' and then obliged it to run for home round Scotland.
Of the 130 ships that had set out, only five were to fall directly to
English action. But another 50 were subsequently lost in storms. The

period 1565 to 1600 was one in which a prolonged cooling trend had resumed in north-west Europe, following a remission earlier in the century. A feature of this resumption is likely to have been a steepening of the thermal gradient that pitches downwards from, say, the latitude of the Azores towards that of southern Greenland. Such a tendency could give rise to deep storm centres that would migrate north-east across the seaboard of north-west Europe. Two further armadas, in 1596 and 1597, were early aborted by gales.[2]

Napoleon's invasion of Russia is, of course, the most famous example of a campaign turned into a disaster by an abnormally early and bleak winter, again part of a renewal of regional and global cooling. Similarly, three severe winters in a row in Europe marked a global return to cooler conditions from 1940. The winter of 1939–40 wreaked havoc with the men and machines of a huge Soviet army trying to subdue Finland. That of 1941–42, described as Russia's worst for a century, badly scarred a German army trying to close in on Moscow and Leningrad.

Another dramatic example of weather bucking the pre-existing trend, thereby presenting an awesome challenge, concerns the Normandy landings of June 1944. The date originally scheduled as D-Day was 5 June, with the 6th as the immediate alternative. The next period of suitably low tides was the 17th and 18th of the month. Unfortunately, the weather in the first week of June did not bring the several days of calm that long-term averages had led one to hope for in the English Channel then. But late on Sunday, 4 June, the chief meteorological officer on General Eisenhower's staff was able to confirm that the weather would be good enough on the Tuesday to allow of the landings and, notwithstanding 'the shake-up in the whole weather situation we are going through', things would be bearable the rest of that week.[3] The German meteorological service, operating with much less information to westward, had failed to recognise the developing ridge of high pressure that was to produce the Tuesday easement. Accordingly, the invasion alert had been relaxed, with Field Marshal Rommel himself leaving briefly for Germany. What is more, the record shows that a postponement to the 17–18 June could have turned out very badly. On the 17th, things did seem to be set fair for several days. But then 19–22 June saw the most protracted Channel storm in that season for decades. As it was, the damage and dislocation along the beaches were bad enough. With a postponed operation only two or three days ashore by then, things could have been far worse.[4]

Just what the connection was between the invasion weather and the climate trend is not clear. But the general point can still be taken. Instabilities in climate may generate weather extremes; and these extremes may do more than military historians always appreciate to shape the fortunes of war, not least when forecasters are misled by pre-existing norms. Napoleon's invasion of Russia was planned on advice from Marquis Pierre Laplace, a brilliant astronomer and mathematician, to the effect that the Russian winter 'really' began in January whereas, in 1812–13, it began in deadly earnest in December.[5] In the run-up to Operation Barbarossa, Hitler's invasion of the USSR, the German meteorological service used long-term averages along with the particular analogues of seasonal fluctuation to judge the prospects of securing Moscow before bad weather set in. After a sharp internal debate, their official advice became that two cold winters in a row presaged a mild one immediately ahead. That judgement proved disastrous.

In certain respects (*eg* icing in cloud and surveillance through cloud) weather bears on military operations much less than it did half a century ago. But it would be wrong to discount it entirely. Take the sophisticated modes of tactical aviation operated by the United States in central Europe. US army commanders were warned in a 1976 doctrinal manual to 'expect a one-third degradation in Close Air Support (CAS) missions during the December–February timeframe.[6] Furthermore, the usual combination of much data and powerful computing nowadays permits regional forecasting 10 to 12 days ahead even in theatres as volatile weatherwise as is the European. Clearly this could enable offensive action to be undertaken whatever conditions are preferred. These will include firm ground and, as a rule, good forward visibility. Meteorology may thus complicate defence and deterrence. However, we must now ask ourselves a grander question. How far will climatic shifts aggravate the economic and political tensions that give rise to war in the first place?

Climate and conflict

Climatic change has been a factor in biological evolution for hundreds of millions of years, not least through those 'nuclear winters' that punctuate the record every few score million years because a giant meteorite has struck or because the Earth's crust is in an acutely convulsive and volcanic phase. One might therefore surmise that vague recollections of these cataclysms linger deep in our psyche, much as a sense of original Creation does. To find a more tangible influence, however, one looks back six to eight million years to the onset, on our ancestral African plains, of much more arid conditions which shrank the rain forests and persisted for millions of years. This dramatic upheaval forced several lines of evolution in the ape world to descend from the trees and spread across the parched savanna, steppe and desert.

Uncertain though the exact progression still is, one of those lines would have been that of our pre-human ancestors. Their generic response to the adversity they faced was to turn largely carnivorous, trapping bigger animals by brave and intelligent teamwork. That in its turn called for high levels of tactical planning and intercommunication, hence the development of sharp and aggressive intellects.

During the last two million years, these proclivities have been well honed as our roving species has grappled with all the vagaries of the Pleistocene ice age. By half way through this epoch the protohumans had evolved into *homo erectus*, a fully upright man with a brain approaching in size that of the modern human, *homo sapiens*. Spreading out of Africa 750,000 years ago, they squared up to the Eurasian icefields by mastering, more or less, the art of controlling fire. The transition to *homo sapiens*, half a million years later, was a further biological response to the endless shifts of climate. Then forty thousand years ago, as things started to cool again, the development of primitive flint igniters enabled them regularly to apply fire to cooking, thereby expanding their dietary range. Thus fortified, our forebears spread still more freely, not least into Alaska and into Australasia.[7]

As the great wave of ideological protest was surging round the modern world, 20 to 25 years ago, an angry debate erupted in academe about whether humanity might not be ineluctably fated to aggression by our genetic inheritance. Certain members of the New Left and counter-culture opined, with a belligerence that was ill-restrained, that we were not inherently aggressive. Only existing society made us so. Never mind that 'existing society' is itself the product of a myriad of human decisions. Nor that warfare has occurred within and between all social systems, not least the Marxian ones. Surely the least that ought to be allowed is that the ancestral legacy of climatic change has seared into our psyche the notion that combative initiative, in whatever mode, is always a precondition of survival. Perhaps this is why arms control seems so ineffably tedious except to those who have made that a crusade. Perhaps, too, it is an added reason for looking askance at the millennial vision of a 'thousand years of peace' (see Chapter 9).

Entering upon what is known as recorded history, one seeks a more precise account of the interaction between climate and human affairs. The multifarious evidence about climate change as such has been subject to analyses of great intellectual power by scholars like Hubert Lamb, Emmanuel Le Roy Ledourie, and Jean M. Grove, following in the wake of such pioneers as C.E.P. Brooks and Ellsworth Huntington.[8] However, the picture that emerges, geophysically and ecologically, is complex and incomplete. Nor have matters been helped by the disposition among historians in general to dismiss climate change (post-Roman at any rate) as either unreal or inconsequential. Apparently, too, this attitude has been reinforced post-1945 by apprehensions that to go to the other way could be to veer towards a geographical determinism that could be prone, however stupidly, to racist exploitation.

Nevertheless, the correlations that have been made, either definitively or plausibly, between climate causes and human historical effects are already numerous. Among the least contentious may be the part climatic fluctuations played in the rise of the first civilisations, especially in the Middle East. Thus before 3500 BC North Africa was moister than now, a circumstance that must have assisted the early colonisation of the Nile Valley. Then a long arid trend began. For perhaps 10 centuries the greater isolation this produced aided the development of the pharonic state. But the political collapse c.2150 BC may have been due in part to extreme aridity.[9]

The Roman world

To a modern student of war, one of the most interesting questions in this sphere may be how climatic change influenced the struggle for survival of the late Roman Empire. Gleaning evidence from writers like Pliny the Elder and Strabo about such matters as the distribution of vineyards, Lamb concluded that the regional climate had started to warm sometime before 100 BC. He further inferred that this trend was sustained until 350 AD or thereabouts.[10] It is an inference that stands in diametric opposition to the view taken by several writers, French and English, in the 18th Century. This was that, around the time the power of Rome was passing its peak, central Europe was significantly colder than in even their own chilly times.

In his magisterial *Decline and Fall of the Roman Empire*, Edward Gibbon noted how frequent and thick winter freeze-ups of the Rhine and Danube afforded the barbarians 'a vast and solid bridge of ice' across which to deploy large armies for offensive action. He also noted that reindeer flourished in the forests of Germany and Poland. He saw Europe then as akin to the Canada of his own day, apparently that much colder because of more forest cover.[11] Two generations later, Dr Thomas Arnold, famous as the reforming headmaster at Rugby School but also a distinguished classical historian, described the Alps of the Hannibal era as far colder and more snow-laden than in Arnolds's own day.[12] This may well be so though judgement on the specific point is made harder by our being uncertain which alpine pass Hannibal's army used to enter Italy.

The conclusion that suggests itself is that, within the context of general cooling, the main climatic belts had swung southwards and that, as a corollary, the anticyclones characteristic of Scandinavia in winter had grown stronger. That interpretation also fits the image we retain of Roman North Africa as an exotic, luxuriant and affluent 'granary' region for the Empire at large. That in its turn completes the picture of the Roman Empire as having fundamentally been, from the time of the Punic Wars, a Mediterranean one. True, we are warned that the customary elements in the said image are either spurious or unproven.[13] But this may mean that it is extravagant, not that it is baseless.

Certain of the early specialists in this sphere were persuaded that the closing centuries of Imperial Rome witnessed more arid conditions across a zone from Germany through much of Russia. Ellsworth Huntington perceived a continual shrinkage of the Caspian from 500 BC to 500 AD, with an acceleration from the first century of the Christian era.[14] Then in the fourth and fifth centuries, according to C.E.P. Brooks, 'many German settlements were established on low ground, now swampy'.[15] Brooks's chronologies were not always too accurate in relation to modern practice. Even so, the indications are of drought sufficient to encourage the *völkerwanderung*, the great tribal migrations that pressed down on the Roman and Persian realms.

Towards an optimum

Soon, however, one begins to move towards the 'Little Climatic Optimum' of the Middle Ages. A pronounced rise in mean temperature occurred between 900 and 1300 AD, across much of North

America and Eurasia. On the glacial margins of Greenland it may have been as much as five degrees. Drift ice became rare around Iceland and the Denmark Strait after 800, and apparently was unknown there between 1020 and 1200.[16] Freeze-ups of the Nile recorded in 829 and 1010 tend to confirm this analysis rather than negate it because they indicate the Azores anticyclone extending strongly across Europe in winter, thereby drawing north-easterlies across Egypt.

One consequence, unnoticed by the outside world but a strategic revolution for those involved, was as follows. Influenced, it seems, by the response to climatic improvement of the whales they hunted, the Thule Eskimos of North Alaska spread east, then south. The Thule culture thus submerged the once dominant Dorset culture that lay in its path, thereby forming a single language group from Alaska through Greenland.[17,18] Much of what we lump together as Eskimo culture (snow igloos, kayaks and so on) is characteristically Thule.

More familiar is the expansion of the Vikings. In 787 AD the first Viking raid burst upon a very tranquil Anglo-Saxon England. Around the turn of that century, they reached Iceland. In 985 or thereabouts, they began what became a colony of 10,000 people in Greenland; and shortly afterwards established a small settlement in Newfoundland. They probably entered the Canadian Arctic as well. Yet within Scandinavia itself they did not actually settle in Finnmark until the late 13th Century.[19] But this could be very much the exception that proves the rule. Greater winter warmth would have weakened if not destroyed the great anticyclonic circulation over Siberia that otherwise locates within that region (at Verkhoyansk, on recent showing) the cold pole of the northern hemisphere in that season. If so, the polar high pressure cell (often rather notional as things are at present) may have reasserted itself, bringing a regular chill to Finnmark.

Historians of the Viking era have little addressed climate *per se.* One thing they seem agreed about, however, is that land hunger played a part, especially in Norway. However, a need for more land may itself be a product of climatic improvement in tribal societies. This is because such improvement eases poverty and so reduces what may otherwise be a horrendous rate (a half of all live births within the first year?) of infant mortality. What does seem certain is that, unlike the Western European age of discovery from the 15th Century, things were not triggered off by the arrival of new marine technology.[20] On the contrary, it was only after the desire to sea-rove had gripped them that the Vikings utilised and improved that which had long been around the North Sea. Thus a large sail was in use in British waters in Roman times. Yet this precondition of oceanic passage was not taken up by the Norsemen until what we know as the Viking Age.[21]

Elsewhere in Western Europe, medieval Christendom reached its zenith between 1100 and 1300. The tree line across northern areas was typically 250 feet higher than it is at the moment.[22] Correspondingly, the frontiers of agriculture widely ascended 200 feet. Great monastic orders were founded. In 1115, St Bernard established the Abbey of Clairvaux in Champagne, which was to be the headquarters of the Cistercians, an order dedicated to pushing the margins of farming outwards and upwards. Hundreds of towns were established during these centuries. In 1241, the Hanseatic League was formed, clear evidence that the northerly Baltic was ready to challenge the Mediterranean as a commercial thoroughfare.

Meanwhile the infant Russian nationhood had been encouraged by the longer growing seasons to shift its centre of gravity from Kiev towards Novgorod.[23] That shift was probably crucial to the very survival, under the shadow of the Tatar branch of the Mongol expansion, of what we have come to know as the heartland superpower. Moscow was founded in 1156.

A cooling trend

Around the peak of this phase, rainfall tended to rise, not least in inner Asia around the Caspian and Lop Nor, the ever-fluctuating lake near the main watershed in Sinkiang.[24] Here again falling infantile mortality, as food became more plentiful, could have come into play. It could have given the Mongols the extra manpower that allowed of the short but dramatic orgy of military adventurism initiated by Genghis Khan (1162–1227). If so, it was a product of climatic change that was very comprehensively destructive. A part of our psyche can hear Liddell Hart when he says of the Mongols that in 'scale and in quality, in surprise and in mobility, in the strategic and in the tactical indirect approach, their campaigns rival if they do not surpass any in history'.[25] None the less, the cultural and political legacy was catastrophic, even apart from the probability that marauding Mongol horsemen casually brought the Black Death bacillus out of obscurity in the eastern Himalayas and gave it on the Asian steppes a base from which to radiate.[26] In 1347, indeed, Tatars besieging the Black Sea port of Kaffa deliberately catapulted into it corpses riddled with this bacillus.[27]

The tragedy was that, although Russia did survive, this was not with its spirit unimpaired. As was noted by Karl Marx among others, it was 'in the terrible and abject school of Mongolian slavery that Muscovy was nursed and grew up. It gathered strength only by becoming a virtuoso in the craft of serfdom'.[28] As Tibor Szamuely put it;

> 'the Muscovy that emerged from the fragments of the old Rus, amid
> the break-up of the Mongol empire, bore hardly any resemblance
> to the free society of Kiev ... The basic Mongol principles of
> unqualified submission to the State and of the universal, compul-
> sory and permanent state service of all individuals and classes of
> society, gradually permeated the Muscovite social structure'.[9]

Likewise, the Mongols inflicted on a hitherto splendid 'Arab Civilisation a blow from which it has never fully recovered', in Meso-potamia at least. They were eventually checked in the Middle East less by the Arabs than by the Turks, the upshot being the establish-ment of the dreary Ottoman Empire across the Arab world. For nearly 500 years that world 'stagnated'. No creative worker or writer or thinker appeared among the Arabs, and they were not awakened from the slumber until the Western nations appeared in the East.[30] But of the two focal points of urbanised Arab culture, Cairo and Baghdad, only the latter city was actually reached and sacked. Added to which Cairo was able to emancipate itself from the Turks sooner. It is a difference in background which may still bear on events.

While the moister phase was making itself manifest, the long-term temperature trend was beginning what proved to be six or seven centuries of unsteady but insistent descent, virtually worldwide though with a time lag in the Southern Hemisphere. Increased vul-canism seems to have been a factor. Between 1025 and 1250, there were remarkably few volcanic eruptions whereas the subsequent record became more like the longer term average with some surges of high activity, notably from 1390 to 1490. Since early in the 13th Century, the crossings to Iceland and Greenland had been getting tougher while the incidence of severe storms and sea floods around the North Sea basin was quite extraordinary. In 1212, for instance, no fewer than 306,000 people were reckoned to have drowned in North Holland.[31] The Mean Sea Level would probably have been well up by then, thanks to some centuries of ice cap melting.

In 1315, after rains so incessant that they were compared with the

Biblical flood, crops failed all over Europe, ushering in widespread famine among populations that had expanded too much in better times. Henceforward famine became more recurrent. Between 1348 and 1351 'a third of the world' of Europe died in the 'Great Mortality' from Central Asia (and, it seems, borne in ships from Kaffa) that we know as the Black Death. As these strains aggravated the contradictions already deepening within the feudal system, the resultant social tensions found expression in the savage millennarianism of such movements as the *pastoureaux* in France and the flagellants in and around the Rhine valley. As part and parcel of this reaction, anti-semitic outbursts also became more commonplace and vicious.[32]

The Viking community in Greenland had died a lonely death by 1475 or thereabouts, isolated from Europe after 1408 and having lost the adaptive resilience to adversity that had characterised its early years. Its members had locked themselves obstinately into a pre-established pattern, 'elaborating their churches rather than their hunting skills'.[33] In this they contrasted markedly with the Norwegians in Finnmark whose farming and fishing positively thrived on climatic adversity until the late 18th Century.[34]

By the end of the 14th Century, tree lines and arable margins were receding across Europe with villages being abandoned everywhere from Iceland to Hungary. Not surprisingly those deserted were mainly in sites that were upland, northerly or otherwise marginal. But to some extent abandonment represented a strategy of concentration in order to take positive advantage of new agricultural techniques and markets. In parts of southern England, for instance, villages were deserted more in the flat and fertile valleys than on the rougher hillsides.[35]

The accelerated cooling of the second half of the 16th Century affected even more than those armadas from Spain. The fact that the Reformation considerably succeeded across sombre northern Europe although it comprehensively failed across sunny southern may well owe something to this. The global trend evolved into the 'Little Ice Age' so famously depicted by the 17th Century Dutch painters of winter landscapes but mentioned in many other contemporary accounts. Across the centuries, bad grain harvests (*eg* in Western Europe in 1313–20, 1594–97, 1788 and 1816) readily led to social unrest. Whether as with the 'great fear' that swept a hungry France early in 1789, this culminated in political upheaval depended on other factors.

To the Dutch people of the last 16th and 17th Centuries, the struggle against climate was a metaphor for the struggle against Spain and *vice versa*. Some fall in the global sea level must have facilitated the great flood prevention projects, while the weakening of Spanish sea power obviously encouraged the independence struggle. Then from about 1675 to 1700 came a quite phenomenal cold plunge. Just before the turn of the century, representative temperatures in central Europe (calculated as 10-year running means) were over half a degree Centigrade lower than anything observable again. The reasons are not entirely clear though several fairly strong volcanic explosions in 1693–94 must have contributed to the worst years. At all events, bad harvests in northern Europe in the 1690s had at least two geopolitical results. A weakening of the Scottish economy left Edinburgh more prepared to accept, however dourly, a political union with London, such as was enacted in 1707. Meanwhile, the loss of a third of the population of Finland in the famine of 1696 had left the Swedish empire with its new king Karl XII strategically enfeebled. The upshot was the formation against it in 1699 of a multinational alliance stretching from Norway–Denmark round to Russia. At a time when the Baltic down to Stockholm was becoming more iced up in winter, a coalition that operated partly from ice-free ports posed a novel problem. Apprehending this, Karl XII had transferred his main naval port from Stockholm to Karlskrona. Yet this was to leave much of his empire very open in the warmer months to sallies from St Petersburg.

The Great Northern War duly broke out in 1700. Sweden finally lost the initiative with the defeat of its expeditionary force at the battle of Poltava, in June 1709, hard upon the same bitter winter as drove the French to make peace overtures during the War of the Spanish Succession. By the peace treaty of 1721, the loss of all Stockholm's Baltic possessions bar Finland was confirmed. A desperate attempt in 1741–42 to restore the balance was to lead merely to the capitulation of a Swedish army broken by cold and disease through wintering in Finland; and hence to the occupation by Russia of Finland.[36] Suffice to add that the inclination of various 18th Century intellectuals, including François Voltaire and Samuel Johnson, to depict Karl XII as uniquely heroic are an exceptionally depressing example of a recurrent tendency among the intelligentsia to offset their own uncertainties by lauding the putative single-mindedness of the man of action.

Research by Chinese scientists indicates that in their country, temperatures were lower from the 14th to the mid-19th Century than they have been in the 20th Century, with the coldest period again being around 1700.[37] What merits further investigation is this: how far did climatic stress heighten the anxiety about internal fragility that induced China from 1430, and then Japan from 1639, to turn towards xenophobic isolation rather than vie with Europe in industry and maritime commerce, something both countries had seemed poised to do?[38] The subsequent interaction between population and resources was complex in China (see Chapter 9). No doubt it was, too, in the Japan of the Tokugawa Shogunate. What can be said of the latter, however, is this. The population doubled to 30 million in the century to 1725. Then it stabilised for a century because of high mortality, in the expanding cities but also on rural margins hit by colder conditions.[39] Famines and peasant unrest became more frequent.[40]

Allowing for a time lag that is typically between three and seven years, glaciers are sound indicators of secular changes in temperature and/or winter precipitation. This applies to the culmination of the Little Ice Age. In China, too, temperatures were at their lowest around 1700. They then rose rather unsteadily until the second half of the 19th Century when the rise becomes more insistent. Glacial recession was to become general from 1880. In Europe, it had done so from 1850.

In Great Britain grain prices rose sharply in the years 1836–41.[41] driven by bad harvest and a secular fall in mean temperatures.[42] During those years, there was considerable vulcanism worldwide, after which the volcanoes lapsed into comparative somnolence for a good two decades. The warmish but very wet Irish summer of 1846 was all too conducive to the explosive spread of a potato blight that was already endemic.[43] Matters were not helped by the fact that it was hitting an agrarian economy stagnating in the aftermath of a series (1839–44) of 'extremely bad harvests' across the board.[44] Overall, Hubert Lamb is probably right to set the end of the Little Ice Age in 1850.[45] For European purposes at least, it is as valid a judgement as any.

The point is important in terms of political instability. The 1840s, the 'hungry forties', became a decade of quite exceptional social stress and revolutionary ferment right across Western Europe. Mass protests in Britain by the Chartists and the Anti-Corn Law League were followed in 1848 by actual insurrections in various continental cities. That year also saw the publication by Karl Marx and Frederick

Engels of *The Communist Manifesto*. By that time, too, Ireland was deep in the throes of her famine crisis. Not till the aftermath of the First World War did such an atmosphere prevail again. That time round, the situation owed nothing to climate change. It figures nowhere in the many explanations of '1914'.

Alternation

Yet, visible and consequential though this long phase of cooling had repeatedly been, the mean temperature in middle northern latitudes had fallen not more than a couple of degrees between the 13th and the 19th Centuries. Then between 1850 and 1940, there was a rather irregular gain of just under one degree. Acting in conjunction with political reforms and other economic changes, that improvement must have helped contain revolutionary pressures quite well, at least until 1917. No doubt, too, the last great phase of Western or European imperial expansion was thus assisted across such territories as the Canadian prairies and Siberia.

Dare one mention, too, the 'Great American Desert'? This bleakly discouraging description of America between the High Plains and the Pacific Cordillera had been afforded by the strangely restless Spanish explorer, Francisco Coronado (1510–44). It seemed to be borne out by the fatalities among that minority of early migrants to California who elected to go overland in wagon trains rather than by clipper round the Horn. But in 1851 Congress indicated a more aggressive approach to the region by ceasing to designate it as one big Indian reservation. The final triumph over the Indians and over Nature was assured by seven successive years of plentiful rains on the High Plains, 1878–85.[46]

There seems to be something like a 20-year drought cycle in the plains. Though the 'dust bowl' in the central and southern plains during the 1930s may have been an event that occurs once every several centuries, there was a more moderate replication in 1950–54. At present the computer programmes are at variance as to what global warming connotes in this region. But long-term soil and botanical damage by industrialised farming may introduce a negative bias.[47] Likewise, droughts lasting at least two seasons tend to occur once every two decades in European Russia, and twice as often in West Siberia. They tend to coincide quite closely with such events elsewhere in the Northern Hemisphere, a positive correlation being observable throughout with spells of global warming – either transient or sustained.[48]

The reversal that occurred around 1940 of the upward temperature trend globally was noticeably abrupt and general. Of the military campaigns thus thrown off balance the most momentous was the German drive on Moscow in 1941. On 8 October, a panzer pincer trapped 650,000 Red Army troops at Vyazma, less than 150 miles from the Soviet capital and over 400 from Brest Litovsk where that sector of the invasion had started on 22 June. In the next three days a deluge of autumn rain destroyed tactical mobility by turning all the roads into morasses until the frosts came around November 7. Then within several days these frosts had utterly disorganised the logistic back-up, based as it was on the railways.[49] Thanks to all these circumstances, plus the stolid courage of its people, Moscow did not fall.

Just as the Cold War was getting under way in earnest came the winter of 1946–47, the bitterest in Europe since 1840 at least. The acute coal crisis which hit Britain in February 1947 accentuated doubts within the ruling Labour Party about a large British military mission being involved in the civil war in Greece. A decision to disengage was taken, thereby obliging the United States to accept the commitment. An immediate outcome was President Harry Truman's enunciation that March of his doctrine of containment of 'direct and indirect aggression', undeniably a major landmark in the geopolitical response to Stalin. The launch, several months later, of the Marshall Plan was effectively a follow-through intended, above all, to stabilise the three Western zones of Germany, the slowness of their recovery from the war having been worsened by the cold weather. Meanwhile, in the USSR the ideological militancy especially associated with the return to Stalin's favour of Andrei Zhdanov, the Leningrad party veteran, intensified as the cold came hard upon a widespread drought.

As Hubert Lamb has always well emphasised, global cooling is very regularly associated with a shift towards the Equator of the sub-tropical belts of high pressure and their steppe and desert landscapes. As this pattern reasserted itself from 1960, the Sahel region of Africa was acutely affected. In the 1950s, the summer rains from the south had tended to penetrate to 20° or 22°N. By the early 1970s, however, their general limit was 19° to 20°. The ecological, and hence the political, implications were serious for everywhere north of 10°,[50] long a boundary of contact and conflict between Black African and Arab. Historians should be left to assess how far drought aggravated political tensions from Mauritania through Chad and Nigeria to the Sudan. Arguably, certain people in the United Nations Environment Programme (UNEP) and elsewhere have had too much of a Coronado-like view of the extent of 'desertification'.[51] What is very evident, none the less, is that drought helped to pave the way for the Marxian coup in Ethiopia in 1974 but then exposed even more starkly than might otherwise have been the case the shortcomings of the revolutionary regime.

Another instance of the movement of a climatic belt generating or exacerbating political tensions is afforded by the confrontations between Reykjavik and London between 1958 and 1976 over fishing rights in Icelandic waters. One fact of life basic to this question was the physiology of the cod in relation to sea surface temperatures. The range within which this staple fish thrives is 4 to 7 degrees centigrade. Few survive below two degrees, primarily because of kidney failure. By the 1940s, the mean annual sea temperature around the Icelandic coast ranged between 3 and 7 degrees, several degrees higher than the nadir of the Little Ice Age, around 1700. Soon, however, a downturn began.[52] The big fishing boom experienced from 1920 was correspondingly curtailed.[53]

An anomalous feature of the new climate phase post-1940 was said to be some weakening of the circulation of the atmosphere in temperate climates.[54] At times, rogue anticyclones (*ie* cells of high pressure) did affect a radical diversion of the prevailing winds, causing harvest failures. Most conspicuously, recurrent shortfalls in rain helped to defeat Nikita Khrushchev's 'virgin lands' agrarian revolution from 1955, and to devastate Mao Tse-tung's 'great leap forward' in the countryside from 1958. In the lower Volga, crop potential, judged in relation to rainfall was a good 25 per cent lower from 1951–60 than over the next 10 years.[55]

Though the cause or causes of the global cooling between 1940 and 1965 are not easy to determine exactly, a Soviet specialist, K. Ya Kondratyev, has enunciated the thesis that the prime culprit is mankind yet again. He argues that the gas nitrogen dioxide (NO_2) is produced by the high-temperature combustion of air and that it readily absorbs solar radiation. He argues that this combustion started to accelerate with increased mechanisation from about 1930 and then much more with the atmospheric nuclear tests of the 1950s and 1960s. However, the validity of this thesis is by no means proven as yet, partly because of uncertainty as to how easily this highly reactive gas ascends to the high altitudes at which it can be effective in shielding the Earth as a whole from the solar flux. Certain related calculations are also questionable.[56] Nor should one overlook the ability of all the nitrogen oxides to act catalytically to produce ozone, a greenhouse gas at low altitude.[57]

If the global circulation of the atmosphere was slacker during those decades and so left room for more freakishness or variability this may have been a follow-through from the previous decades of global warming. By the same token, we might expect this trend to have been sustained with the strong resumption of global warming from 1965: some 0.25°C in the 1970s and as much again in the 1980s. As yet, however, this is not evident. According to Working Party 1 of the IPCC, however, there has lately been no clear evidence of an increase in variability.[58] In the study already cited of central England temperatures (1810–1990), there does seem to be some tendency for monthly temperatures to become more variable as of the last 15 years. But taking the series deployed as a whole, the correlation between warming and variability looks weak.[59]

In the USSR pre-1941, one of the themes that was seen as symbolising 'socialist man's drive to victory over the forces of nature' was the development of the Northern Sea Route, along the coast of Siberia through the Behring Straits to the Pacific. After the war, this declined in importance relative to the expanding rail network, especially *vis à vis* north east Siberia. About half the trade into the region was seaborne in 1950 whereas less than 10 per cent has been of late.[60] A marked increase of ice, between 1950 and 1970, probably helps to explain this precipitate decline. But the USSR is preparing to develop a new cargo line from European ports through the Behring Straits to Japan. The service may level out at somewhere between 10 and 30 vessels a month, depending on what ecological pressures are thus engendered.[61]

What the more modern histories of climatic change show above all is the extreme complexity of it, as seen over time or between places. What also is suggested is that alternations in climate have quite often had a discernible effect on human affairs. Swings in mean temperature of one or two degrees Centigrade in the course of several centuries have affected the fortunes of individual societies and politics. Gradual upward shifts have usually appeared benign, while downward movement has generally been adverse. But a strong trend in either direction may be detrimental not least because of the associated disruption of rainfall patterns. Nevertheless, the evidence specifically concerning the effect of climatic change on the biological environment, and hence on human society and politics is both intricate and incomplete. Furthermore, shifts in climatic norms have rarely been at all rapid within the span of recorded history. The resultant impact tends to be most apparent on rural margins that were barely above destitution at the best of times.

Clearly, there is much more historical research to be done in this area, not least at regional level. But underlying all such enquiry will be the question as to whether our emergent world society can adapt to very rapid climatic change better than that of our forebears might have; and if not, how readily a lack of adaptability will pitch us into a new era of international violence. At the strictly technical level the answer does appear positive, this for a whole variety of reasons. With respect, Jean Grove seems to me misguided when she allows that it 'is now recognised that the more efficiently farming is organised to make optimum use of "normal" weather conditions, the more sharply production is likely to fall if the climate deviates markedly from this norm'.[62]

Yet translating technological virtuosity into a global grand strategy may be even more difficult today and tomorrow than it proved for John Kennedy's New Frontier or, for that matter in several major wars. At the societal level, we may be more fragile partly because we are so globally interactive and interdependent about everything from curbing pollution to fighting crime to preserving military security; and partly because of a cultural commitment to consumerism and hedonism that is currently growing stronger, thanks in part to the collapse of Communism. Moreover, our fragility may be further taxed by the tendency for climatic change to impact differentially between and also within major regions.

Nor may the sort of international containment strategy most widely being canvassed (based on a 20 per cent reduction of CO_2 emissions by 2025) delay the doubling of carbon dioxide equivalent levels by more than 10 to 15 years.[63] Besides which, climate is far from being the only environmental problem we face. There would still be a major ecological crisis even if climate were entirely stable. Out of that broader crisis could come a good deal of armed conflict.

8

Ecology and Conflict

ALREADY A cult of computer-driven numeracy thrives within the planetary debate. If the enthusiasts are to be believed, 'objective analysis' can predict not only the geophysics but also such human consequences as the flow of 'ecological refugees'. Nevertheless, historical narrative may also have much to contribute. History, after all invites comparisons with other times of paradigmatic change: the Renaissance and the Reformation; the collapse of Rome and the rise of Christianity; the intellectual and spiritual awakening, from Greece to China, of the sixth century BC. It may make us literate as well as numerate about the impact of climate on human affairs. It teaches us, in effect, all we know of war and preparations for war, including military sociology and the psychology of conflict, two subjects which may be of growing significance for our defence planning (see chapter 11). It has vast materials about our impact on Nature. It is a rich storehouse of philosophical thought, not least political philosophy.

It reminds us, above all, how few arguments are new. Certainly this is so with environment. As the industrial revolution gathered pace in Britain two centuries ago, an anxious debate developed about the impact not globally but nationally, on town and countryside. Thomas Malthus, for instance, discussed population growth very much from what today would be seen as an ecological perspective.[1] Soon, the wider debate was to influence such aspects of public policy as agricultural protection, railway development and industrial working conditions. To which one might add that one is today unlikely to develop a full planetary consciousness – if you like, a global patriotism – without some sense of world historical development.

Unfortunately, however, many people growing up around the modern world have links with history that are desperately tenuous.

The vagaries of educational fashion apart, the reasons are several-fold. A lot of contemporary architecture owes nothing to local traditions, partly because all the logistical factors work against them. Much archaeological evidence is eroded or swamped. The generation that knew the deeper-rooted world of pre-1939 is beginning to pass from the scene. Part of the reason why communalism has once more to be regarded as a menace to general peace is that its roots in terms of a 'sense of place' have actually become less secure.

What one must hope is that this loosening of ties will not leave those concerned too susceptible, in what could be a more stressful future, to historical mythologies of the more vicious kind. It is a hope made all the more earnest by a recent suggestion that history is already at an end, thanks to the 'unabashed victory of economic and political liberalism' over its fascist and bolshevik opponents. The author of this conclusion, Francis Fukuyama (who is deputy director of the policy planning staff of the State Department) avers that the liberal West can well absorb the other foreseeable threats to its own nature and situation, these being identified as religious fundamentalism and traditional nationalism. The post-historical phase will, so we are told, take longer to embrace those smaller nationalities with unresolved grievances ('Palestinians and Kurds; Sikhs and Tamils ... ') but 'large-scale conflict must involve large states still caught in the grip of history and they are what appear to be passing from the scene'. Fukuyama views with a Kiplingesque blend of satisfaction and sadness the prospect he depicts.[2]

As with much of the more thought-provoking work, the ultimate allegiance of author or article is hard to identify except, in this case, via a fulsome appreciation of F.W.G. Hegel for his insistence on the primacy in history of thought and ideas: a point of departure that Fukuyama gladly contrasts with the cult of economic determinism lately subscribed to not just by Marxists but also by Wall Street and its acolytes. Since his own lineage is otherwise ill-defined, however, he has come under attack from more or less all quarters.[3] But without wishing to join the hue and cry, one cannot but express surprise that somebody so committed to ideas as lead factors should make no allowance for paradigmatic changes in outlook. The current celebration of economic liberalism, pure and simple, may well have to give way quite sharply, at some point, to a new ethic geared to ecological preservation.

Indeed, it may have to. Let us think of the sort of ecological degradation that would go on even if greenhouse warming ceased.

Species would continue to vanish at an alarming rate. Neither acid rain nor ozone depletion would go away. Augean amounts of toxic waste would still be generated. And so on. What is more, many of the negative tendencies are continually getting worse and are acquiring more of an international dimension.

Population pressure

At the centre of this sombre scene is the human population explosion. On this front, the outlook is worse again, partly because birth rates are being controlled less tightly in post-Maoist China and because they remain well in excess of falling death rates all across Africa. The estimated growth of population has only dropped in percentage terms from 2.05 in 1965 to 1.73 in 1990, which means that the absolute rate of growth has been accelerating. The United Nations Population Fund (UNPF) projection of world totals shows a rise of from three to five billion between 1960 and 1987 and a fore-cast rise to seven billion by 2010.[4] Among the countries said lately to show at least three per cent growth were no fewer than 16 in Africa; Mongolia and Pakistan in Asia; five countries in Central America and three in South America; and Jordan, Iraq and several Gulf states in the Middle East.[5] In the light of such figures, Dr Nafis Sadik, the executive director of UNPF, has said that she fears that the total by the end of the next century could top 14 billion instead of the 10 to 11 officially predicted as of now.[6]

To a disturbing extent, the population explosion remains an urban implosion, not least in the developing world where the urban per-centage of the population increased from 17 in 1950 to 31 in 1985.[7] The mechanisation of farming may push young people towards the towns. So may agricultural decline, for climatic or whatever reasons. If not, the colour, diversity, tumult and relative absence of social constraints may draw them thither. Among all age groups, however, much bitterness, leading either to anger or to apathy, is engendered by the filth, congestion and inchoate ugliness of the shanty town environments so grimly characteristic of, to borrow another of Barbara Ward's graphic phrases, 'the cities that came too soon.' In Francophone West Africa, the shanty districts are colloquially named after the surplus *bidons* or steel drums much used in the construction. For the *bidonvilles* of Dakar read the *bustées* of Calcutta or the *favellas* of Rio de Janeiro.

Perhaps some authors have too glibly equated urban congestion and a disposition to mass unrest.[8] All the same, there is no denying that a total syndrome of deprivation can give rise to political insurgency especially where communal tensions are also endemic. In his tract, *Minimanual of the Urban Guerilla*, Carlos Marighella (the quasi-mythical Brazilian terrorist leader who was eventually killed in a gun battle with Saõ Paolo police in 1969) identified a whole series of tactical options: assaults, raids, strikes, the occupation of factories, kidnapping, sabotage, propaganda, raising false alarms, and turning mass demonstrations into legal confrontations through the use of snipers and bombers.[9] The scope for this tragedy is enhanced by the extent to which urban influx tends to focus on metropoli and other large cities. The population of Bangkok, for instance has risen this last half-century from 0.5 to 8.2 million.

Recently, insurgencies have tended to be either singularly urban or else decidedly rural. An example of the former was that against the British in South Arabia, 1963–67. For it was very largely confined to Aden and its suburbs, with the exception of the Radfan district along the Yemen border. An example of the latter pattern is South Vietnam, 1959–75. Here the cities were little afflicted by violence until the Tet offensive of 1968, itself a case of Viet Cong and North Vietnamese cadres storming in from outside, in breach of the Tet truce and usually with little in the way of tactical success. Certainly, in 1966 – a 'hinge of fate' year in both situations – the scattered villages of South Arabia were politically soporific; and, while downtown Saigon strongly had the aura of a city at war, there were few bombings in the bars and no bullets in the streets.

Viewed in the round, however, the problem of instability is always a rural-cum-urban one. As much is evident when one considers a basic resource, such as water. Global water use doubled between 1940 and 1980, and it is expected to double again by 2000, with two-thirds of the projected consumption going into irrigation.[10] Rivers that have already been the subject of international tension include the Zambesi and Niger; the Ganges; the Rio Grande and Colorado; the Nile; the Tigris and Euphrates; the Jordan; and the Danube. Water competition may be the least tractable obstacle to an accord between Israelis and Palestinians, particularly because both communities are irresponsible about population growth.

Take, too, the Colorado, a water system under desperate pressure from rising demand. Under an international treaty signed in 1944, after a half century of wrangling, Mexico is formally guaranteed a fixed volume of water per year. However, the treaty provisions for allocations during drought are ambiguous and never yet tested. Needless to say, too, there have been no negotiations to cover the very real possibility of decreased rain as the Mexican desert shifts northwards.[11]

Renegotiation of this matter could be further complicated by illicit migration to the United States. Already three to six million illegal migrants are north of the border. That in its turn reflects the parlous economic outlook for Mexico as a whole. Here again, metropolitan growth is alarming. The latest UN projections for Mexico City are for a growth from 17.3 to 25.8 million between 1985 and 2000.[12] Compare those figures with one million in 1940. In many situations, urban implosion coupled with international migration, licit or otherwise, threatens to assume major proportions against a background of ecological change.

Nor are there any technological fixes that are both available and painless. The desalination of seawater, though much talked about, cannot be the answer as far as the more extensive margins of agriculture are concerned. Suppose one wanted thus to provide enough water per year to a country of 2,000,000 square kilometres (roughly the size of Mexico) to equate to 25 centimetres (roughly 10 inches) of average rainfall. Then one is talking about 500 billion tonnes of freshened water annually. For that to be produced by distillation (*ie* evaporation), would entail a power input of 100,000,000 megawatts, whereas the electrical capacity of the whole world is only 12,000,000 MW at the present time. In other words, it is farcically far beyond the bounds of possibility. True, a desalination technique based on 'reverse osmosis' has been developed; and since it does not involve evaporation, it is much more economical with energy,[13] each megawatt of input yielding perhaps 500,000 tonnes a year. What is more, the energy efficiency may be poised to improve more.[14] Even so, the proportions remain hopeless in the terms just described.

They come more into line if one talks instead about supply to large cities. Take an urban area of 25 million (*eg* Mexico City as it is expected to be) consuming a modest 20,000 litres of water per head per year. That works out at 500 million tonnes, suggesting a level of power consumption that will be feasible exceptionally. By 1989, the city state of Kuwait had made itself critically dependent for its drinking water on desalination facilities. Similarly, Riyadh, the capital of Saudi Arabia (population now 1.5 million), was consuming 30 million tonnes of freshened water per annum, about 10 per cent of the world total. Reverse osmosis facilities can be less massive, therefore less inviting as military targets.

Ecology and Strategy

Yet, irrefutable though the proposition may be that the history of human ecology is not at an end and does threaten peace and security, the international security community will never find it easy to effect a meeting of minds about grand strategy with not only economics but environmentalists as well. To an extent, of course, it will be a question of differences in political balance. Both strategies and environmentalists extend across quite a range of opinion. Nevertheless, it would be fair to say that not only the former accommodate, albeit uneasily, the far Right; and that only the latter embraces the more utopian Left, complete with its arbitrary anti-militarism, its Manichean attitudes to nuclear energy in whatever form and its quasi-Maoist obsession with how the big powers 'compete and collude'. Attempts at communion between these ways of thought could easily degenerate into a re-run of the polarising dialectic of the early 1980s between the multilateralists and the unilateralists. We are still talking, after all, about many of the same actors.

The dichotomy of attitudes is exemplified by *Politics for Life*, the most recent manifesto of the Green Party in Britain, known as Ecology Party before 1985. The 'Roots of War' are delineated simply in terms of weapons development and economic growth (pp. 6–7), the view implied being that all mass societies are equally aggressive, regardless of their political systems. The best answer is deemed to lie first and foremost in a complete rejection of nuclear weapons together with withdrawal from NATO and from the European Community. Western and Eastern Europe should be encouraged to come together in a 'genuinely defensive alliance' (p. 9). Arms exports should cease unconditionally. Then 'in the more decentralised society that we envisage, we shall be able to reduce our dependence on military power and develop non-violent means of defence' (p. 9). All the same, the country 'must be able to defend itself against attack or invasion or any infringement of our rights under international law, and should therefore continue to possess conventional weapons systems suited to a defensive role' (p. 9). We are promised elaboration later but get nothing extra except a commitment to abandon *in toto* applied nuclear research (fusion apparently included) (p. 29); and either the abolition of civil defence or else its being focused on damage-limitation against conventional attack and radiation drift from elsewhere (p. 27). There is almost nothing at all on general foreign policy except a bemoaning of the Falklands expedition as 'a terrible human tragedy' (p. 7) and a proposed declaration that Antarctica is 'a world reserve' (p. 27).

The comments on civil defence (like some of those on ecology) offer food for thought. Otherwise, the utopianism is incredibly callow. How could anyone have hoped for a stronger international regime in Antarctica if Galtieri had taken over the Falklands? What about such vexed questions as the desirability or otherwise of a Palestinian state or continued sanctions against South Africa? Should we uphold the territorial integrity of the USSR within existing boundaries? What about Britain's peacekeeping obligations within the UN Security Council? Are there any overseas contingencies for which the Greens might favour a military response, given their adamant opposition to the Gulf intervention of 1990–91? If so, could this response be made by means of whatever may be identified as 'defensive weapons'? How would a Green government prepare people psychologically for the cruelly daunting task of non-violent defence of the home territory? And so on.

What we are talking about, of course, is a political movement that looks upon military preparedness much more as an ecological worry than as a security guarantee. It is an attitude that intertwines closely with feelings that, if one must prepare for war, one should do so through reliance on (a) light weapons rather than heavy ones, (b) weapons that incorporate stable and non-exotic technology and (c) those that hopefully can be characterised as defensive. Evidently, these attributes would overlap to an extent, thus permitting what would be presented as a distinctively 'non-provocative' military posture. In addition, we would be proffered less vulnerability through the promotion at a national level of 'a stable eco-system' and a concept of economic 'self-reliance' that combines 'self-sufficiency in essentials with an equitable exchange of other goods/services'.[15]

All of which was foreshadowed, vaguely at least, by the way in which, through 1968 and subsequently, environmental impact became, certainly for the New Left, a central part of the ethical and aesthetic case against involvement in Vietnam. Nor is there any denying that the widespread use of defoliants and of very heavy applications of firepower did torture extensively the landscapes of Indo-China.[16] Nor again, is there any doubt that in an era in which certain of the more obvious military threats have receded while environmental anxiety is on the increase, this political challenge is sure to wax stronger, and to do so in regard to military training less than to actual hostilities.

So if those of us with a continuing interest in defence *per se* do not wish to be marginalised in policy debates, we will do well to examine afresh a long, if imperfectly upheld tradition of environmental restraint in war. The destruction or poisoning of water supplies has been among the strongest and most general taboos, though siege warfare affords not a few ugly exceptions. Incursions by the Mongols were liable to devastate elaborate systems of regional irrigation though even this may have been the result of general impact as much as specific intent.[17]

Granted, also, the Korean War eventually proved a grim case in point. Between 13 May and 18 June 1953, the United States Air Force bombed a quarter of the 20 big dams in Haeju, the 'rice bowl' area of north Korea. This threshold was crossed just after the rice seedlings had been planted out. It marked the climax of a two-year evolution of United Nations policy in that theatre as regards strategic bombardment, air and also naval. To start with, the overall purpose was 'Operation Strangle', an attempt so to rupture communications as to effect the logistical isolation of the Communist Forces in what had become a very stable front across the waist of Korea. Through 1952, however, it became more of a counter-society campaign.[18] This legacy may help explain why the North Koreans have since been unable to emerge from the exceptionally venal and vicious dictatorship of Kim Il Sung.

It was soon claimed that the bombing of the dams must have been what induced the Chinese and North Koreans to abandon, some time between 7 May and 4 June, a precept they had previously been adamant about: namely, the repatriation of prisoners of war regardless of their stated preferences.[19] What is not in doubt, in any case, is that this concession did pave the way for the armistice in July. However, such acute economic pressure is best seen as complementary to a tough warning that, unless the negotiating deadlock was thus broken, the USA would widen the war's horizons and perhaps resort to nuclear release as well. Though this warning was conveyed covertly via New Delhi, the Formosan Straits and the peace talks at Panmunjon, one is bound to say that, given the mood prevalent today, neither this initiative nor the bombing of the dams would be accepted at all keenly by Western public opinion in 1991. Ecological anxiety would be a prominent reason for doubt. Indeed, ecological concern gives a lot of resonance throughout the contemporary West to Mikhail Gorbachev's *obiter dictum* that the world is now too small for war.

Addressing the World Climate Conference in November 1990, King Hussein of Jordan opined that a war in the Gulf would be a world disaster environmentally, not least because of 'an increase by at least a factor of 100' in the global rate of emission of carbon dioxide. Though this was the wildest of exaggerations, the Gulf region itself could be polluted terribly by acid rain and the marine spills. Meanwhile the soot emissions could strengthen the Indian monsoon, perhaps causing in consequence excessive floods in Bangladesh.[20]

In June 1991, a round table conference took place in London, sponsored mainly by Greenpeace International and by the Centre for Defence Studies at London University. It considered a 'Fifth Geneva Convention' covering environmental problems in time of war. Without wishing to prejudge the final outcome of this initiative, may one just comment that, to be effective, any such accord should rest on neat definitions and have aims and objectives compatible with legitimate military operations. What this probably means is that it should focus sharply on making belligerents liable for environmental damage to neutral territories. Even this precept has its difficulties, one being that by no means all climate disturbances will be harmful to everybody. Nevertheless, such a provision might still be suitably restraining, not least on the manner and extent of any nuclear release.

Otherwise, the clash between environmental protection and miliary activity has lately been at its most acute in regard to operational training facilities in Western Europe. This has especially applied to the impact on the environment, in the fullest sense, caused by low-level and high speed tactical flying by NATO air squadrons. Force reductions as such are unlikely to ease this problem sufficiently.

Air commanders like to insist that a strike sortie as practised in peacetime bears a '90 per cent' resemblance to a similar mission in wartime: the skills required are that comparable while the mental milieu is much the same. Clearly, this will be an overstatement. Nor is there any doubt that, for aircrew at any rate, the peacetime ambience can be made to correspond to the wartime one more readily than with, say, an infantry battalion attack. However, maximum realism would involve some approaches to target being made, by night as by day, at altitudes a hundred feet or so above the surface at speeds that may sometimes exceed the sound barrier. Similarly, helicopter crews need to be attuned to 'nap-of-the-Earth' flying at any time of the day or night.[21]

For many years past, however, the NATO military authorities have had to make big compromises. Take, for example, the scope for tactical flying as presented of late to allied air squadrons in Germany. In a few limited areas, planes have been allowed to descend as low as 250 feet. But generally, the minimum ceiling has been 500, which might now be much too high for active operations into well-defended hostile air space. That high up you might be far too susceptible to being shot down from above as well as from below. Helicopters have also been severely circumscribed, particularly on account of the noise they make. Often altitude minima have been higher still at night.

Then in the summer of 1990, things took a sharp turn for the worse from the military standpoint. They did so when the federal authorities in Bonn rather peremptorily announced that the minimum altitude for flying training was to be 1,000 feet above ground level except for one designated RAF squadron (perhaps working up for the Gulf) and certain special permissions. Manifestly, this decision came as and when it did because a Federal election was approaching against the background of a more casual public approach to defence and a more anxious approach to matters environmental. All the same, it was not a very good study of how to blend the planetary and the geopolitical.

In the light of which, it is all the more surprising and gratifying that coalition air arms flew so low so well in their war against Iraq. Ground-based simulators can these days provide realistic training of a kind; and several weeks or months of pre-combat desert flying will have helped in this particular situation. Besides, the air arms mainly involved were well versed in strategic mobility exercises of a relevant kind, witness the deployment of RAF Tornados to Oman in 1986.[22]

Planetary concern

Quite promising, on current showing at least, are the prospects for a planetary-geopolitical dialogue about resource and ecological constraints as an underlying threat to peace. As much was indicated early on by the work of the Independent Commission on International Development Issues, under the chairmanship of Willy Brandt, from December 1977. Historians will have to judge what influences the report, formally presented to the UN Secretary-General in February 1980, had on the actual behaviour of governments hamstrung at every turn by the worst world trade recession for half-a-century. But its broader influence can be gauged in the translations into over 20 languages, the mass rallies (notably in The Hague and London) in support of its recommendations, the parliamentary debates in many countries and so on.

In his introduction to the report, informally named after him, Herr Brandt wrote:

> War is often thought of in terms of military conflict or even annihilation. But there is a growing awareness that an equal danger may be chaos – as a result of mass hunger, economic disaster, environmental catastrophe, and terrorism. So we should not think only of reducing the traditional threat to peace but also of the need for change from chaos to order.
>
> At the beginning of a new decade, only 20 years short of the millenium, we must try to lift ourselves above day-to-day quarrels (or negotiations) to see the menacing long-term problems.[23]

It was probably unhelpful here to draw a distinction between the 'traditional' threats to peace and those which stem from social chaos. After all, the order that succeeds chaos may be of the despotic sort; and despotisms are always too prone to wax bellicose. Never mind, the overwhelmingly important thing in this passage in the first Brandt Report (a second such was published in 1982 by a reconfigured commission) is that it broke out of the false dichotomy between development studies and strategic studies. A whole succession of events in the Middle East alone had shown how readily economic, social and political stresses add impetus to an arms race and yet, in their turn, are accentuated by that tendency and its violent culminations. To put the point still more starkly, if our population explosion were to terminate in a 'population crash' (a sequence by no means unknown in other species of animals and plants), that crash might take the form of a pandemic, another Black Death. But it might well take that of a nuclear war. Indeed, the former might follow the latter.[24]

A strong awareness of the interaction between 'sustainable development' and peace informed the World Commission on Environment and Development, the body that Gro Harlem Brundtland (lately Prime Minister of Norway) was invited by the UN Secretary-General to chair. The Brundtland report, *Our Common Future*, was submitted to the UN General Assembly in the autumn of 1987. This study (which is quoted above, FNs 7 and 10), devotes its 11th Chapter to 'Peace, Security, Development and the Environment'. Yet with the customary exception of South Africa,[25] it nowhere alludes to the way political repression can threaten peace. It mainly conducts a sombre assessment of the 'arms culture', this on the basis of a ritual impartiality as between different political systems.

Nevertheless, *Our Common Future* is a further step towards the formulation of a comprehensive 'grand strategy', albeit a step taken by a body comprised of people who severally are (a) in or close to government, (b) specialised in developmental or ecological questions, (c) liberal (in the Leftist American sense) on economics, environment and most likely defence and (d) committed to far-reaching though evolutionary change in the planetary ambience. This World Commission (like those under Willy Brandt) epitomised the rather Whiggish liberalism exhibited by that ascendant species in modern Western politics, the 'great and the good'. Therefore it is gratifying to see convergence similarly under way from the other direction as well, from within circles that are geopolitical in their general perspective and principally or largely concerned with the formulation of national defence policies.

Green geopolitics

Thus in March 1990, the White House published a report entitled *National Security Strategy of the United States.*[26] In what a preface by President Bush presented as an invitation to 'the American people and Congress' to dialogue, (p. *v*), there is no mention at all of 'greenhouse warming' or other ecological threats to peace. Nevertheless, there are various references to the peace-threatening connotations of global poverty in what is termed 'our economic agenda'. In particular, attention is drawn to the fact that a Third World debt now aggregated at well over a trillion dollars necessitates annual interest payments of $70 billion; and that this 'is a tremendous burden on struggling democracies and on the ability of many friendly countries to maintain their security' (p. 21). Emphasis is also placed on the proposition that the 'international trade in illicit drugs constitutes a major threat to our national security and to the security of other nations' (p. 7). Likewise, Secretary of State James Baker said at the UN Drugs Conference on 20 March that 'drugs pose a serious threat to global security'.[27] Several months earlier, they had likewise been given prominence in the special edition of *Survival* (the bimonthly journal of the International Institute for Strategic Studies) on 'Non-Military Aspects of Strategy'.[28]

In June 1990, Senator Sam Nunn, Chairman of the Senate Armed Services Committee, joined with several other of its Democratic members to urge the creation of a Strategic Environmental Research Programme. Their notion was that, while our extensive research capability on matters appertaining to national security ought to be retained within the Pentagon and the Department of Energy, a sizeable fraction of it should as a rule be directed to the tackling of environmental degradation. Part of the benefit might be access to military data of environmental relevance. An example might be thickness of polar ice as measured by nuclear submarines.[29]

Yet even before the present wave of concern, more individuals could be identified than one might have expected who had combined a firm commitment to military defence with an active concern not just with economic development (a duality exemplified by Robert McNamara's movement from the Pentagon to head the World Bank) but also with ecology. At the beginning of the Gulf crisis of 1990, Sir Crispin Tickell was UK Ambassador to the United Nations. In 1975–76, this professional British diplomat (now head of Green College, Oxford, and President of the Royal Geographic Society) had been a Fellow at the Center for International Affairs at Harvard. The monograph that resulted was seminal in the way it highlighted the human impact on climate, especially through 'greenhouse warming', and the need for an international framework of institutions and understandings to check these perturbations.[30] Also, Tickell chaired the round table conference in June 1991, referred to above.

Most striking of all is how, in the years in which the greenhouse effect was being ignored or discounted by the great majority of professional climatologists, it was being solemnly warned against by the two men so often spoken of as being the fathers of the American and Soviet hydrogen bombs respectively. In 1958, Edward Teller and a colleague noted that, if the combustion of hydrocarbon fuels drove up the level of atmospheric CO_2, this would act like 'the glass in a greenhouse', with a melting of the ice caps the ultimate result.[31] Ten years later Andrei Sakharov was warning that CO_2, 'from the burning of coal is altering the heat reflecting qualities of the atmosphere. Sooner or later, this will reach a dangerous level'.[32]

When Franklin Roosevelt appointed his first Cabinet in 1933, he made a little-known Chicagoan called Harold Ickes (1874–1952) his

Secretary of the Interior. Working through organisations like the Civilian Conservation Corps, Tennessee Valley Authority, Bureau of Reclamation and National Park Service, Ickes strove to ensure that (unlike in the 1920s) environmental restoration went hand-in-hand with economic recovery. He was also strong for minority rights, especially of those most native of Americans – the Indian peoples. For both these strong thrusts, he is still celebrated by much of American liberal opinion. But as the incumbent from 1941 of the new office of petroleum co-ordinator, he charged himself with getting secure access long-term to Middle East oil. This geopolitical aim was not very successfully pursued, partly because of doubts from the liberal wing. Nevertheless he stayed with this theme post-1945, seeking to guarantee the long-term supply of a wide range of minerals including coal. Though his main emphasis was on new sources of production, he also advocated recycling, a remedy that is sound ecologically as well as geopolitically.[33]

Charles Lindbergh (1902–74) is an example of somebody evolving from geopolitical primitiveness to ecological sophistication. This veteran aviator made isolationist speeches from 1939 on behalf of the America First Committee. A visit to the *Luftwaffe* had convinced him *pro tem* of the invincibility of Nazism and of its geopolitical value as a bulwark against Communism. In 1945, he described the underground tunnels at Nordhausen in which V-2 rockets were produced, largely by slave labour, as the 'height of human accomplishment and the depth of human degradation'. Later on, he was directly involved in the planning that brought into operational service the first generation of US strategic missiles. But then 'with Atlases and Titans in position and Minuteman and Polaris under way', he came to see the 'greatest danger facing modern man' as the way civil technology was 'breaking down human heredity and the natural environment'. He was especially exercised by the urban spread across the countryside, as evidenced 'when flying over the United States on a clear night. Huge areas that once lay blank glowed with electrification'.[34] The late Sir Peter Scott, himself a fine naval commander in wartime as well as a quite outstanding conservationist, paid tribute to how Lindbergh then headed 'extremely effective conservation missions to a number of countries such as Madagascar, Chile and the Philippines'.[35]

However, it is Theodore Roosevelt (1858–1919) who, not least-when in the White House, personified most monumentally such a confluence of attitudes. With him, it is to be observed in several directions. His urge to be close to the primeval was expressed as a farmer, as a game hunter in Africa, and through fighting as a 'rough rider' in Cuba in the Spanish-American war. Also he battled for the homesteaders, promoting irrigation through a Reclamation Act and reviving the federal strategy of 'trust busting' monopolistic capitalism. At the same time, he was committed to geopolitical expansion, and concerned to protect America's forests for strategic as well as ecological reasons. Deep contradictions remained throughout but the personality in question seemed big enough to accommodate them.

In various countries at different times, albeit most conspicuously in the Britain of the early 19th Century, the economic protection of farming has been driven by a coincidence of interest between (a) rural landowners and related interests, (b) national strategists anxious about food supplies, and (c) those concerned to protect the beauty of the countryside, of 'Nature' as they have known it. Against that some will protest that environment issues now transcend the nation-state in general and national defence in particular.[36] But that it is just as true of military security. Never have the two themes come together more dramatically at a multinational level than in the Gulf War of 1991.

Two other individual life stories may be taken, not exactly to prove an underlying unity but to illustrate it well enough. The one is about Hiroo Omado, the soldier from the Imperial Japanese Army found still wandering in a Philippines jungle in 1974 because nobody had ever ordered him to surrender. Now he has founded the Omado Natural Academy in Fukusima Prefecture, a reserve intended to inculcate into children a sense of reverence, stability and peace. The only thing is that the venture is under some strain because modern Japanese youngsters expect their creature comforts, even deep in the forest.[37]

The final example leads us to the etymology of 'holistic', a term that came much into vogue in the New Left and counter-culture days of the 1960s as connoting an all-embracing quasi-mystical view of the natural world, a view that stood in welcome contrast to the narrow deductive logic of technology-driven scientific enquiry. We have it on good authority[38] that the word was actually coined in 1926 by Jan Christian Smuts of South Africa in order to connote the 'whole-making' balance of nature. At all events, the book he wrote that year was entitled *Holism and Evolution*.

Field Marshal Smuts was a distinguished Boer commando leader who came to serve in the highest councils of the British Empire in two World Wars. David Lloyd-George credited him with being the father of the Royal Air Force, created as an independent service in 1918. He was one of those who then struggled wisely but in vain for a conciliatory peace with Germany as a good foundation on which to build the League of Nations. His credentials as a grand strategist of heroic vision would be impeccable if only he had addressed himself better to intercommunal relations at home and so to ensuring that his United Party (which he led as Prime Minister from 1919 to 1924) developed a coherent non-racial alternative to what became *apartheid*. In planetary strategy no less than in strategy of a more traditional kind, the stability of the home base is an absolute prerequisite. But that truism strengthens the hope that there may be confluence between the two streams of thought.

9

Strategy Unbound

THE GIST OF my argument throughout has been that strategic studies must now incorporate wholeheartedly several disciplines it has thus far treated as incidental or extraneous. But this must not exclude further development along existing lines. Three themes, in particular, ought to be addressed more fully. These are rationality, persuasion and the action-reaction phenomenon. Each would be fundamental to the formation of a new grand strategy.

Dissuasion and persuasion

An assumption of rational behaviour was early built into the theories of deterrence. Even when, as in the exotic surmisings of the late Herman Kahn,[1] irrationality was allowed to figure, it was as and when a rational advantage was sought by affecting maniacal tendencies, the 'game of chicken' scenarios.[2] The notion thus conjured was of a 'strategic man' closely akin to the profit maximising 'economic man' of classical economic theory: a person who is fully informed, totally logical and utterly single-minded.

Nor may this depiction be that far from the realities of most crisis management to date. Undeniably, attitudes that are irrational on almost any definition often play a part in initiating or sustaining aggression. But one need not be too hard a cynic to observe how often aggressors become more rational and circumspect once their own homelands are being savaged and when they themselves, and their friends and relations, are liable to be killed.

This truism is borne out well enough by fascist behaviour in the Second World War. If in 1941 Imperial Japan had paused coolly to reflect, she would have seen how much wiser it was to agree to

withdraw from China than to wage war against Britain, The Netherlands and the USA. Yet that December, she adopted the latter
course, despite grave doubts within her own ruling circles about her
ability to withstand a counter-offensive. To heighten the absurdity,
there was never any desire in Tokyo to see an outright victory by a
Nazi regime committed to Teutonic world supremacy. Therefore
the best the authorities there could hope for was their country
becoming the arbiter of a German-American stalemate, a balance
almost certainly too delicate to achieve and patently too delicate to
last.

In 1944, a savage air offensive began against the imperial homeland, the offensive that was to culminate in the dropping of two
nuclear bombs. Evidently, the fascist leadership could have fought
on a while, using prisoners-of-war and occupied peoples as hostages.
This time, however, it decided with some alacrity to 'endure the
unendurable', a capitulation far more total than that called for in
1941.

Similarly, Nazi Germany was in desperate straits by late 1944. On
the other hand, she did have stocks of shells and bombs loadable with
nerve gas. Moreover, she had already proved herself ready to use
poison gas without pity or remorse on millions of Jews, gypsies and
other deportees. Yet not even the vengeful Hitler could bring himself
to authorise its use against the invading Allied troops or their
homelands. An Anglo-American ability to retaliate in kind is generally adjudged a factor in this restraint.[3]

Since 1945, fears of desolation through 'total war' have largely
related to nuclear weapons. The usual reckoning is that some 200
distinct wars, half of them with an active international dimension,
have occurred in the interim. Yet fewer than 10 have done so in
Europe, not one as between the Atlantic alliance and the USSR.
Granted, various influences have contributed to this veritable revolution in the fortunes of a traditionally war-torn continent. Among
them must be the tight lid kept, till recently that is, on the communal
tensions so long endemic in what we now again call the Balkans. But
nowhere has the nuclear confrontation been as dense and direct as in
the European theatre.

All the same, it would be foolish to assume that this rational respect
for deterrence will hold good everywhere throughout this era of paradigmatic change. The behaviour of Saddam Hussein is ominous in
this regard. So is the degree of popular support he has attracted in the
Arab and Muslim world. Meanwhile, we could soon face, in respect

of the USSR, the chaotic disintegration of a thermonuclear state, with what that could connote for the for the wildcat release of the most terrible of weapons. It is a danger posed for the second time. The first was with China when, as Theodore White put it, half a century 'of torment bred madness'.[4] He was referring to that extraordinary orgy of hatred dignified as 'the Cultural Revolution': rabid xenophobia, industrial chaos, shattered universities, desecrated churches, teachers terrorised by crazed children, thousands of casualties in street violence, millions exiled to the countryside, ferocious repression and high mortality in the labour camps, and the gleeful destruction of cultural relics. In China today, this era is defined as extending from 1966 to 1974. but the most ferocious phase ended in 1969 with the intervention of the military. It was in 1967 that the country exploded its first thermonuclear warhead ie hydrogen bomb.

With the USSR today the risk of irrational excess is accentuated by the communal factor. In late 1990, reports came in of theatre nuclear missiles being withdrawn from certain of the more unruly non-Russian republics. So did there of a possible military takeover at Kremlin level. A collapse of nuclear control is made the more imaginable by the fact that hundreds of the USSR's intercontinental missiles are positioned in peripheral republics.[5]

In any case, the causes of irrationality extend both deeper and wider. Suppose the world does become a lot more stressful, this largely on account of trends extrinsic to nuclear deterrence as such, trends in the realms of sociology, economics, ecology and climatology. Might not reason and reasonableness be gravely stretched? Might not many take leave of rationality in the positive, life-preserving sense? Much stimulated by the New Left and the counter-culture, a body of literature had burgeoned these last three decades along the lines that, though nuclear deterrence may conform to a kind of narrow logic, it is hopelessly irrational in a more holistic sense. The ICBM is seen as the apex of an unstable pyramid, institutional and technological, mindlessly erected by urban mass society.

Alas, this literature has been stronger on imagery and allusion than on sequential argument. The authors in question leave the impression that they read each other avidly but never read anybody else. They have advanced a clutch of untestable hypotheses about the 'bomb culture', even placing on it the blame for any lapses in their own inspiration.[6] Their understanding of arms technology is always rudimentary. Thus E.P. Thompson thought Ground-Launched

Cruise Missiles, although fired from road-mobile platforms, were 'fire strike' weapons, the introduction of which would 'signal a point of no return'.[7] In fact, these weapons would have been less geared to nuclear first strike than, say, warplanes poised on very destructible runways. He further opined that the introduction into strategic missilery of solid rather than liquid fuels implied acceptance by those concerned of 'launch-on-warning'.[8] Never mind the stability then offered by the hardened Minuteman emplacements (see Chapter 2). Nor that another consequence of this minor revolution was that it allowed such weapons to be borne in submarines far out at sea.

None the less, this school of thought is now receiving a fillip from the realm of eco-concern. A youthful Anglo-American contribution puts the point with evocative lucidity. Bill McKibben interweaves a solemn warning and stern indictment in the manner of biblical prophecy. The gist of his judgement is that, by depriving 'wild nature' of any separate existence, we have unhinged ourselves. Above all, by 'changing the weather we make every spot on Earth man-made and artificial. We have deprived Nature of its independence, and that is fatal to its meaning'. A corollary will be the divorce of religion from naturalism, thus exposing us to 'a siege of apocalyptic and fanatic creeds'.[9] Reason thus jettisoned at the religious or philosophical level could hardly survive at the societal or, indeed, the geopolitical level.

However, pursuance of a strategy of environmental control on the international plane will depend on recalcitrant states being persuaded, perhaps with economic and political coercion. The crux of the problem thus presented is his. Dissuading a regime form unwelcome action is rarely easy, even if one can boast *force majeure*. But it can be even harder to induce it to launch out on such policies as one sees as constructive. Writing 25 years ago, Thomas Schelling, one of the founding fathers of strategic studies, introduced the term 'compellence' to cover this requirement as it might arise within the context of a nuclear showdown.[10] He warned against trite applications of behaviourist psychology, trying to reward conduct that was welcome and punish that which was not.

A key question now is how best to use economic and political pressures to secure environmentalist ends. Here one may note the emphasis Schelling famously placed on preserving 'face', not false pride but a reputation for due responsiveness:

> Few parts of the world are intrinsically worth the risk of a serious war ... but defending them or running risks to protect them may

preserve one's commitments to actions in other parts of the world
and at later times.[11]

Perhaps the same applies to non-violent modes of persuasion.

Action-reaction

It has been well said that action-reaction is a useful formulation,
provided it is not raised to 'a virtual iron law of international relations'.[12] It is most applicable to military rivalry where it is driven not
just by the stark reciprocation of hostility between one side and 'the
Other' but also by what J.F.C. Fuller called the Constant Tactical
Factor, arms races sustained by technological rivalry and – so he
thought – endless cycles off defensive and offensive advantage. President Kennedy was exercised about this, most notably in the speech to
the American University in June 1963. Robert McNamara followed
suit, as in September 1967 when he sought to justify Anti-Ballistic
Missile deployment on just a minimal basis.

When hostilities threaten, Theodore Roosevelt's advice to 'talk
softly and carry a big stick' will almost always be pertinent. So far as
actual war is concerned, the highest expression of statesmanship may
be found in what Churchill used to speak of as fortitude in combat
followed by magnanimity in victory and goodwill in peace.

What needs also to be remembered is that, especially in confrontations that are well below the threshold of armed violence, each side
will have its more hawkish but also its more dovish elements. Mutual
reinforcement by the respective hawks partly covers what President
Truman was getting at when, in February 1950, he quipped that
'anti-Communist' witch-hunting by Senator Joseph McCarthy had
turned him into 'the Kremlin's greatest asset'. On international environment questions, the hawks will be, first and foremost, those
imbued with too narrow a sense of national advantage.

Countless examples could be cited of polities of all kinds having
been treated, in foreign policy analyses, as more monolithic and
immobile than they are or were or could ever be. This probably used
to be the case with the USSR. It is conspicuously the case still with
Israel. So many times she has been discussed by supporters and
critics alike as if her political attitudes were totally homogenised, not
least in relation to the Palestinians. Everyone ought to know they are
not. All else apart, absolutely crucial differences have emerged
between the leadership of the Labour Alignment and that of Likud,
the dominant bloc in the present government coalition.

Likud very much draws its inspiration from the aggressive Revisionist Zionism of the late Vladimir Jabotinsky. The two Prime Ministers it has thus far provided, Menachem Begin and Yitzhak Shamir, came to national politics via terrorism, as the leaders of the Irgun and the Stern Gang respectively. Correspondingly, Likud was prepared to resort to orchestrated hooliganism against its Labour opponents in order to retain power in the pivotal general election of 1981; and so to time an attack on the Iraqi nuclear facility as to serve that same end. The ambivalence that Prime Minister Shamir displayed all through 1990 about the offer of elections to the Palestinians in the occupied territories and about the settlement in those lands of immigrant Soviet Jews is only too consistent with a Likud ethos that remains altogether too morbid. One further recalls how badly Menachem Begin compromised Anwar Sadat, at Camp David in 1977, by refusing to have the Egyptian-Israeli peace agreement provide for more than the briefest of halts in Jewish settlement of the occupied territories.

The Labour party, on the other hand, is rooted in the social democratic philosophy of the Zionist mainstream. Though never soft on Israel's basic security, Labour had been cramped in recent years by the rise of communal passions throughout the Levant. One hope must therefore be that a younger generation in Likud will gradually come under more expansive modern influences, much as has lately happened within the Nationalist Party in South Africa. Portents can be seen in the attitudes towards peace currently struck by two younger members of the present cabinet, David Levy and Dan Meridor.

All the same, the return to power of a Labour Alignment will almost certainly have to be a feature of any sustained revival of what we sanguinely refer to as 'the Middle East peace process'. Contributory to this will be curbing of fascisto-Marxist extremism within the Palestinian movement, not to mention Damascus. Another will be for the West bluntly to warn the Israeli people that Likud's ideology resembles old-time *apartheid* too closely for the modern world to accept. Only then may Zionism evolve the partnership between Jew and Arab that the more progressive of the Zionist pioneers, and above all Albert Einstein, always looked towards.[13]

Where commentators in the West, not least those with Leftist credentials, long failed even more blatantly to back dovish tendencies was the Republic of South Africa. Few could ever bring themselves to take advice simply to be fair towards the Whites:

This does not mean the abandonment of principles not the removal of pressures. It does mean the abandonment of double standards and the practice of continually shifting one's ground and raising the ante: practices that convince Whites that their critics want to punish, not reform, them and that exacerbate their fears, which are a major obstacle to further progress'.[14]

Instead, as the debate about sanctions and *apartheid* became more intense in 1986 (with the reciprocal introduction in South Africa of a wide-ranging State of Emergency), the strictures became more hysteric than ever. In Britain, no less a figure than Denis Healey opined that 'South Africa today suffers from a news blackout far more complete than any Communist country has ever known'.[15] Did it? Albania under Enver Hoxha? Cambodia under Pol Pot? China during the Cultural Revolution? North Korea? Russia under Stalin? When a political intellectual is so wound up as to skew reality that badly, he convinces the conservative hard core in South Africa (White and non-White) that the rest of the world is not worth listening to. He does so the more if there are no countervailing assurances.jo In the speech just cited, these were omitted apropos everything from necklace murders to the modalities of majority rule.

The audit of environment

Since when, South Africa is more visibly part and parcel of the paradigmatic change that the information explosion is inducing, however confusedly, across the modern world. Even so, it would be crassly naive to rest the hopes for democracy there simply on the stature of Nelson Mandela and F.W. de Klerk. Their qualities will avail nought without economic development on a scale unsustainable just by an internal redistribution of income and private inward investment but which might be ensured by a Capricorn Marshall Plan offered to South Africa (and the other 'front-line' states) in exchange for those concerned committing themselves to authentic majority rule.

Manifestly, it would be within the capacity of the Atlantic Alliance and Japan to finance an official aid programme along these lines allowing as well for the renewed flow of private capital that official loans or credits would encourage. After all, we are talking about aid sufficient to meet, year to year, a few per cent of the national incomes of recipient states. The Gross National Product of South Africa is one part in a hundred of the aggregate for the Atlantic Alliance and

Japan. If the other front-line states are added in, the ratio becomes one in 75.

At all events, a big inflow is needed especially to the Republic of South Africa. Nobody should presume that, since she exports a lot of gold, her streets must be paved with it. The average income of the Republic (including the four 'independent Black Homelands'[16]) is a fifth that of Canada's. Certainly, South Africa does need a drastic redistribution of economic power internally, as a foundation for a truly democratic political order. But this might best be a monitored concomitant of multinational aid, not a precursor of it.[17]

What lends urgency to this is the likelihood that, by the turn of the century even, global warming will be reducing South Africa's aggregate production of grain by several per cent.[18] Moreover, this effect will not be at all even across the country. A strong argument in favour of the unitary state favoured by the African National Congress and against the federative solution customarily advocated by White liberals now has to be that the former may the better adopt a synoptic response to climatic adversity. But this in its turn means that the constitution of a democratic south Africa would need to incorporate (a) a solid network of local government and (b) a Bill of Rights, something like that drafted by the KwaZulu-Natal Indaba in July 1986. There will also be a need to explore what can constructively be provided by way of international guarantees.

Similar arguments apply in the Levant. Early in 1986, Shimon Peres, speaking then as Labour Prime Minister of Israel, urged that a quasi-Marshall plan, led by Europe and Japan, be launched across the Middle East to offset falling oil prices. He told European and Japanese officials that if they wanted to guarantee the oil supply in the future, 'you should invest not only in refineries and pipelines but in political infrastructure'.[19] The following month Mrs Thatcher was to make what was, in terms of personal impact, a most successful visit to the region. With something of a presentiment of the *intifada*, she called on the Israelis to give the Palestinians a constitutional alternative to violence by allowing, after a nine-year hiatus, mayoral elections in the West Bank and the Gaza. In a rejoinder, Defence Minister Yitzhak Rabin pooh-poohed elections, saying that no Arab state ever held genuine ones. Then on a more positive note, he suggested Europe be more ready 'to assist in the welfare of the people who reside in the West Bank and the Gaza strip'.[20]

Here, too, inter-communal tension could worsen as rainfall declines as the sub-tropical anticyclonic belt moves northwards. Yet even now the competition for water supplies is extremely acute as between the Israelis and Palestinians; and in the occupied territories involves severe discrimination by the former against the latter. As much has recently been demonstrated in a thorough survey in the *Journal for Palestine Studies* by a legal counsellor at the Washington office of the UN High Commissioner for Refugees.[21] This journal, founded some 20 years ago at Kuwait University and the Institute for Palestine Studies in Beirut, soon established a good reputation for germane but objective scholarship.

The connotations of all this are tough for both Israelis and Palestinians. One is that the hydrological imperative makes Israel and the territories more or less inseparable politically, no matter what this implies for the traditional Zionist vision of a Jewish democracy or for current Palestinian notions of acceptable statehood. For the Israelis, it means tight constraints on immigration from the USSR or wherever. For the Palestinians, it has to mean a big drive for family planning. My impression when on the East Bank in Jordan, in 1972, was that the country had generally adopted a most constructive approach to economic recovery since the 1967 war; and yet, although family planning was already practised by a high proportion of the more educated, there was a manifest disinclination to encourage it officially. Whilst this may have stemmed in part from a desire not to clash head-on with the Muslim Brotherhood and other conservative factions, it was also the product of a desire not to lose out in the numbers game with Israel. But what did comparative head counts really do for the moral weight of Palestinian claims or, indeed, to the military equation? Were these the most basic questions to ask, in any case?

About a formulated response at global level to environmental pressures, this much has to said. One plank in any strategy has to be the restrained use of the hydrocarbon fuels, coal and wood especially. More efficient energy usage always commends itself, even if one clings to the sanguine assumption that the 'greenhouse' threat has been exaggerated. It helps block off other adverse trends, such as acid rain. It can be made attractive to entrepreneurs in terms of energy supply and demand, actual or prospective. Energy lends itself well to government intervention in the market, when required.

However, the attractiveness of this approach means that many projections of future energy demand and supply already assume a continuation of the trend towards higher efficiency evident ever since the Industrial Revolution but accelerated by the 1973–74 'oil shock'.

Yet often those same projections indicate a renewed energy shortage, early on in the next century. Natural gas will boom but oil will most likely peak out. Firewood certainly will. Coal will be ever less acceptable environmentally, partly because it is rich in carbon rather than hydrogen. Therefore its waste products include less water but more carbon dioxide.

Contributors to the energy debate, especially from the Left, tend to depict the closure of an anticipated 'energy gap' as hinging on a choice between nuclear power or the 'renewable' sources (winds, tides, hydroelectric, solar . . .), the latter being much preferred. In several respects, however, the two approaches are similar. Both are capital intensive, too much so to get us through the next half century unaided. Even so, the economic prospects for both will improve as and when oil again becomes dear. None the less, both will always have environmental drawbacks, aesthetic or ecological or both.

The special problem of the disposal of the waste products of nuclear fission appears manageable, technically speaking. The decommissioning of fission reactors probably is as well. A tougher aspect, partly because it is so political, is how to inhibit the diversion of Plutonium 239 residues to military ends. The fact is that just one year's high intensity operation by a small power reactor (one with a thermal rating of between 25 and 30 megawatts) can yield the six to eight kilograms needed for a Nagasaki-type bomb. However, the correct inference to draw may be that what probably is a needful nuclear fraction of the global energy budget ought to be provided within the advanced industrial nations, especially those that already are military nuclear powers.

What should also be widely addressed is the part controlled nuclear fusion may play in curbing 'greenhouse' tendencies through the second half of the next century. An otherwise thorough Greenpeace review of the greenhouse problem entirely ignores this dimension.[22] Yet the very reason why we are today in such difficulties is because, during the first three-quarters of this century, we failed to think far enough ahead about energy, environment and the interaction between them.

It has been my good fortune to observe development work in controlled nuclear fusion in several of the lead centres in the field: Birmingham, Canberra, Culham, Naka, Osaka, Princeton and Tokyo. Clearly, an economically-viable commercial reactor will not appear for several decades, if ever. The nub is the difficulty of confining the hydrogen plasma in position long enough and at a high enough density and temperature for fusion to take place. Two approaches have been adopted: the use as a 'bottle' of a magnetic field (usually 'doughnut shaped', in a design known as a torus or tokamak) and inertial confinement via bombardment by converging beams, either laser or nuclear particle. Their fortunes have fluctuated, compared with one another and with the exacting ultimate goal.

Still, international collaboration between fusion scientists, not least Soviet ones, has been exemplary for more than 30 years. What can also be said is that fusion researchers as a community have been admirably cautious and objective in their discussion of the possibilities. Unfortunately, however, their repute has been marred by several premature claims, these mostly driven by extraneous factors. In 1951, the fascistic regime of Juan Peron in Argentina claimed that an Austrian immigrant scientist, cited in connection with Nazi war crimes, had achieved controlled fusion. Five years later a premature claim came from a Britain, then rather desperately casting about for symbols of greatness (*eg* the role of sterling in world trade) to offset her retreat from Empire. This claim, made by the then director of the nuclear research establishment at Harwell, was of a '90 per cent' probability that fusion had been achieved in the ZETA facility there. Similarly, after the Princeton Large Torus came into service in 1975, there was heady talk of commercial application within 20 years. Nor was the launch of the Fusion Energy Foundation by that roguish eccentric, Lyndon La Rouche, helpful in this regard. Then, in 1989, a highly precipitate assertion came from the Universities of Southampton and Utah, this to the effect that 'sustained fusion' had been achieved 'cold' (*ie* at room temperature) in a laboratory.

Never mind. We would do well to back fusion research more firmly as a hope for unlimited power that would not cause too much pollution (radioactive or otherwise) and need not greatly facilitate the proliferation of nuclear weapons to states that do not currently possess them. In fact, the only danger in this particular respect comes from high-energy lasers developed for Inertial Confinement Fusion (ICF). These just might be applied to the triggering of hydrogen bombs in static prepared sites: a variant of the 'doomsday machines' that the late Herman Kahn dolefully envisaged.

Charles Maisonnier currently heads the encouraging programme for Magnetic Confinement Fusion (MCF) the EC has undertaken with its Joint European Torus at Culham in Oxfordshire. He warns that fusion cannot possibly produce commercial electricity before the year 2040; and that in the interim it will require a total expenditure in excess of £30 billion. But he backs perseverance.[23] Meanwhile, Japan is emerging as a strong candidate to host the International Thermonuclear Experimental Reactor (ITER): the next generation MCF programme being sponsored by the USA, the USSR, Europe and Japan herself. Her claims rest on a sound technology base and considerable experience with both MCF and ICF.

Calculations proliferate about the economic burdens liable to be incurred through 'greenhouse' and other ecological threats. The 'greenhouse' increase in world agricultural costs in the next century, with a 'business-as-usual' scenario (ie no attempt to limit climate change) would likely be between 5 and 15 per cent of their present level.[24] Also, the World Watch Institute has estimated the total cost of achieving sustainable development globally through the year 2000. It allows for the maintenance of topsoil, reforestation, slowing population growth, raising energy efficiency, the development of renewable energy and 'retiring' the debt burdens of developing nations. Two annual figures it has come up with, at constant prices, are $46 billion in 1990 and $149 billion in the year 2000.[25]

Granted, even the latter will be under one per cent of world economic output, for the year in question. However, there are many measures against diverse forms of pollution that could as well have been included. All in all, it is safe to say that an adequate global strategy for ecological management could absorb most or all the 'peace dividend' looked for from an easement of the arms burden. At present, world military expenditure is around a trillion dollars a year, perhaps five or six per cent of the economic output.

Limits to growth?

But the ultimate question is whether the concept of 'sustainable development' that has become a veritable dogma in the United Nations and elsewhere is itself sustainable. May we not have ultimately to accept that there is a finite limit to how much more human activity this planet can accommodate. Surely, we can no longer applaud the sanguineness behind projections such as that of the Hudson Institute in 1977, which showed world energy consumption per year rising over 14 times between 1975 and 2176.[26]

The absurdity, within the confines of this small planet, of attitudes so bullish is well demonstrated by reference to a constriction that owes nothing to complex interactions, physical or biological. Instead, it is almost entirely a function of geometry. What is alluded to is the near critical congestion of Space vehicles and debris in Earth orbit. These man-made objects and remnants, moving at speeds of at least six miles a second, have mostly congregated in the 300 to 1,200 miles altitude zone; and, more narrowly, around the geostationary level. At this height, some 22,300 miles above the surface, the angular velocity at which a body revolves is exactly in phase with that of the Earth itself. Therefore if that body is in the equatorial plane, it will always be above the same equatorial point. Since this has great merit for communication relay, parts of this geostationary circle are even now very crowded, a state of affairs that may lend itself only partially to technical amelioration.

But let us focus on the lower zone of congestion. A comprehensive tracking of Space objects conducted from the ground by the North American Aerospace Defence Command (NORAD) has so far only registered, even in the lower orbits, objects a least several centimetres across. But it is from this size range that the risk of catastrophe through collision mostly comes. NORAD's catalogue of such items has expanded from 1,800 in 1970 to 7,500 in 1989. Assuming the list continues to grow at 500 per year, the likely number of collisions has been given as four by 1995 and 12 a decade later. However, there is the serious complication that a single collision between, say, a discarded rocket case and a four centimetre fragment could create another 10,000 particles at least a centimetre across, not to mention millions of tinier ones.[27,28]

This particular crisis has come quite suddenly upon us. It can be remedied, if at all, only be international planning facilitated by technical advance. Meanwhile, a feeling is abroad that our planet is filling up in a wider sense, a feeling not unlike the mood endangered through the turn of the century as the great age of exploration and moving frontiers seemed abruptly to end.[29] Many people today would see that change-around as one more of appearance than of substance, certainly as compared with the many ways our world is 'shrinking'. Even so, it has been adduced as contributing to the build-up of tension that led to the First World War:

> The very process of imperial activity had simultaneously furnished occasion for clashes and crises, and served the function of safety valve for the overflowing energy of Europe. There was, in 1914, no more room in the world for fresh conquests.[30]

What one may well be saying is that, if acute tension is to be avoided, fairly tight limits to economic growth may ultimately be imperative. Yet what should also be admitted is that this would certainly be damnably difficult; and therefore productive of tension itself. Since the Renaissance at least, a majority of people in the West (and, ever more so, those elsewhere) have seen material progress as usually feasible and always desirable. Nor did the dramatic turning inwards of the two great civilisations of East Asia, China and Japan, in the 15th and 17th Centuries respectively (see Chapter 7) actually involve for either a cessation of growth and development. All else apart, the curbing of civil unrest led in both cases to prosperity and hence a population boom. In Japan, there was a doubling to 30 million in the century to 1725. For China, the standard interpretation had been that the population hovered around 50 to 80 million in the 15th and 16th Centuries but was then to more than double by the late 18th. It now seems probable, however, that a sustained rise began rather earlier.[31]

In terms of contemporary politics, there was something very facile about the way the New Left and counter-culture in the 1960s celebrated the prospects of limits to growth, invoking as they did so half remembered traditions within political thought and literature about prehistoric 'noble savages' loping carefree through an unspoilt 'state of Nature'.[32] At the practical level, virtually the only country in the modern world to adopt an ideology at all close to 'limits to growth' has been Tanzania. In the Arusha Declaration of 1967, President Julius Nyerere committed his people to socialist 'self reliance' largely on the basis of rural co-operative communities, within a framework of one-party rule. By the time he retired from the presidency in 1985, impressive advances had been made in health and education. But the economy was faltering despite large and diverse injections of foreign aid; and today, population growth is still 2.8 per cent a year. Besides which, there has been, since 1975,[33] a steady shift away from ideology and towards pragmatism Western-style.

Eternal vigilance

The warning famously delivered by John Philpot Curran in 1790 that 'The condition upon which God hath given liberty to man is eternal vigilance' is applicable enough to Western consumerist democracy in 1990. A tough external challenge lies ahead in terms of evolving a global political economy that can sustain us through the next century. Even as things stand, tough internal challenges arise from the contemporary social turbulence. Not the least is armed violence by communalist or ideological extremists.

Looking back over the last 20 years, however, we can feel some pride and satisfaction at the resilience of open societies in the face of such insurgent threats. Overall there has been little in the way of abject appeasement or of an 'action-reaction' backlash of violence against disaffected minorities. None the less, since 1983, over 50 members of ETA, the Basque extremist movement, have been killed, either in Spain or the South of France, by GAL, a Rightist 'counter-terror' group. Investigative journalism has unearthed strong indications of GAL's having backers within Spain's police, Interior Ministry, army and civil guard.

In Ulster, too, there has been a fair amount of counter-terror against the IRA by illicitly 'loyalist' paramilitaries. On the whole, however, Ulster Protestants have displayed amazing stability in the face of an orgy of violent intimidation, involving since 1969 well over 2,000 deaths. So, too, have the great mass of Roman Catholics in the province. So, one might add, have the people of mainland Britain, except for some police perversion of the course of justice. On the other hand, the emergency legislation and associated changes in juridical practice have considerably undermined individual rights within Ulster. Private homes can be entered at any time without warrant and suspects can be held for a week without going before a judge. The presumption of innocence may also have been compromised. Likewise, in Italy the Red Brigade has obliged the authorities to secure much wider powers of search, arrest and detention without trial. In Spain, the case for Basque partial autonomy was probably conceded too readily (see Chapter 3).

Another major challenge to the liberality of Western democracy may soon be much stronger pressures towards international migration as populations explode, cities implode, and ecosystems degrade. But so far at least, so good. Over the last 30 years, the countries of Western Europe alone have received 20 million immigrants. Yet although the associated social problems have been considerable, they have led to little in the way of overt communal strife, even during the post-1973 recession. Meanwhile, the immigrants have done much to underpin economies and have begun to enrich the cultural scene.

But how will perspectives change as the crowds at the borders grow? Not quite a quarter of the 20 million just mentioned have come from either North Africa or Turkey. Today the population of the 14 Mediterranean countries not within the EC is 200 million.

Three decades hence, it could well be 350 million, French demographers have visualised the consequent departure of 25 to 30 million from the Maghreb alone within 30 to 40 years; and such projections mayor may not take due account of climatic change (see Chapters 6 and 10). Yet, as President Mitterrand has surmised, a 'threshold of intolerance' may already be close.

Two aspects especially liable to sear the liberal conscience are illicit immigration and political asylum. The familiar case of Mexican 'wetback' immigration into the United States has already been referred to (Chapter 8). Spain, Italy, and Greece probably host between them over a million foreigners from outside Europe and residing illegally. Switzerland estimates she has 110,000 illegal aliens; and even Japan is thought to have 50–100,000.

Whereas only 20,000 people from around the world in search of asylum were in the West the mid-1970s, another 600,000 came in 1990 alone. Maybe a fifth of all arrivals these days are truly in flight from actual persecution. Many of the rest are as concerned with economic opportunity as with political refuge. Yet four-fifths of them stay as regular immigrants anyhow, partly because the alternative procedures are too involved.[34]

Most fundamentally, however, the resilience of a parliamentary democracy will depend on its maintaining a vigorous but constructive dialectic between the Right and the Left of the political spectrum. However, the democratic Left has lately lost inner confidence and a sense of direction. Throughout the years of Cold War, it repeatedly fissured over defence and East-West relations. Yet now, it seems no more assured. Though particular reasons can be adduced in particular countries (*eg* the USA, Britain, Israel, India and Japan), there are more general explanations. One is simply that the Left's policy-shaping tends to be too drawn out for a time of unprecedented change. So do its endeavours to recast its political philosophy, not least in regard to whether anything of value remains in the Marxist tradition. Another is that the worldwide resurgence of liberal democratic ideals, these last 10 to 15 years, has gone hand-in-hand with a marked restoration of regard for the political as well as the economic merits of the free market. As clear-cut a measure of this as any is that, by 1986, over 50 governments were involved in the drive to privatise public assets.[35] Likewise, though the new Eastern Europe has yet to settle down politically, the indications to date have been that market-led consumerism is pitching it well to the Right.[36] What happens in the former East Germany may prove crucial in this regard.

Meanwhile, the 'new frontier' argument that only progressivism can defeat Soviet Communism seems totally to have lost its force.

There are, in any case, other conceptual dilemmas. Among them is how to respond to the progressive erosion of communal identities that seems inevitable if society is to become ever more open and fluid. In Britain, for instance, the Left has regularly insisted (correctly, in my view) that the Whites in South Africa have to accept not only the abandonment of political supremacy but also a cultural convergence, not least through educational desegregation: a process at last under way.[37] However, the British Left's declamations along these lines would ring truer if they were less often interlaced with wan pleas on the home front for the preservation, intact and indefinitely, of the distinctive cultural attributes of Celtic nationalisms, coal-mining villages, immigrant communities or whatever. Much the same has been true, through this century, of the Democrats in the United States; witness John Kennedy's *A Nation of Immigrants*, a book first published in 1958 and heavily retrospective in its general pitch.[38] The roots of such social nostalgia lie in a genuine but naive concern for the oppressed nationalities of Europe. One thinks of Woodrow Wilson and Lloyd George at Versailles; and, well before them, Gladstone on the 'Eastern Question'.

By much the same token, the democratic Left has so far reacted to, more often it has led, the upsurge of ecological concern; never mend that this is bound, in due course, to cast afresh some of the classic arguments for public intervention in the market. The fact still remains, however, that a good dialectic within the parliamentary democracies is essential if we are to head off what could otherwise be disastrously negative reaction to a deepening world crisis on the part of the more radically-minded in the West and, even more so, those further afield.

False millennia

The allusion here made is to the millenarian tendency that has all too often found expression, either religious or political, during times of stress. The central vision, usually as focused through a great leader who has arrived or is imminently anticipated, is of the approach of History's last great struggle-the dark valley of apocalyptic crisis and near catastrophe that must and will be traversed to reach the celestial city on the hill, a thousand years of peace. This decidedly non-rational notion waxed strong in Christian Europe as the anguished

10th Century drew towards its close. It died away, with good results for true enterprise and real progress, once the year 1000 had passed.

These days we may flatter ourselves we will be less entranced by the mystique of the 'perfect number' as expressed in one particular year. What this may mean, however, is that for quite a long time after the year 2000, those of millenarian inclination may be fortified by this extra manifestation that History is at a turning point: a time of taxing conflict, to be followed by lasting tranquillity.

A very recurrent and dangerous deficiency in millenarianism is its impatient indifference to exactly how 'the thousand years of peace' is to be created and sustained. Another may be the special strength of its appeal to those who obsessively feel themselves to be 'outside the system' in whatever sense. Henri Focillon advises us that the chiliastic prophesyings of the 10th century are nowhere to be found in the official documents and chronicles of church or state in the era.[39] Likewise, Norman Cohn points out that the successive millenarian outbursts in central Europe over the following centuries (which often were vicious, not least towards Jews) drew their support from the 'amorphous mass of people who were not simply poor but who could find no assured and recognised place in society at all'.[40] Unless democratic participation can be made solidly to flourish at precinct level as well as at national level or above, there may be hundreds of millions of such in the 21st century: not least in the shanty towns of the developing world, the *bidonvilles* and the *bustées*.

In our generation, millenarian protest in the West may come in cycles of perhaps 15 years and may all too readily turn to some degree of violence. Philosophically, it may have a variety of different configurations, depending much on circumstances and more than a bit on chance. The Campaign for Nuclear Disarmament (CND) has always had a millenarian streak. Thus its once cherished slogan, 'Better red than dead', took for granted that a world covered with Marxist regimes would at least remain at peace with itself. As George Orwell would have been quick to remind CND, however, the probability was that such regimes would go to war more often. Not a few times, we have seen actual hostilities between various Communist states: Yugoslavia and her neighbours; the USSR and Hungary; the Warsaw Pact and Czechoslovakia; the USSR and China; Vietnam and China; and Vietnam and Cambodia. Nor should internal strife between rival Marxist factions be ignored. So first Red and then dead?

Certain Green movements could also prove sufficiently apocalyptic to be susceptible to millenarian takeover,[41] a hard-core test in each particular case being the reasonableness or otherwise of its critique of applied nuclear energy and especially of controlled nuclear fusion. Utopian socialist traditions, such as that of Anarchism in Spain and elsewhere, can likewise assume this pattern. So, to quite an extent, does classical Marxism-Leninism with the party as an 'elect' and the doctrine of the 'historic inevitability' of violent upheaval in place of the more obvious kinds of prophecy. Among the big religious traditions, Shi'a Islam is always the one that can most readily be mobilised against the West in this way. A further facet of the millenarian mentality can be its penchant for blending schools of thought that appear, in principle, incompatible: Marx and the counter-culture, let us say. In which connection, we ought not to make as much as we often do of the 'irreconcilable' conflict between Marxism and radical Islam.

Under certain circumstances there could, of course, be action-reaction in terms of a millenarian backlash in the West, from the radical Right and related religious influences. Hints of it can be seen in the way some American televangelists were speaking only a few years ago about the 'inevitability' of armageddon against Soviet Communism. The Lyndon La Rouche school went so far as to suggest, *inter alia*, that 'Chernobyl' might have been wilfully contrived to sap the West's nuclear resolve.[42] The Unification Church, still quite an influence in Korea and Japan, used to have similar proclivities and probably still does.[43]

A prime purpose of the West's grand strategy has to be to ensure that the new world order we may be creating is never again exposed to such destructive gyrations to extremism. In the 1950s, people in NATO used to talk of their conventional 'shield' and their nuclear 'sword'. Today, we should be shaping a planetary sword, along with a geopolitical shield. The struggle of adaptation we must thus embark on seems destined to go on deep into the next century. Hopefully, we can thus avoid the 'end of History' in the apocalyptic sense so feverishly prepared for by millenarians of whatever hue. What seems sure to me is that we are a long way from the 'end of History' in any other sense.

10

Geopolitics and Beyond

ONE GEOPOLITICAL tradition was to depict as 'crush zones' or 'shatterbelts', regions that were fractured politically and subject to intrusions by rival blocs.[1] The world today is too kaleidoscopic to draw such neat distinctions. A quarter of a century ago, China, Indonesia and Nigeria looked fissiparous. Today, their unities seem assured. Then the USSR and Eastern Europe appeared as one solid 'heartland'. Today, this heartland could face complete fragmentation. Canada could fragment if Quebec secedes, this in a vain attempt to restore an 'identity' otherwise undermined by inward migration and cultural melding. A European bloc may arise the while. Arise and then fragment?

So establishing the right geopolitical framework for effective planetary management is no easy task. Meanwhile, however, one or two regions do stand out as persistently fragile. Southern Africa is certainly one. Moreover, the backwardness of the continent as a whole is confirmed by an economic growth rate of but 0.6 per cent per head per year these last 30 years.[2] An appreciable rise in this index in the 1960s gave way to a levelling off from 1970 and an actual fall in income per head after 1980. What this could presage is indicated by a speech Robert McNamara made in Montreal in May 1966. He said that 32 of the 38 states listed by the World Bank as 'very poor' (average yearly incomes then below $100, or about $350 today) had 'suffered significant conflict', internal or external in origin, since 1958. So had 60 per cent of the poor nations and 48 per cent of those with middle incomes. Of the 27 nations classified as 'rich' ($750 or more at 1966 values), only one had known internal upheaval.[3]

Granted, those were Cold War years with much external promotion of insurgency, 'indirect aggression' in Harry Truman's phrase.

These days, however, economic or social deprivation may engender an uprising more spontaneously, given that the spread of information into all but the most tightly closed societies invites comparisons between what is and what might be. Thus the outlook for peace and democracy in Southern Africa will be bleak unless poverty can be tackled together with social and ecological stress. A dynamic approach to birth control and to public health in general will be a precondition.

Another zone that, even while the Cold War has waned, has continued to command attention is that which embraces the Levant but also such other foci of stress as Kashmir, the Kurdish home territories, Cyprus and the Horn of Africa. Within it, most upheavals are caused less by unremitting poverty than by the tensions caused by uneven development. More than once regimes have been overthrown even as they cashed in on an oil boom. Examples are afforded by Iraq in 1958, Libya in 1969 and Iran in 1979.

In the 19th century, the British used the term 'Near East' to cover South-West Asia and North-East Africa. Occasionally, India was included.[4] After all, British commitments in the Gulf were managed from New Delhi, an overriding concern there being Muscovite expansion. Quite often, too, the Balkans would count as 'Near East Proper'.[5] But with the collapse of the Ottoman Empire and of Tsarist Russia at the end of the First World War, so wide a definition seemed less useful. By 1940 it was superseded by 'Middle East', in British Commonwealth parlance if not yet in American. An indication of what this embraced was afforded by the Middle East Supply Centre set up by Britain in 1941. Its ambit extended from Malta and Libya, east to Iran and south to the Somalilands.

Yet by 1970, that same term was often applied just to Israel and the 'front-line' Arab states. Originally, this usage served to play down the urgency of addressing the Arab-Israel conflict. But that connotation weakened after 1973.

As new crises broke in Afghanistan and Iran from 1979, Washington reverted to an older term, 'South-West Asia'. This was intended to affirm the importance (some said the primacy) of the Gulf in regional strategy. It further commended itself as standing in apposition to 'North-East Asia', another potential locus for superpower confrontation.

However, any symmetry within Asia as such has little lasting relevance. The true bounds of the zone identified above are surely set as follows. To the west, Libya must be included, certainly as long as

Gadafi remains. As things stand, the Maghreb might be left out, given its detached though sometimes interlocutory relationship with the Middle East proper.

To the south, the Arab-versus-Negro divide always looks critical, especially against the background of climate shift. Witness the unease engendered in Black Africa when Libya tried to grasp in Chad the kind of leverage it had once sought through Idi Amin in Uganda. To the east, the entry into Pakistan of several million refugees from Afghanistan showed those two countries still to be part of the same arena. Yet if Pakistan is reckoned in, then Kashmir has to be. Yet for some purposes the Indian subcontinent is a strategic unity.

To the north, one would hardly include Turkey without Greece because the two remain in conflict over Cyprus and the Aegean; and also because each is in NATO and either in or looking to join the European Community and the Western European Union. Twenty-five years ago, Saul Cohen pointed out that the Bureau of Near Eastern Affairs in the State Department managed its Greek desk; and that the purview of the United Nations Commission to Foster Economic Development in the Middle East stretched from Pakistan through to Greece.[6,7] Perhaps parts of the Balkans merit inclusion once more, not least because of the Islamic factor.

Like most clichés, the one about the Near East as the 'crossroads' of the world has a deal of truth in it. Also Israel's conflict with the Palestinians has a resonance across the world much greater than has always been evident from media coverage in the West. This is partly because Occidental Jewry has so often been the butt of Christian communalism, yet also because of the prominence assumed by Jewish people in the commercial, political, academic and artistic life of the West, especially in this century. Meanwhile, the Arab and Muslim concern with the 'Zionist dagger' still owes a bit to recollection of the Crusader occupation of Jerusalem from 1099 to 1187. On both sides of this divide, in fact, folk memories run deep of many wars between Muslims and Christians, from Spain across to Central Asia. Meantime all parties could heed more than ever they appear to that Palestine is the Holy Land.

Throughout the Near East, communalism aggravates instability. The effect is accentuated by the way the porosity of various international borders allows outside interests to sustain, with arms and in other ways, the fanatics within rival communities (see Chapter 11). So is it by the uneven pace of economic development; and by a rate of cultural change that sometimes compresses a span of a thousand years (chattel slavery to satellite television, let us say) into one generation or so. In the nearby case of India, the communal geography is so complex that it has thus far underpinned democracy by making monolithic dictatorship almost unimaginable on any enduring basis. In general, however, the communal antagonisms are inimical to democratic government emerging and surviving. In Pakistan the progress of democracy is unsteady and unsure; and in Turkey and Greece, it has lately been so. Across the Arab world democracy is still weak. Even the recent advances in Jordan and, indeed, Algeria are under threat from an Islamic fundamentalism that the 1991 Gulf war has accentuated.

In the scale of its weaponry, the Near East rivals Europe and outstrips the Koreas. Granted, its panoplies will shrink if the West and the USSR can establish a new regimen based on arms limitation. But that may not itself lead to greater political stability. Besides which, indigenous capabilities have been increasing in regard to the 'weapons of mass destruction'. Israel is believed to hold dozens of nuclear warheads. Nearby, India tested a nuclear 'demolition charge' in 1974; and an ulterior motive is confirmed by the way both her nuclear and her Space programmes evolved in response to changing perceptions of the strategic threat from China.[8] Lately, Pakistan and Iraq have come close to the military nuclear threshold. As regards stockpiles of poison gas weapons, Iraq, Syria and perhaps Libya have come well to the fore by world standards. Moreover, the region includes the only three theatres post-1918 in which poison gas has actually been used in the field. These are Ethiopia, 1935–36; the Yemen, from 1965 to 1967;[9] Ethiopia again, 1975–76; and Iraq (against the Iranians and then the Iraqi Kurds) from 1984.

Meanwhile, the Near East is bound to remain nodal in more than the strict geometric sense. It is always central to the religious life of the world. So is it to global oil supplies. It will command between a third and a half of the world's exploitable reserves, with production costs that will long be exceptionally low. What could lend extra significance to this situation is a concerted drive to have oil and gas replace coal more completely, this for 'greenhouse' reasons. Indeed, unless peace can be brought comprehensively to this region in the aftermath of Saddam's adventurism, it is hard to see how a unity of purpose on planetary management can be achieved as between the West and the developing world as a whole. So it is in a comprehensive sense that the Near East remains a singularly pivotal shatterbelt within the emergent planetary order, a crossroads in time as well as spatially. An 'Eastern Question' will have to be answered, regardless of what happens next in Moscow.

A UN Concert?

None the less, the underlying argument remains. It is that virtually anywhere in today's world might, at quite short notice, prove pivotal to the fortunes of all mankind. Take the Falklands conflict of 1982. An outline map of the world, unearthed by one British television channel to serve as a backdrop for studio discussion, did not even have those islands inscribed on it, so low had their relevance once been rated. Nevertheless, success for the Argentinian *junta* would have had grim repercussions worldwide. A precedent for the triumph of *force majeure* would have been set in respect of dozens of other disputes. In addition, the effects on Britain and hence on the Atlantic Alliance would have been mortifying. So how much, under these circumstances, for planetary management?

A confluence must therefore be sought between the geopolitical and the planetary streams of thought. Evidently, each can agree that, since peace is indeed indivisible, the world must be treated as a unity. Accordingly, it is desirable that the United Nations be upheld as a framework for a global survival strategy. Were the UN to collapse for whatever reason, it might be desperately hard to reconstitute or replace. The history of Europe and the world since the Thirty Years' War (1618–48) shows that formal understandings for the regulation of the international order are likely to be reached only in the wake of a general war – 1648, 1815, 1919 and 1945. We could hardly wait upon that or upon a comparable ecological catastrophe.

It is a matter for some relief that the waning of the Cold War has allowed the UN to revive, especially at Security Council level. In his opening address as President of the General Assembly in 1989, Joseph Garba of Nigeria observed how 'an emerging atmosphere of trust' enabled the UN to put its 'dog days' behind it. Likewise, Javier Pérez de Cuellar, the Security General, spoke of a new 'collegial spirit' within the Security Council. This, he felt, afforded fresh scope for the resolution of political conflicts as well as for tackling the ecological and social problems of an 'ailing and exhausted Earth'.[10] The previous year, 1988, had been a turning point, with the UN playing a key role in the resolution of three major conflicts: Afghanistan, Iran-Iraq and Namibia. That autumn the General Assembly adopted a new agenda with several novel items. Among them were the conservation of climate as part of the 'common heritage' of mankind.

In the light of these and more recent developments, the United Nations looks almost too strong to be broken by any one setback. Evidently, however, its authority still has to wax if it is not to wane, not least as regards the agonies of the Near East. In 1989, acute tension developed between the United States and Israel on the one hand and the rest of the membership on the other over an intended US ban on the admittance to the UN headquarters of a PLO observer mission; and then over the denial of a visa to Yasser Arafat, a move that led to the General Assembly debate on Palestine being switched to Geneva.

Cyprus is another place where the UN has become deeply involved in a communal or inter-state conflict without thus far effecting a resolution. In the years following the establishment of a United Nations Force in Cyprus (UNFICYP) in 1964, some of us apprehended that it would merely have postponed, and thereby aggravated, a major conflict.[11] Turkey's seizure of over a third of the island in 1974 seemed to vindicate this fear. However, the invasion and the events which brought it on ought not to overshadow completely the countless occasions UNFICYP mediation has prevented local tensions between the embattled communities, Greek and Turk, from escalating out of control.

Even so, movement towards a long-term remedy is liable to require the co-ordinative intervention of the recognised world powers; meaning, above all, the permanent members of the Security Council. Evidently, too, what applies to Cyprus must apply as well to other political conflicts and, indeed, to planetary management. Yet however desirable such co-ordination might be, it has attendant dangers. Take the last time such a remedy was sustained with vigour, the Concert of Europe from 1818 to 1825. This was mooted as a framework to contain post-Napoleonic France. But at the initiative of Britain, France was immediately admitted. Ironically, though, all that liberal move did was raise to the top of the Concert's agenda the aims of a Holy Alliance newly forged by Russia, Austria and Prussia. In essence, these were repeatedly to intervene against Leftist radicalism throughout Europe and beyond. Britain could not prevent France, with Alliance backing, restoring absolute monarchy in Spain in 1822–23. However, she did protect democratic developments in Latin America, and also Portugal. Hence the demise of the Congress system.

The *modus operandi* of the new concert of powers in unlikely to settle into any kind of pattern for some years yet. Uncertainty in Soviet affairs has to be one reason. Another concerns doubts about the European Community. A third unknown is how 'globalist', and in what sense, the United States will wish to remain, not least as regards the Near East.

The American heartland

As of now, the talk, so modish of late, about American 'imperial overstretch' looks to have been premature. American involvement has lately been decisive in resolving issues as far-flung as independence for Namibia and the reunification of Germany. From last August, the United States deployed troops to the Gulf twice as fast as she deployed them to France in 1917. Throughout, she acted in a manner akin to that of 19th-century Britain, exercising benign or coercive influence one-on-one on many individual countries within a wide international constellation. She did so with mounting assurance. Hegemonic power can thus become, once for London and now for Washington, greater than the sum of its component parts. With each hegemony, too, nodality within firm borders has been basic. Britain was pivotal to the Eurocentric sea-going world of the 19th century. Today, the United States bestrides the one area at present able to rate as a continental heartland, presuming the Soviet alternative has to be excluded awhile.

So how long will she wish to stay as active abroad as her ascendancy could allow? Will she turn isolationist instead? What isolationism has meant historically is an illiberal rejection of a trans-Atlantic interdependence with Europe in favour of a less trammelled paramountcy in the Caribbean and the Pacific. The political divide betweened the Atlanticists and the 'Pacific Firsters' has customarily been in the middle of the centre-to-Right spectrum of Republican opinion. Inside the Reagan administration, the two approaches were in conflict, at least until 1987. Those more to the hard Right were disposed to deplore Britain's expedition to the Falklands; support Menachem Begin's advance to Beirut; empathise with the Taiwanese regime and maybe the South African; and undercut Gadafi and Castro, as well as the Sandinistas in Nicaragua.

Those inclined more to the centre dissented or demurred from these stances. Nor were they as positive towards ballistic missile defence as some Rightists were, even before the Presidential launch of the Strategic Defense Initiative (SDI) on 23 March 1983. Soon there were to be acute though semi-covert differences over whether the West could or should assist the USSR through the crisis of liberalisation that Gorbachev had precipitated.

To my mind, a fuzzy yet salient turning point came with the departures from the administration during 1987 of the Pentagon's five SDI stalwarts: Frank Gaffney, Fred Iklé, John Lehman, Richard Perle and Caspar Weinberger. Each in turn gave his own reasons, business or family or whatever. Nevertheless, their all going marked a shift away from the headier visions of Space-based defence, with their connotations of 'Fortress America'. That shift has continued under President Bush and Secretary of Defence, Dick Cheney.

Not that the battle lines could be discerned as clearly as they might once have been. Looking at the five resignations, one finds that Fred Iklé and Richard Perle are four-square on the Right. But what of Caspar Weinberger? This renowned Anglophile had tended to adopt liberal Atlanticist perspectives on, for instance, regional conflicts. Correspondingly, he had cautioned against SDI being allowed to engender 'illusory fortress' notions. But between 1985 and his retirement in 1987, he repeatedly pressed for the early deployment of whatever SDI elements seemed ready enough. Yet to have proceeded thus might well have been to cut across 'the need for closer consultation with our allies' recognised by President Reagan in the speech of March 1983. The formulation of a true alliance policy would require all concerned to stand back at some point and take a synoptic look at all options.[12]

Early into the 1990 Gulf crisis, a debate erupted within the Republican Right. Jeane Kirkpatrick and Edward Luttwak were among those stressing that the United States was not one of the countries with a vital 'national interest' in the flow of Gulf oil. On the other hand, Richard Perle and the *Wall Street Journal* were toughly interventionist, the latter talking of the installation of 'a MacArthur regency' after the fall of Baghdad.[13]

As to the further outlook, it is tempting to invoke the long-running debate about alternating cycles in American public attitudes. Two versions command attention. The one, first enunciated in 1951 by Frank Klingberg of the University of California,[14] divided American history since 1776 into phases of 'introversion' and 'extroversion', the former averaging 21 years and the latter 27. Though his definitions were not well-founded, Klingberg certainly scored with his prediction that the period of extroversion which had begun in 1940 would give way in the late 1960s to one of retraction. During its onset, 'it is quite possible that the major problem ... will carry heavy moral implications: the aspirations of the people of Asia and Africa could well furnish the chief cause ... along with repercussions from America's own racial problem'.

Duly, the first signs of a retrenchment appeared in 1967, exactly on schedule on a straight extrapolation of the median Klingberg cycle and in circumstances akin to his surmise. Among these signs were the USA's refusal to get too much involved in the internal conflicts raging in Nigeria (see below) and the Congo or over Egypt's closure of the Straits of Tiran. At the same time, criticism of the Vietnam War had begun to burgeon, one contentious issue being the high proportion of young Blacks drafted under the Selective Service Act. To all of which one might add that the 1987 *démarche* over SDI could be said to betoken the end of the rather unilateral globalism of the early Reagan years. On that loose but perhaps apposite interpretation, the timing fits well again.

The other cycle to note is that perceived by Arthur Schlesinger, the laudatory biographer of John Kennedy. Looking back down the 20th century, he sees a 30-year cycle of alternation between 'public purpose' and 'private interest', with another phase of the former due in the 1990s. He discerns little difference between the two in terms of likely war involvement but judges a 'public purpose' era the more likely to incorporate into foreign policy ideas of democracy, reform, human rights, civil liberties, social change and affirmative government.[15] Evidently, environment control should now be added, especially as regards global warming.

Of the two analysts, Schlesinger is the less persuasive because he is the less persuaded, indicative perhaps of the difficulty the Democrats in the United States have in coming to terms with the flux of the modern world in general and the legacy of Vietnam in particular. In the near term, however, the American willingness to play a lead role is bound to depend heavily on the final outcome of events in the Gulf. Wars do not come in cycles but may well abort cycles in other realms, political or economic or whatever. Any very profound disillusionment could drive the United States back to introversion and, indeed, private interest. Economic and ecological policies would be starkly affected.

Yet as and when she does turn inwards again, this can hardly be to isolationism in the 'Pacific First' tradition. All else apart, the United States' view of Japan, as a political partner but commercial threat, would now be too complicated to allow any coherent theme to develop along such lines.

A Japanese superstate?

What is little in doubt is that, however stultified her party politics, Japan is poised to assume a higher profile on the world stage. When the long overdue revival of political philosophy takes place in the West, those concerned will do well to study her as a polity that to all appearances is on course for boundless prosperity coupled with a superior social ethic. Among the outward signs are low levels of individual crime. So, too, are amazing progress in public health; cities clean and tidy to a fault; and high attainment in the high schools, notably in science and mathematics. Above all, Japan remains a very consistent model of vitality and proficiency in the workaday environment.

She promises a number of technology breakthroughs in the 1990s (*eg* in artificial intelligence, mass transit, automatic translation ...),[16] no matter that her technology base is not yet as strong across the board as is the American.[17] Armed with good mathematics, Japan may also generate a lot more of the fundamental scientific thought she has thus far been judged backward in.[18] As regards ecological control at global level, one of her major contributions will be how to limit carbon emissions. When gross domestic products are compared on the basis of purchasing power parity, her emission per unit of output is half that of the USA. The contrast with the EC is less sharp but still positive, seeing how industrialised Japan is.[19]

Until recently, her pattern of overseas aid has been narrowly geopolitical in its overriding concern with securing markets and supplies around the Pacific. At last, it is starting to branch out.[20] At the same time, Japan has become a key actor in world finance. During the crash of October 1987, Tokyo was a calming influence. Through 1990, on the other hand, the world was exercised about an ill-founded boom in her property market. This was so because 'eight of the world's biggest banks are Japanese; they account for almost 40 per cent of all cross-border bank loans and a sizeable chunk of domestic lending in America and Britain'.[21] All this being so, Tokyo's continued 'reluctance to allow yen outflow and to encourage its use as a global reserve currency is coming to look feeble. Ceding some control over the domestic economy would, of course be the price.[22]

Hesitant over the assumption of responsibilities in the financial sphere, Japan is even slower to contribute to strategy in the military sense. Nevertheless, she does have two irreducible defence tasks. The one is to stand guard, alongside the United States, over the social experiment that she herself represents. The other is to act as a logistic support area for the Republic of Korea, as she did in the war of 40 years ago. The military balance on the Korean peninsula may come to appear less stable if its politics become more fluid.

A confederal Europe?

The unity in freedom of Europe may again hang in the balance. If so, this is because of too uncritical a twinning of two very different principles. The one is that the members of the European Community must urgently forge a unity that is complete economically and therefore far advanced in the political sphere as well. The other is that any European country can accede if it sees membership as conducive to its own stability and development; and provided it can present itself as sufficiently liberal, economically and politically.

This concurrent pursuit of deepening and enlargement would not so long ago have been seen on almost all sides (a few fanatic federalists perhaps excepted) as a contradiction in terms. The late Chancellor Adenauer and his successor in Bonn, Dr Kiesinger, cautioned against the EEC growing so large as to be at best unwieldy and at worst amorphous; and President de Gaulle was, on sundry occasions, firmly explicit about this danger to his vision of a closely co-ordinative *l'Europe des patries* centred on France. In July 1969, President Pompidou warned at a press conference that Britain's joining the EEC 'could not but mean the membership of a number of other countries' and therefore must involve 'profound changes for the Community'. Seven months later, he reiterated the point in the United States. In 1977, the Gaullists and the Communists orchestrated strong initial hostility within France to the Iberian applications for membership, this stemming partly from fear of agricultural competition but also from more general considerations. The outcome was to be decided, however, by a general conviction that, in the post-fascist era, democracy would be most secure in a Spain and Portugal set within this wider Europe. That is to say, the argument hinged on the implications for the applicants rather than those for the existing Community. Much the same applied with Greece.

In her speech at Bruges in September 1988, Prime Minister Margaret Thatcher pugnaciously posited a straight choice between making the Community ever closer-knit and extending it geographically, including the eventual accession of such countries as Czechoslovakia, Hungary and Poland. She also made it clear that her government favoured the latter course. In other words, it upheld a customary British preference for a loosely confederal Community, one with wide bounds not tight bonding.

Much the same had been evident in 1976 when Harold Wilson's government enthused over Greece's application because it might further the building of 'a new and wider Europe'. Indeed, the said preference can be tracked back to the 1950s, to the attempt by the Macmillan administration to promote a wide European Free Trade Area as an EEC writ large. In the end, London had to settle for a peripheral European Free Trade Association (EFTA).

All of which relates to the highly distinctive character of the United Kingdom, perhaps the most structural aspect being the high ratio of urban dwellers to rural. But in a sense, too, it continues a British tradition of strategic operations of the flanks of Europe; a tradition built by Churchill, Nelson, Wellington and Marlborough. Being themselves set so axially in the centre of Europe, Paris and Bonn were almost bound to think differently.

But now we are all poised to get either the best or the worst of both worlds. In 1992, the European Single Act will come into effect; and the Community will, if President Jacques Delors has his way, be *en route* to a single currency. Then in 1993, enlargement will resume. Neutral Austria and neutral Sweden can expect to join by 1994. Most or all of the other four members of EFTA are likely to become members soon after. The application by Turkey, formally made in 1987, will succeed more slowly because of economic backwardness, shakiness on human rights and the continuing occupation of two-fifths of Cyprus. An application is also coming from Cyprus while several East European states wait more distantly in the wings.

The hazards are multiple. A Community of 20 states might find it hard to reach a common position on anything, be it a long-term plan or a short-term crisis. Nor might it be any wiser flatly to circumvent the individual sovereignties through the creation of a single currency. Unlike the Exchange Rate Mechanism (ERM), it would foreclose any option of withdrawal. Yet that could never prevent a non-licit and therefore utterly disruptive withdrawal by any country that felt hopelessly disadvantaged by whatever monetary policy was being followed by the European central bank. Nor can this be ruled out, considering that a Community much expanded would embrace economies that vary greatly in their adaptiveness. How things go will turn a lot on Germany. This decade, she may be weighed down with her own political fusion. After that, her position, size and economic culture could make her growth very dynamic, especially within a big single market.

Perhaps the best way to avoid secessions from a Community subject to internal stress would be not to make them *ultra vires* in any juridical sense. Stop short of a single currency in order to preserve the bargaining process. If valid it be, this argument draws extra strength from the likelihood of climate change. If climatic belts swing polewards on account of greenhouse, much of northern Europe will benefit from warmer weather and most of southern Europe suffer from its being drier. A mean temperature rise of five degrees Centigrade, say, could lead to an average northwards shift of a 1,000 kilometres[23] in the successive zones of vegetation. Viewed in more detail, however, the prospect is, yet again, rather uncertain and very complex. Take a prediction derived from the model used in Britain's Meteorological Office. This anticipates that a doubling of carbon dioxide equivalent, leading in the Mediterranean to a four degree mean rise and a 15 per cent reduction in summer rainfall, would cause a biomass decrease of only five per cent in Italy yet no less than 36 per cent in Greece.[24] Even allowing for what may be done globally to retard greenhouse, such prognoses are alarming.

Nor may the other contradictions within the EC be eased by the initiative Delors launched in January 1989: namely, the commitment to create by 1993 a European Economic Space (EES). What this is intended to involve is the free circulation of goods, services, capital and people as between the EC and EFTA. Delors himself has indicated that he sees a prime purpose of the EES as being to enable EFTA to serve as a stepping stone to the EC, especially for applicants from Eastern Europe. But the established EFTA economies will not get on easily with the erstwhile Comecon ones.

If national sovereignties are largely surrendered to Brussels and its affiliates, a desire will wax strong for new modes of representative government lower down. But the response to this aspiration will require careful thought in view of (a) historical differences between EC member states as regards the devolution of power to regional, provincial or local bodies, and (b) persistent tugs of loyalty within states, e.g. those in Italy between the provinces and the cities. Unfortunately, discussion is likely to be vitiated by callow romanticism, not least on the Left, about the apparent resurgence of traditional communal or national identities. In Britain, for instance, members of the Liberal Democratic Party regularly extol the prospect of a federal United Kingdom in terms that jar oddly with the success they themselves often make of devolutionary politics at the more local level where it can really mean something, not least to the young.

None of which is to deny the likely material gains from the EC's enlargement and development, in terms of environmental management plus a near-term increment of several per cent in average output.[25] Nor that there can be big social and cultural dividends, again with special reference to a younger generation that sees a European consciousness as the way through to a planetary one. Nor, indeed, that there may be the makings here of a powerful economic, and hence political, bloc. After all, 25 per cent of all foreign trade takes place within the EES boundary as presently envisaged; and the aggregate foreign trade of member countries is over 40 per cent of the world's total.[26] Nor should one forget that, ever since the Marshall Plan, the internationalist stream of opinion dominant in modern America has welcomed, in principle at least, the prospect of a European 'twin pillar' within the Atlantic Alliance. However, the formal neutrality of at least three actual or applicant members (Ireland, Austria and Sweden) has to be reckoned with. So does the strategic nuclear question.

As is now widely appreciated, the key to building 'twin pillars' now lies in accelerating the revival of the Western European Union which began in 1984. What has to be admitted, however, is that, in terms of bureaucratic muscle, WEU is a long way behind the EC. The latter has 22,000 full-time civil servants. WEU has barely 50 people at its London headquarters; and only a few hundred with any kind of assignation. EFTA, one may note, has 73 in its secretariat.[27]

The battle for Moscow

In any case, Europe could never 'twin' the United States in any very equivalent sense: this for a number of reasons, most of which stem from her lack of a heartland location. So the question that has thus been accented is how far we should encourage the revival, under President Gorbachev or his successors, of Soviet strength and influence. Let us recognise again the dangers in that endeavour. Even analysts who would back it, on one definition or another, freely acknowledge them.[28] Our efforts might either be entirely futile or counterproductive or else would revive a Muscovite polity that was sufficiently strong to aggress but insufficiently stable not to.

Nor can one just forget the damage ill-gotten Soviet influence has done in the past. The spurious prestige accorded by certain academic circles even to Stalin's Russia led to the suppression throughout much of 'Soviet studies' of creative imagination and hence of basic integrity.[29] Other branches of the humanities were also affected. No doubt it further delayed, in fields like political philosophy, the due integration of observation and theory, something the natural sciences have practised ever since the Renaissance.[30]

The fact of the matter was that the Bolshevik takeover of the Eurasian heartland lent enormous prestige to its avowed creed. Unfortunately, however, Marxism-Leninism has been a poor guide to progress on the part of under-privileged peoples. It puts blinkers on History and ignores Geography. Its obsession with private property as **the** fount of power, wealth, status and life style is pre-electronic as well as pre-Stalin. Karl Marx's vision of life beyond the great divide of revolutionary upheaval is just as rosy and vacuous as that of other millenarian cults. His episodic disquisitions on the primitive communism by which early man was presumed to have lived merely recast the 'noble savage' myth. He bothered little about future relations between states, socialist or otherwise,[31] or even about the existing colonial order.

Correspondingly, the once numerous devotees of Vladimir Lenin's attempt to put some kind of flesh on Marx's skeletal ideas about imperialism rarely became aware of his crucial debt to J. A. Hobson. Yet Hobson was a British liberal economist who concerned himself little with Marx and whose impassioned condemnation (in 1902) of empire-building stemmed from a well-founded conviction that it was not an absolutely ineluctable outgrowth of high capitalism in crisis.[32] One can hardly be surprised therefore that the Marxian version of 'historical inevitability' has led down false trails with a depressing regularity. Most disheartening of all, especially apropos the 1930s, was the way various of the West's literati saw the fascistic inclinations of the Kremlin under Stalin but chose to shroud them in euphemism.[33]

Such interactions could occur again under certain malign circumstances. On the other hand, the impact of Moscow on the world might be very different 15 years hence, say, if it was at last on its way to being the capital of a prosperous, pluralist and devolved democracy: a model of political redemption on the part of a developing nation.

However, a likely precondition would be the Soviet Union's standing complete within its existing borders. An analogy can be drawn with Black Africa where what has been called the principle of 'extantism' has very generally been upheld: the principle that the statehoods as defined at independence shall not be disturbed. An early application thereof was to be seen in the support most members of the Organisation of African Unity (OAU) gave to the Nigerian federal government from 1967, as it insisted that the precept of self-determination did not allow the secession of those who had, with a fair measure of popular backing, seized power in the Eastern region, 'Biafra'. Britain and the United States gave the Nigerian Federation their support, as did the USSR. Those countries that took the opposite tack and channelled arms supplies to the rebels (i.e. France, Portugal and Spain) made the resultant war far more calamitous.

Now the secession of any constituent republic of the Soviet Union could trigger off a 'domino effect' whereby all the non-Russian republics successively tried to withdraw, not to mention some of the autonomous territories. Nor could one even be sure disintegration would stop there. It is not hard to imagine fissiparous strains then appearing, perhaps along the Urals or in the Far East, across the Russian Soviet Federative Socialist Republic (RSFSR). It is only too easy to imagine whoever retained power in the Kremlin then being totally consumed by action-reaction xenophobia, evident at its most stark in anti-Semitism and a lack of interest in global *détente*. At the same time, newly independent regimes might well unleash national or communal antagonisms, especially in the Caucasus and maybe Central Asia. In the latter region, indeed, tensions could be accentuated by climate change, as greenhouse warming took hold. The zonal shift referred to above could be one factor; and another the drying of continental interiors (see Chapter 6).

Yet any actual warfare in any such locations could constitute a precedent for similar conflicts elsewhere. Also, it could place an awesome burden, politically and also logistically, on the peacekeeping capacity of the United Nations, this at the very time when the UN's authority needs shoring up in pursuance of planetary management. Let us recall, too, that the first big failure of the League of Nations came with the Vilna dispute between Lithuania and Poland from 1920 onwards. Nor should we ignore the possession and control of strategic nuclear assets. Nor the likelihood that the end result would be to leave the United States in what might be a bitterly envied yet deeply unenviable role of sole superpower in a world beset by novel problems.

To apprehend such developments is to suggest that the West might more actively seek to help the central authorities in Moscow keep the boundaries of the USSR intact, at least as long as the quest for democracy and prosperity still has some chance of coming good eventually. Undeniably, however, such a strategy would always involve much agonising especially in the absence of Gorbachev. How does one assess the prospects for democracy and prosperity in so fraught and fluid a situation? If the inter-German border can be abolished, cannot other boundaries be shifted? Are not the Baltic states seen as a special case, particularly in Northern Europe, on Capitol Hill and in the Vatican? Should not the interplay between national secession and individual emigration be explored? Yet perhaps the ultimate question to ask is whether one should passively accept the balkanisation of much of the Eurasian heartland, this in deference to ethnic inclinations that might otherwise be expected to weaken over time but which could, in the meanwhile, divert us from the global problems.[34]

If one does decide against passivity, however, one has to come up with a countervailing strategy. One approach which could be adopted, as one 50th anniversary succeeds another in the battle honours of the Red Army, is to encourage a fuller recognition, in the media and academe throughout the West, of the contribution made by the USSR as we have known her to the defeat of Hitler. The Soviet leadership itself has extolled ever afterwards the achievements of the 'Great Patriotic War', as one way to preserve an all-Union consciousness. Now, in their travail, Western Marxists have started to focus more on the epic struggle on the Eastern Front as the supreme achievement of the Bolshevik experiment. As Eric Hobsbawn has put it, 'Perhaps History, in its irony, will decide that the most lasting achievement of the October revolution was to make the 'developed world' once again safe for "bourgeois" democracy.'[35]

Yet even on this subject it is easy to pour scorn. Huge defeats in the first several months of the Nazi invasion stemmed considerably from poor strategy and worse man-management. Throughout the conflict, far too many brave young men were sacrificed in mindless frontal assaults. Too much material privilege was sustained in the upper reach of army and party. Discipline for the lower ranks was much cruder and crueller than in the *Wehrmacht*. Among the populace at large, the invaders were not unwelcome in the Baltic States and, initially, the Ukraine. Many thousands of Soviet prisoners of war were persuaded, albeit rather forcibly, to enlist either in the *Wehrmacht* itself or in quisling formations. After liberation from the Nazis, the powerful partisan movement that had grown up in the Ukraine (perhaps 200,000 by 1943) fought on for five to seven years, this time against Stalin rather than Hitler.

For Russia itself, psychological mobilisation was largely based on a nationalist appeal akin to 'old believer' xenophobia, political and religious. While the behaviour of the victorious Soviet forces on entering Germany was orgiastically primitive, in Poland it remained callously expedient. Nor can the Nazi-Soviet alliance (1939–41) be justified entirely in terms of Munich and other Western lapses. Besides all of which, the West might well have won, in any case, by dint of being first to the nuclear bomb.

Yet still the facts remain that 75 per cent of the *Wehrmacht*'s war casualties were incurred on the Eastern Front and that many episodes in the Soviet war record would count as utterly heroic in any hall of fame. Historians of the era all remark with awe on how, as the *blitzkrieg* slowed in the face of the wintry weather of late 1941, a downtrodden Red Army drew fresh inspiration from the mud and then the ice.[36,37] Outstanding among many epics were the dour resilience of Leningrad during its 18 months of all but total siege; the defence for eight ferocious months of the fortress city of Sevastopol; and, of course, the hinge of fate at Stalingrad.

What the West ought also to recognise is how large a part verve and enterprise played in the great resurgence to victory. In a recent analysis of armour at war, the contribution of the Soviet tank forces, 1941–45, has been written by a retired British paratrooper. He well emphasises that it

> required skill of no small order to command, control, move and supply powerful strike groupings so that they could first concentrate on small breakthrough sectors, then smash through deeply echeloned defences without formations getting in each others' way and snarling the whole operation.[38]

A similar virtuosity was evident in tactical aviation. Thus in 1945, some 7,500 planes were assigned to the Battle for Berlin; and, at times, more than 2,000 of these were committed to 'quite narrow sectors.' Meanwhile, Soviet aircraft production rose from just over

10,000 in 1941 to a peak of 40,000 in 1944;[39] and this on the basis of good and improving design work, electronics excepted. Taken at face value, that is no more of an industrial miracle than Britain or Germany were achieving and lags well behind the United States, where 96,000 military aircraft were produced in 1944. But it looks uniquely impressive against the background of a huge relocation of industry eastwards in 1941–42 under the shadow of the *blitzkrieg*.

The oddest aspect is the relationship between this industrial heroism and Stalinism. Aeronautical development, for instance, largely took place at 'aircraft prison centres', their staff being a mixture of prisoners (A. N. Tupolev was a famous example) and free citizens. Ethics apart, this was a grossly inefficient way to harness creative talent. However, Soviet science had boomed so well during the more pragmatic years of the New Economic Policy (1922–28) that sufficient talent could survive and even thrive.[40] All in all, victory in the Great Patriotic War was more in spite of Stalinism than because of it. Furthermore, the horrendous human cost, including over 20 million war-related dead, left Stalin all too free a rein after liberation (see also Chapter 7). Nevertheless, that victory was a stupendous achievement for the Russian and Soviet people; and merits more fulsome acknowledgement.

Meanwhile, the channelling through Moscow of food and other economic aid can be a very tangible form of support, provided it is effected in such a way as to further *perestroika* within distribution and other economic sectors. In addition, stronger international links between scientists can help sustain Soviet liberalisation, particularly if the West is alive to both the constraints and the possibilities.[41] Controlled nuclear fusion was one area mentioned in the Reykjavik summit communiqué in October 1986, albeit with little or no prior consultation on either side with the scientists operationally involved. On the Magnetic Confinement Fusion (MCF) side, an early fruit of international collaboration was the sharing by the Soviets of their invention of the tokamak in the 1960s. This has been the progenitor of modern torus designs – notably at Culham and Princeton.

So far as Inertial Confinement Fusion (ICF) by lasing is concerned, however, a direct clash could have occurred between a wish to collaborate and a concern to protect the research into SDI. The lasers for ICF would probably work best on wavelengths similar to those for the Free Electron Lasers that a fully-fledged SDI canopy might heavily rely on. There might also be a broad correspondence in required 'brightness' and perhaps in pulse lengths, too.[42] But in April

1991, an international conference on 'Drivers for Inertial Confinement Fusion' was held at Osaka University. Unlike a few years ago, the contributions from the United States were not impeded by security considerations.

Surprisingly enough, there has always been less risk of so acute a tension between planetary and geopolitical considerations in regard to collaboration in deep Space research. So it was that, even in the early years of the Space age when the dominant thrust was towards open rivalry in Earth orbital and lunar missions, there was already a preparedness, on the American side at any rate, to consider the possibility of joint ventures further afield. In his inaugural address in January 1961, President Kennedy urged that 'the two sides in the Cold War come together to explore the stars'. At the otherwise glacial Vienna summit with Khrushchev that June, he was to air the option of their two countries going to the Moon together, an overture he was to repeat at the UN in September 1963. He had committed the United States itself to 'go to the Moon within the decade' on 25 May 1961.

Subsequently, the tendencies towards co-operation in the Space realm strengthened or weakened erratically. Then as Mikhail Gorbachev began to establish himself as the new-style Soviet leader, there was a marked resurgence of interest in joint exploration. An accord signed early in 1987 provided *inter alia* for the co-ordination of unmanned reconnoitres of the Moon, Mars and Venus. At the Reagan-Gorbachev summit of May-June 1988, the two leaders cautiously described 'scientific missions to the Moon and Mars' as 'areas of possible bilateral and international collaboration'. Since then, however, less interest has been expressed by either side. Those concerned are more aware that, until the Kremlin has beaten the bread queues, such essays in technological virtuosity can do its domestic standing more harm than good.

So one is driven back to the conclusion that the most solid assistance the West can lend the more progressive forces in the Soviet Union during this critical juncture of the early 1990s, is to block all tendencies towards outright secession. Perhaps it ought to indicate, as overtly and collectively as possible, that no breakaway by any constituent republic will be welcome as long as fair hope remains that *glasnost* and *perestroika* will generate at federal level the right conditions for democratic and devolutionary pluralism, as prosperity approaches and communication extends. Any republic (including the RSFSR) that may wish to defy this advice will find itself faced with multiple means of dissuasion: non-recognition, no sponsorship for UN membership, no financial aid or other economic favours, no arms exports, the withholding of security guarantees . . . . However, this would be a hawkish way to bolster the more liberal inclinations within the Soviet leadership and would entitle the West to look for reciprocity. Firm adherence to a Shatalin-style programme of constitutional and economic reform would be the other side of the deal. The decollectivisation of Soviet agriculture could be a key part of it.

The developing world

The importance of a redeemed Moscow assuming a lead role in a dialogue with the developing world is confirmed by the part the latter has to play in planetary management. This applies to the upholding of international law against outright aggression, diplomatic abuses, political terrorism and syndicated crime. It also applies to making sure that renunciations of the large foreign debts so many developing countries have run up never cause a collapse of the world financial system. So does it apply to family planning. So does it, too, in relation to mineral reserves, including those of oil and of non-ferrous metals, the latter being a resource sector that may figure too little in the academic and public debate.[43] It conspicuously applies as well to the preservation of the rain forests. So does it to the control of AIDS and other potential pandemics.

Nor are the developing countries unimportant in terms of the increasing part they play in carbon emissions through commercial energy consumption. As of 1989, four developing nations (Brazil, India, Indonesia and, above all, China) were producing nearly 1,000 million tons a year between them. The USSR is reckoned to yield just over 1,000; the USA just over 1,400; and the EC 740.[44] Another relevant yardstick could be that China alone possesses a fifth of the world's coal reserves. Both she and India would be reluctant to switch heavily to oil.

For all these reasons then, we need the active co-operation of the developing world at governmental level and more widely. Unfortunately, however, its willingness to enter into constructive dialogue in pursuit of planetary management could be lessened by the fact that, in terms of the usual criteria of power politics, its bargaining position *vis-à-vis* the West has been declining sharply of late, a truth only too well symbolised by the debt crisis and by Iraq's abject defeat in war. Therefore for those many issues for which 'compellence' can be nothing but a bad last resort, our bargaining position is weakened reciprocally.

Certainly, one factor in the decline is that nobody in Afro-Asia and Latin America can so freely play rival blocs off against one another as these compete for geopolitical leverage through arms supplies or economic aid or trading opportunities. Even if relations between Moscow and the West were to sour once more, it would still be a long time before anything like that pattern resumed, seeing that Moscow no longer has the East Europeans to act as surrogates.

A more intrinsic weakness of the developing world, less remarked but very limiting, is a persisting failure to generate a corpus of political and general thought that even begins to match up to modern problems. This is in spite of the expansion of its education base, especially since 1950; the depth and richness of many of its traditional cultures; and the vitality of much of its contemporary life, literary and artistic. There has certainly been too little political philosophy, socialistic or otherwise, and what there has been has owed too much either to a warmed-over Marxism or else to cultural chauvinism. The result has too often been to undermine the hopes of constitutional democracy and to encourage authoritarian excesses, undue militarisation most certainly included.

Needless to say, some of the worst examples have come from men who have established or been working towards the establishment of personalist dictatorships. An early case in point, *Towards Colonial Freedom*, written by Kwame Nkrumah in 1942,[45] was little other than a quasi-Leninist diatribe of bitterness. The *Philosophy of the Revolution* by Gamal Abdel Nasser was heavily anecdotal. Nor did one glean much enlightenment from the opinion of Muammar Gadafi that 'all methods of education prevailing in the world should be done away with through a worldwide cultural revolution to emancipate man's mind from curricula of fanaticism and from the process of deliberate adaptation of man's taste, his ability to form concepts and his mentality'.[46]

Another bathetic example was afforded by someone who himself has been held in much more regard in the West than Colonel Gadafi. Confirmed evidence of the subhuman treatment in custody by the South African police of Steve Biko just before he died in their hands from brain damage in 1977 was a chilling example of the manic extremes to which those will be driven who would preserve communal separatism in the face of all the tendencies towards convergence that are the very 'warp and woof' of the modern world.[47] What also has to be said, however, is that Biko's own testimony failed to draw a qualitative distinction between 'White racism' and his 'Black Consciousness' movement.[48] He well identified positive traits within traditional African culture (pp. 55–61). He stressed the urgent need to free 'the mind of the oppressed' (p. 82). But his bitter sneer at the 'myth of integration' (p. 36) betrayed a total lack of awareness of how dangerous, in the modern world, is a pseudo-retreat into the kraals of yesteryear. So did his castigation of modern education as just a cultural threat (p. 36).

There are, of course, brighter spots. Certain elements within the African National Congress – including Oliver Tambo and Nelson Mandela – have more of a renaissance outlook than what has just been described. Nor can the Tanzanian experiment be dismissed out of hand. Then again, the liberal democratic tradition has resilience still in India, despite the current upsurge of communal extremism. Likewise, in Latin America it regularly reasserts itself against the caudillo tendency. There are, in any case, many fine political economists and the like working within the public service in the developing world. Even so, it is hard to demur from a judgement such as that, on the overall record to date, 'African socialism and Arab socialism share far more specific traits with paradigmatic fascism' than with the pristine visions of the European socialist pioneers of the last century.[49] Sombre talk by Western Marxists about 'lumpensocialism' is cast in a similar vein.[50]

A most disturbing aspect throughout has been how ready many of the political intelligentsia have been to reject one authority structure only to crave for another.[51] The upshot has been a Rousseauish obfuscation whereby the notion of individual freedom gets intermingled hopelessly with that of psychological liberation through the mobilisation of the 'general will', perhaps in pursuit of the instant millennium. For all his professed love of the simple life in small but stable communities, the anti-cosmopolitan and anti-rational egomania of Jean-Jacques Rousseau (1712–78) provided a conceptual tap-root for the xenophobic totalitarianism of Robespierre, Hitler, Stalin, Mao Tse-tung, Kim Il-Sung, Saddam Hussein and all their ilk.[52] In other words, Rousseau and his 'general will' represented the beginnings of a sinister break with the rich Euro-American milieu of liberal rationalism, the milieu within which the 13 colonies were winning their independence from Britain to form the USA.

Where the liberal rationalists failed, however, was in not acknowledging the costs of progress, socially and ecologically. The case has been well made that a salient truth about the great era of European imperial expansion, launched on a tide of renaissance optimism five centuries ago, is that it successively destabilised what had mostly been societies in a tolerable state of equilibrium with themselves and with Nature.[53] Yet despite a strong background of naturalism in many traditional cultures, from Shinto Japan to pre-Columban North America,[54,55] the developing world has been slow to take up the ecological theme in its modern mode. It has preferred to follow the lead of the late Indira Gandhi who accepted the importance of environmental protection but insisted that the key initiatives had to be taken by those nations that had already broken out of the poverty trap.[56] She in her turn may have been reacting too strongly against the utopian anti-modernism of Mahatma Gandhi, with his hopeless cult of the cottage spinning wheel and ostensible rejection even of Western medicine.[57] Meanwhile, the Christian Marxian 'liberation theologians' of Latin America followed rather than led over matters like conservation of the rain forests.

A particular theme to address is the consolidation of liberal democracy, the advance of which began afresh around 1975, was extolled by Presidents Carter and Reagan, and has markedly gathered pace these last several years, fuelled by the information explosion. Witness democracy's emergence or re-emergence in places as far-flung as Argentina, Pakistan and the Philippines, not to mention Algeria and Jordan and what we used to call the 'Soviet bloc'.

However, in politics as in war gains made rapidly may be insecure. Communalism fired by economic and social instability is an endemic threat to democracy, not least in the Balkans and the USSR. Then again, the events in Tiananmen Square in June 1989 heralded months of dark reaction in China, a country now facing a dubious future even though communal conflict as such has lately surfaced only in Tibet. In South Africa, the Chris Hani/Winnie Mandela tendency could still triumph within the ANC. Likewise, democracy's consolidation in Latin America may wait upon a much more resolute extension of social justice.[58] Moreover, the corpus of democratic theory may still lack enough solidity to commend itself universally,[59] partly thanks to the feeble input of late from the West. On that score, *inter alia*, H. G. Wells is still right.

In the medium term, much may depend on how well environment and resource constraints can be accommodated, in terms of operational management but also at a philosophical level. Failure could open the way for a resurgence, across much of the developing world, of militant authoritarianism, Red or Blue or millenarian or hybrid. The information explosion as such is by no means a guarantee against this, any more than the first Renaissance excluded Henry VIII and his kind.

Institutional links

The official linkages between the West and the developing world in the field of planetary management run through a myriad of channels. Of special ecological importance are certain of the UN special agencies. Sadly, the ragged character of this side of the UN shows how far off still is any very deep sense of planetary community.[60] Meanwhile, controversy gathers round the application by the World Bank of the philosophy of environment protection it newly enunciated in 1987. The controversy has centred on a dam scheme, the Sardar Sarovar in northern India, that involves the displacement of 90,000 rural poor.[61] Yet this in its turn serves to show how unsure we now are about basic objectives. The building of the Aswan High Dam in Egypt, opened in 1969, engendered fierce controversies: geopolitical, economic and ecological. Since when, big dams in general have more and more been called into question. Yet half a century ago they were held to be the supreme symbols of the transformation of Nature through progressive planning: the New Deal and the Tennessee Valley Authority or the Soviet Five Year Plans.[62]

Regional security

On the geopolitical side of things, new frameworks will be needed for regional security. A strategy that is 'grand' in that it embraces every requirement from economic development to guarantees against nuclear blackmail should be reflected in these arrangements. Indeed, the grouping for all purposes might usefully be into what could be termed 'ecological regions': entities closely akin to what the geographers have defined as 'natural regions' but with more account taken of the legacy of human intervention.

As a rule, that stipulation need not be too contradictory or otherwise unmanageable. A coastline, say, is a boundary that is basic ecologically but also for defence. The same applies to a mountain range. Rivers can be contrary examples in that they can be effective as military barriers but are otherwise expressive of a local unity. But modern equivalents of the 'watch on the Rhine' are not much in evidence, the Jordan excepted.

As often as not, the trick may lie in a positive action–reaction: the locking into a mutual security matrix of powers that otherwise would gyrate towards confrontation. Countries like India, Israel and South Africa might eventually become accepted as lynchpins of regional security rather than as prime threats thereto. A good model was afforded with the signature in 1971 of the Five Power Defence Arrangement (Britain, Australia, New Zealand, Malaysia and Singapore) for the defence of Commonwealth South-East Asia. After Singapore's enforced secession from the Federation of Malaysia in 1965, anxious talk was to be heard about possible hostilities between that city-state and the federation, a risk which intertwined with that of ethnic hostility within Malaysia between the Malays and the Straits Chinese. In 1969, in fact, some 200 people (over 80 per cent of them Chinese) were killed during five days of rioting in Kuala Lumpur. Since 1971, however, this tension has markedly receded. Vigorous economic development, within a tolerably democratic setting, has undoubtedly contributed. But so, too, has the interlocking of defence preparations.

One proposition that commands wide support, in the United States as elsewhere, is that work must proceed on a new and comprehensive security structure for the Near East in the wake of Iraq's expulsion from Kuwait. What is acknowledged, too, is that the drive to create this structure must be underscored not only by the adjustment of economic imbalances but also by the advance of democratisation all round: with the Palestinians under occupation; in fascisto-Marxist regimes such as those of Iraq and Syria; and in the more conservative regimes of Arabia and the Gulf. That in a region of such rapid cultural change, things will get more repressive where they do not get more liberal is all too well indicated by the 1991 Amnesty International report on Bahrain.[63]

As regards the still hoped-for renaissance of a war-wracked Kuwait, the effective restriction of the franchise to members of families who have resided there for two or three generations will have to be replaced by a more expansive dispensation, linked to the return of the many innocent people obliged to flee Kuwait, in the aftermath of Iraq's expulsion. A needful precursor is the relaxation by the Al Sabah family of its monopolistic grip on ministerial posts. Important, too, would be a reversal of the *démarche* of July 1986 whereby the National Assembly was suspended and a draconian press law introduced. It was a response to a rise in Shi'ite militancy over the previous year and, more specifically, to insurgent bombings of the Ahmadi refinery two weeks before. All this was against the background of an escalation of the Iran-Iraq war. But now, in the aftermath of Saddam's latest inglorious adventure, the political atmosphere is as dark as the soot-laden skies above. The whole situation in this city-state has given a new and ugly twist to John Ruskin's notion of the 'pathetic fallacy'.[64]

Even without further such conflicts, it will take years of active involvement to transform this region politically. What also is indicated is that if 'strategic studies' is to revive on a more interdisciplinary basis it will do so most usefully through application to such regional perspectives.

11

Defended Peace

WERE RELATIONS with the Soviet Union to sour again, she would still be unable to present the main threat the West has prepared against these last 40 years: the overland *blitzkrieg* to the channel ports or, in its tempered version, 'the grab for Hamburg'. As Mackinder would have put it, the heartland has lost its grip on Eastern Europe. As noted in Chapter 4, however, the Soviet Union retains other avenues for military adventurism. Moscow is also likely to remain a significant arms exporter. Therefore, the quality of her military equipment, actual and future, remains of interest, not least in relation to its mediocre performance in Iraqi hands.

Tactical aviation usually affords a good indication as to the balance of advantage in this regard. Since 1945, Soviet design bureaux have continued to produce machines that are impressive aerodynamically. What they have never been able to incorporate are electronic systems that are sufficiently compact and dexterous. This is why Soviet-built aircraft have so consistently been worsted in combat: Korea, 1950–53; the Formosan Straits, 1958; the Arab–Israel borders, 1956, 1967, 1973 and 1982; and the Gulf, 1991.

All round computer performance has likewise fallen short. In 1970, *The Economist* spoke of a general lag of 10 to 15 years behind the West, in concept and in quality.[1] In 1978, it reckoned seven.[2] The year before, an OECD report put the current lag behind the USA at 5–10 years, with little reduction (except perhaps in software)[3] the previous 10 years. In 1982, the first edition of an annual Pentagon assessment of the entire Soviet panoply suggested that, whereas in 1965 'Soviet development and production of microelectronics and computers was about 10 to 12 years behind US capability', nowadays the gap was 2–7.[4] However, the 1987 edition found 'quality control difficulties' unresolved and software very adequate. The Soviets still trailed a decade behind the West in civil/industrial applications.[5] Few would alter that verdict for today.

Few would doubt that bureaucratic stultification within a command economy was largely to blame. Nor 'can it be a coincidence' (as Marxists used to say) that this malaise most afflicts personal computers, since a dislike of the innovative diversity their development needs goes hand-in-hand with a dread of the devolution of data-handling that their procurement connotes. Only in the late 1970s did Soviet planners overtly acknowledge the importance of the microprocessor.[6]

Those of us who attach importance at this juncture to Soviet economic and political stability are bound to feel some ambivalence about this state of affairs. Even in terms of military advantage, however, euphoria seems unwarranted. Industrial espionage, often focused on military applications, may narrow particular lags by several years.[7] Witness how 'the apparent ease with which the Soviet Union cloned Intel's chips ... has never been satisfactorily explained'.[8] Besides, prediction is made all the more chancy by big sectoral variations in Soviet technical prowess. Thus the USSR's achievements in radio- and radar-astronomy have long belied general notions of backwardness. So have those in controlled nuclear fusion.

Evidently, too, *perestroika* can especially assist electronic restructuring. On the other hand, certain consequences of *glasnost* could lengthen the West's lead. The breaking away of Eastern Europe is one. The emigration of Jews, Germans and other Soviet citizens, often of high talent, is liable to be another. Then as regards the military-industrial complex as such, there has been pressure to extend faster its deepening involvement, evident through this last decade, in non-military production.[9] Correspondingly, objections have been more vocally raised against the priority given to weaponry in Soviet research and development – 70 per cent of all the personnel, according to Roald Sagdeev, the leading Space scientist and politician reformer.[10] And what of the imperative need for more international interdependence, as high technology becomes more diverse?[11] Will not this enable the West to lengthen its lead? Among the less remarked but important trends of late has been the incorporation of Japanese electronics in US military systems.

More fundamentally, every gauge of time lag ought to be related to the 'extended-S' or sigmoid curve so characteristic of technological evolution. The notion is that, within a given sector, performance will improve very gradually for some time but then become rapid. Later on, it will slow right down, as the said technology matures. Both acceleration and retardation may onset abruptly, with any quality lags as between countries and alliances being widened by the former and narrowed by the latter.

A systematic rendering of this model was published by OECD in 1967. Among four alternative patterns also depicted was that of an indefinite 'exponential increase with no flattening in the considered time frame'; and this, it was suggested, is 'exhibited by a variety of functional capabilities, among them the representative maxima for aircraft speeds'.[12] Yet it was virtually at this very moment that (as noted in Chapter 5) the levelling off of the speed of warplanes began. This concurrence served to confirm the wide applicability of the S-curve concept.

Arguably, indeed, it covers the entire realm of human progress, general economic growth included. Never mind that the ultimate transition to a stationary state cannot be harmonious without 'a world movement potent enough to meet the challenges'. Otherwise the planetary prospect may be catastrophic 'regardless of the long-run reassurance implicit in the S-curve'.[13] Social scientists and population biologists ought actively to debate this prognosis. Does it imply early limits to economic growth? How does it relate to theories about historical 'long waves'?[14] What it does for us now is emphasise how basic this pattern is.

In some aspects of electronics, a levelling out is already in train or in sight in the West. Radar as such has become quite stable. The compaction of the silicon chip will be near its limit by the turn of the century. Stealth may exhaust its possibilities within a similar time frame. Beam guidance of tactical missiles can already be deadly accurate if ambient conditions are good.

On the other hand, lasers will develop a lot further yet in terms of quality and versatility, Gallium arsenide will soon come into its own as a semi-conductor. It will do so as one in which electrons flow several times as fast as in silicon oxide and which, indeed, favours the use of fibre optics – a medium in which electrons are replaced by photons. The latter are faster still and are, in addition, impervious to Electro Magnetic Pulses (EMP), the acute radiation bursts that nuclear explosions cause. Much more powerful computers will become available these next few years. Electronic Warfare (EW) will get ever more sophisticated. So an electronic revolution will continue through the year 2010 for sure, thus accentuating the quality lead in military equipment of the West over the USSR.

A war-torn developing world?

Likewise, many developing countries will lag further in terms of any ability indigenously to sustain a full panoply of weapons and support systems, a prospect all the more significant now that the USSR and the West seem less inclined to assist respective clients in this regard. Even at the best of times, technical education and operational training present problems. Nor does a good tradition of staff work easily take root. The most crucial constraints, however, concern systems development and production.

For purposes of illustration, the case of Turkey can very fairly be taken. She now has, after all, a population of 56 million, and a steel output of over seven million tons a year. Her martial tradition stretches back through the Middle Ages, when her soldiers well confronted the Crusaders and the Mongols. By 1914, she was producing small arms under a Mauser licence. Faster industrialisation under Kemal Atatürk, post-1918, was partly in pursuance of ordnance self-sufficiency, a Directorate of Military Factories being established in 1921. By 1935, the Turks were assembling a fighter-bomber under a Polish licence and a basic trainer under a British licence. Today their country ranks as a major power regionally. Though prominent within NATO, it has been concerned to retain some freedom of action.

Yet despite so conducive a setting, progress to date has been modest. A lot of maintenance and some modification work is done on a whole variety of systems. Contrary to an American recommendation made in 1982, the final assembly of F-16 fighters destined for the Turkish air force is being done locally; and similar provision is now being made for their engines. A limited number of army lorries is also manufactured as, under licence, are certain of the simpler kinds of electronics, such as combat radios and scramblers. There the bounds are likely to be drawn for some time ahead.[15]

However, a technology gap often matters less in a constrictive environment: urban, jungle, mountain, archipelagic or whatever. So does it when like is not pitched against like. With all respect to F. W. Lanchester and his Square Law, subtle differences in electronic dexterity can be very decisive when one squadron of combat aircraft, say, in engaging another. But surface-to-air missiles or surface-to-surface ballistic missiles do not need to be as good as their counterparts on the other side, merely good enough to accomplish given tasks. As much applies to nuclear bombs and chemical warheads and to sea mines. Moreover, the last four categories are sometimes easier for an emergent industry to cope with than are more elaborated systems. So it is that President Bush has advised that over 20 countries are now able to make chemical weapons.

To a large extent, the prospects for truly independent capabilities within the developing world hinge, this next two or three decades, on the procurement of surface-to-surface ballistic missiles. In 1989, William Webster, then Director of the CIA, warned that at least 15 such countries could be constructing these systems by the year 2000.[16] Later that year, Assistant Secretary of State Richard Clarke told a Senate hearing that 20 'third world' states could soon be.[17] This thrust contrasts with a near impasse in respect of the production of even a minimally adequate general mix of weapons: aircraft, armoured vehicles, warships.... Only nine developing states are currently credited with some such ability: Argentina, Brazil, China, Egypt, India, Israel, North and South Korea and Taiwan.[18]

In the Near East, several countries have available, or almost so, ballistic missiles with ranges of at least 800 km (500 miles). China has supplied Saudi Arabia with some 30 of its CSS-2s which carry perhaps 2,000 km. The *Jericho* 2, on the brink of entering service in Israel, carries 1,500. Before confronting the world in Kuwait, Iraq had started to deploy the *Al-Abbas* of 900 km range: an extended version of the *Al-Husayn*, a model developed with Egyptian and Soviet-bloc assistance and used towards the end of the war with Iran. Baghdad may also have had some Soviet *SS-12*s.[19] Beforehand, President Mubarak had pulled out of the Condor missile development (range, 800 km), a project led by Argentina with Egyptian assistance and Iraqi funding.[20]

In judging the likely accuracy of indigenously-produced ballistic missiles, it may be helpful to review the corresponding debate about Soviet systems. Doubts have regularly been expressed as to whether any of the latter have achieved standard accuracies (Circular Error Probability or CEPs)[21] below 200–300 metres; and there was nothing about the Iraqis' use of the Scud in the 1991 Gulf War to suggest that they had. Yet even without chemical or nuclear warheads, even that inexactness could be acceptable against certain military targets. Simulations indicate that a salvo of six to eight

*SS-23*s (Soviet ballistic missiles with ranges of 500 km) would be 90 per cent likely to close for a while an 8,000-ft runway.[22] Ultimately, of course, all such accuracies might match those the West already registers with its on-board inertial guidance. The Pershing 2, the US ballistic missile cancelled under the terms of the Intermediate Nuclear Forces (INF) treaty of 1987, was designed to achieve a CEP as tight as 30 metres over a range of up to 1,800 km.[23]

Between 1983 and 1987, however, seven of the advanced industrial states (Britain, Canada, France, Federal Germany, Italy, Japan and the United States) successfully negotiated a Missile Technology Control Regime (MTCR). Its stated purpose is 'to limit the risks of nuclear proliferation by controlling transfers that could make a contribution to nuclear weapons delivery systems other than manned aircraft', this hopefully being achieved without impeding the legitimate use of rockets in Space research. Capabilities identified as of special concern are payloads of not less than 500 kg delivered across distances of not less than 300 km.[24]

Buttressing the Non-Proliferation Treaty (NPT) of 1968 has to be another element in this aspect of grand strategy. So must the evolution of more systematic and ethically-sensitive policies apropos arms exports. The chief questions to ask in given situations may be these. Might an embargo on exports to a war zone, actual or prospective, work lopsidedly, as did the proscriptions the League of Nations applied to China as well as Japan (1931–33) and then to Ethiopia as well as Italy (1933–36)? What distinctions can be preserved between defensive and offensive weapons or between internal security and external? Is the internal security to bolster licit and beneficent authority or is it to sustain repression? How far would arms supplies encourage the growth of a country's military establishment and what does this connote for its overall development? Might the associated supply of spare parts and ammunition afford opportunities for constructive political leverage? Is weapons standardisation important for defence co-ordination? Would a withholding of arms induce the would-be recipients and maybe others to turn to less scrupulous exporters? Or might it encourage them to develop their own arms industries? Might the output from these include weapons of mass destruction? How does one crack the international mafia of illicit arms dealers, in Brussels and elsewhere? And if more responsible policies are thus pursued in regard to arms exports, will these be in the context of a grand strategy that is suitably reciprocal, not least as regards arms control?

Nor must we forget how readily authoritarian regimes may resort to indirect aggression, by smuggling arms and in many other ways. How the action-reaction phenomenon may thus be exploited to exacerbate enmities, communal or ideological, in more open polities was shown by Libya's huge shipments of arms to the IRA, especially after the US air strikes against her (partly from British bases) in April 1986.[25] Before these attacks, launched to curb Libyan sponsorship of terrorism elsewhere, the IRA had been losing out comprehensively. Sinn Fein, its political wing, was to win just one out of 17 Ulster seats in the British General Election of 1987; and to secure a paltry 1.5 per cent of the popular vote in the 1989 election in the Irish republic. None the less, those extra shipments served to reverse awhile the collateral trend within Ulster towards diminished political violence. The deaths thus caused numbered 55 in 1985 and 62 in 1986, but then were 93 in 1987 and again in 1988. Yet again, the placid resilience of the Ulster people took the strain well; and the death rate was to drop again to 62 in 1989 and 76 in 1990. Undeniably, however, some extra clout had been given to an organisation with a hard-core 'active service' membership of only about 80.[26] By 1990, the IRA probably had a 'bigger reserve' of ordnance than ever before. Large finds by the security forces had included the French interception of a cargo ship in the autumn of 1987.

Questions were raised as to how strong the case was for singling Libya out for blame rather than Iran, Syria or, of course, Iraq.[27] Questions might also have been raised about whether the Reagan administration ought not to have set such action within the context of a more purposive strategy for the Near East as a whole. But the chief point for the moment is that, having thus embarked on a compellent strategy, Washington might usefully have persevered sufficiently to discourage this indirect aggression against Britain. At all events, the dying away of the Cold War should make perseverance more feasible against future such challenges. Protection against them may be a precondition of the progress of liberal democracy, especially within the developing world.

What is very hard to decide is whether one should ever retaliate in kind, countering subversion with subversion.[28] Could this represent the time-honoured principle of an 'eye for an eye', applied with a minimum of fuss or palaver? Across the decade 1965–75, for instance, a variety of intelligence services operated on canvases that were broad in more senses than one, especially in the Near East. Not all the political effects were well judged. Bad examples to the contrary were Mossad's arming of the EOKA B extremists in Cyprus in 1973; and the decision of US and British intelligence not to warn the royal authorities in Libya against the coup that brought Colonel Gadafi to power in 1969.[29] Nowadays it may be more difficult to subvert from the outside a regime that is prepared to be totally repressive, perhaps using the subversion threat as its excuse and new forms of information technology as its instrumentation. Nor may covert operations readily find a place in the world order if this is stabilised by a new concert of powers, operating via the very open diplomacy of the United Nations.

The covert collection of information is about as easy to exclude as sin itself; and is, in any case, good on balance for the peace of the world. Perhaps, however, the covert sponsorship of particular parties, journals, radios, research programmes and the like is better left for situations in which an adversary power is already acting thus. Certainly, the promotion of internal violence should never be undertaken except against a polity that has posed an active threat to general peace. Nor should it be undertaken except in the aftermath of a formal declaration that a state of confrontation exists. A quarter of a century ago, the late Herman Kahn asked what the Atlantic Alliance should do if the Warsaw Pact took over West Berlin. His own reply was that it should declare war, thereby presenting itself with a host of more specific options. The stratagem is one the UN Security Council could usefully bear in mind.

Force projection

In his televised speech to the American people on 16 January 1991 about the war then looming, George Bush quoted the phrase, 'These are times that try men's souls', words uttered by Thomas Paine, the fiery English radical who became a fierce partisan of the American revolution. In the course of that partisanship, Paine stressed the difficulty the Royal Navy faced operating on the opposite side of the Atlantic Ocean from where its home ports were situated. He averred that American naval strength would therefore prevail over British even if the latter were 20 times as great on paper.[30] Allowing for some hyperbole at the time and much logistical change in the interim, the general point can still be well taken.

Even so, the merits of naval force projection as a means of resolving regional crises may be rather greater than is immediately evident from the 1990-91 confrontation with Iraq. An offshore naval presence is especially valuable when (a) it is not clear which side has been or may be the prime instigator of hostilities, (b) key overflight permissions have been or may be witheld, and (c) the strike facilities ashore stand exposed to pre-emption. None of these circumstances (except contingently the last) has applied in this latest episode. To which one might add that sea-delivered cruise missiles will have great salience in the future, though maybe as borne in flotillas of function-built and smallish vessels more than in renovated battleships. Among the former might be submarines.

Other instruments forged in a rather distant past that have acted in this crisis as pointers to the future are the B-52 strategic bombers the USAF has flown on non-nuclear missions to the Gulf, staging through Britain or Diego Garcia, the Anglo-American facility set deep in the Indian Ocean. They illustrate the role of, and confirm the need for, a sizeable fleet of Long-Range Combat Aircraft able to deploy from operating bases up to several thousand miles from the main battle area, bases that may enjoy considerable immunity on that account. Depending on the variant, their capabilities might include electronic warfare, reconnaissance, free-fall bombing, stand-off missile strikes, anti-submarine operations and air-to-air missile defence. Some priority might be given to the creation of such a force, albeit with any implications for strategic arms control duly in mind.

In the years ahead, the debate about the 1991 Gulf war will focus very frequently on the exercise of air power. Any attempt here to comment more definitively would be premature. But this much may perhaps be said. The aircrews flying tactical missions on behalf of the coalition faced a challenge almost unprecedented in its complexity. All through each mission they had to sustain a high level of technical virtuosity and, above all, dexterity. Yet at the same time, they had to be utterly single-minded in their basic resolve.

These two behaviour patterns are not easy to blend. Very consistently, however, those young airmen achieved a synthesis magnificently. This is how they kept their own losses, from air defences that were quite sophisticated and sometimes extremely dense, down to the astonishing level of one per thousand sorties. In raids over Kuwait, they shattered the army of occupation, morally as well as materially. Over Iraq itself, they crippled her air force and navy; battered and bogged down her army; and dislocated her potential for the production of nuclear and chemical weapons.

At the same time, they went to great trouble and no little risk to minimise collateral damage to residential areas as such. On the other hand, the targeting schedules presented to them did embrace the infrastructure for electric power, urban water supply, oil refining and petrochemicals. Such targets had military significance only indirectly and in the longer run. But their relevance to the health and well-being of civil society was very direct and on-going. The decision to attack them seems to have derived from the assumption that civilian discomfiture would lead rapidly to the collapse of the regime.

In actuality, the immediate effect may have been to persuade many ordinary Iraqis, in the capital city at any rate, that Saddam Hussein was right to say that the coalition was waging a war to destroy their country and with it Arab honour and dignity. The longer-term effect may have been to make it harder to promote in Baghdad a successor regime that is at once authentic, stable and reasonably liberal.

Two other questions arise in relation to this having been a coalition campaign mandated by the UN. One is whether it might not have been possible to depose Saddam Hussein before the cease-fire, while still keeping a sufficient consensus in the Security Council. The other concerns the extreme reluctance of the coalition military command to confirm that the Iraqi military dead numbered over 100,000.[31]

The Atlantic citadel

One precept that events in Eastern Europe have well vindicated is the NATO doctrine of flexible response, including graduated nuclear response. They have done so in the retrospective sense that firmly sustaining deterrence helped bring about changes in the Soviet bloc that may still work out very much for the best. They have also done so in the forward-looking sense that we are now free of the threat to which flexible response was most closely geared yet operationally least well adapted, that thrust across the inter-German border. Given the nodal importance of this sector and the likely dynamic of any East-West war across it, the toughest of questions were perennially posed about how nuclear flexibility might relate to frontal defence well forward and to a collateral need for crisis bargaining. Never mind the problem of West Berlin.[32]

The threats that contingently remain are all ones that flexible response can more readily encompass. Thirty years ago, General Laurie Norstad, then Supreme Allied Commander Europe (SACEUR), warned that only tactical nuclear weapons could check a heavy attack on Northern Norway.[33] Then again, Admiral Sergei

Gorshkov (who, in December 1985, retired after three decades as C-in-C of the Soviet navy) reckoned that, in the First World War, the manpower the Allies dedicated to retaining sufficient control of the North Atlantic was 20 times that deployed by Germany via her U-boat fleet. For tonnage lost, the ratio was close to 100. Nor were things much different in the Second World War.[34] For this reason alone, the West could not possibly sustain another Battle of the Atlantic against a large and modern submarine fleet. The choice under these circumstances would lie between tactical nuclear recourse and outright surrender. So would it in the event of a blockade of our ports by means of sea-mines that could be far more sophisticated than any seen in the Gulf these last few years.

Moreover, maritime threats of this sort could also develop outside the NATO area, a prospect that makes even more absurd any notion that the West could and should commit itself to nuclear 'no first use' as a matter of absolute principle. The same applies to possible scenarios to landward, not least in the Persian Gulf and Korea. Nor dare we discount the dissuasive value of nuclear firepower, at any rate in a world not gone completely crazy. Nuclear compellence may also figure. On the negative side, it may do so as a form of blackmail to some illicit end. On the positive, it may sometimes do as a uniquely persuasive means of effecting the early cessation of hostilities.

Yet none of this amounts to an argument in favour of national nuclear forces being run on an entirely autonomous basis, within the Atlantic area or anywhere else. The argument is rather for collective deterrence. Take the strategic nuclear forces of France and Britain. At present, each basically consists of submarines bearing 16 strategic missiles apiece, four such boats in the British case and six in the French. May one say yet again that it would be quite straightforward so to co-ordinate their patrol schedules and targeting matrices as to ensure that together they could the more convincingly fulfil the basic task assigned to each: that of ensuring overwhelming retaliation against any full-scale onslaught on their national territories, probably within the context of a general offensive against Western Europe as a whole. It is a capability that well complements that for flexible response against more local or selective threats, the latter being afforded within NATO largely by the big and diversified American deterrent.

Such an Anglo-French arrangement would need little in the way of bi-national command. Therefore it need not exacerbate anxieties still felt, in Paris but also in London, about any pooling of military sovereignty. If, on the other hand, the political climate evolved aright, it could be the basis for a revival of the Atlantic Nuclear Force (ANF) proposal of 1964-65. This would have involved the creation, within NATO, of a multinational command for the control of a fair number of assigned nuclear strike weapons, strategic and theatre. Some of the constituent formations might have been 'mixed': that is to say, composed of troops from more than one country. Essentially, the aim was to underscore the American guarantee and to exclude a separate European deterrent as unsound in terms of both political and military geography. Put more widely, it was to prevent polarisation between a Rightist isolationism in the United States and a Leftist nuclear neutralism in Europe.

As regards the perennial question of the modernisation of forces in being, the most crucial issue pending may be the introduction of several calibres of Anti-Tactical Ballistic Missiles (ATBMs). Many on the Left, in the USA at least, judge ATBMs entirely in terms of how they might undercut the existing ABM treaty, a document so far treated in such circles as a sacred text never to be modified.[35] Meanwhile others, particularly in Europe, adhere to the classic disarmers' axiom that all military innovation undermines stability. Yet, as Hedley Bull demonstrated in his classic text, everything depends on the objective facts in each case, and how adroitly these are responded to by those working for arms control.[36]

The current inclination when defence reductions are being planned (through arms control or otherwise) is strongly towards the destruction of the weapons platforms to be withdrawn, rather than their mere translation to inactive status in a more remote location. This approach ought to be reviewed for three reasons. A major war in somewhere like Europe might involve platform loss at a very high rate. These days, certain kinds of platform take a long time to build from scratch, perhaps 18 months in the case of a strike fighter. On the other hand, modern techniques of modular improvement (eg the installation of new electronics or guided missiles) can sometimes make the modernisation of older platforms more efficacious than before. The renovated American battleships remain an instructive case in point. So allowance might usefully be made in arms control accords for the 'mothballing' of selected platforms, as a precautionary measure. The same could apply to other defence reductions.

What ought to be resisted is a revival (likely in Europe, these next few years) of what amounts to the 'small is beautiful' approach to defence: the approach broadly favoured by militant 'greens' and their *alter ego*, the millenarian nuclear neutralists. This will usually envisage the replacement of existing armies with militias. These will be depicted as having a 'non-provocative' weapons mix built around light guided missiles, anti-tank and anti-aircraft. Conceivably, so simple a panoply would have some limited value against a mass tank charge backed up only by helicopters. Certainly, it could be useless against any other armed thrust. Nor could such militias sensibly be the basis for guerilla resistance of Titoist or Maoist hue. Our modern mass society is ill-adapted, in this generation at least, for a style of war so savagely pervasive. Its lack of that much toughness is most recently evidenced by the collapse of international tourism in 1991, this in the face of what was only a minimal threat of Gulf-related air terrorism.[37]

What could be most relevant, on the other hand, is a restructuring of armed forces around the concept of volunteer reserves at the ready. Young people might be invited to serve for two or three years with the colours, this to be followed by perhaps nine years in an active reserve always ready to come to war status in a week or so. Historically the record of reservists at war has been mixed. But when volunteer reserves have been properly selected, trained, equipped and organised, their prowess has often been high, not least when operating in independent formations.

Moreover, this can still apply as much to air arms, a sphere in which one might have thought proficiency would these days depend on long engagements with the colours. With the USAF there are currently 92 squadrons of aircraft in the Air National Guard (ANG) and another 37 in the Air Force Reserve (AFRES). The air defence of the continental United States (CONUS) is provided by one regular air division with 18 F-15 Eagles and by eight ANG squadrons with a total of 48 F-4 Phantoms and 90 F-16 Fighting Falcons. Ever since 1961, in fact, the ANG has been integrated into the round-the-clock programme of runway alert.[38] However, it may be harder to train aircrew, in particular, for the full round of tasks involved in tactical air support, tasks often carried out fast and low. In 1976, an official Australian defence review made the point that, even in regular service, the amount of flying training feasible could be what set the limit on the multirole use of modern warplanes.[39] On the other hand, a cadre reserve system could provide thorough initial training; and could allow of extended recall for full-time retraining at times of high political tension.

In an era in which instant readiness for a major European war will no longer be a constant requirement, recourse to this recruitment philosophy might save a deal of money while keeping flexible the manning levels available for unforeseen contingencies. To this actuarial consideration must be added the more subtle but utterly vital question of military motivation. Standing armies might not be easy to motivate adequately these next 20 years if (a) the Soviet threat does diminish more or less continually, (b) the social milieu is unfavourable to some key elements in the traditional martial ethos and (c) the whole notion of adequacy has to be shaped by the much greater ferocity a major war may now be waged with. On the other hand, acceptance of the principle of using regular cadres to train intensively volunteers who are first on short-term colour service then on ready reserve may be good for motivation all round, not least because of the wider social and economic value of much of the training provided. Meanwhile, society at large may come to appreciate this more as it swings away from anti-institutionalism and towards 'a rediscovery of honour'.[40]

What is more, such a restructuring could enable the continental European members of the Atlantic Alliance to ease themselves out of traditional reliance on standing armies based on conscription without losing entirely the connotations of the 'nation at arms'. These connotations the European Left, in particular, has long felt to be sounder, politically and socially, than what has sometimes resulted from armed services becoming closed and isolated communities of long-term regulars.

A further attraction of cadre reserve is that it could be a way of bringing the manpower structure of Britain's armed forces into line with that of her continental neighbours. Her reversion, from 1957, to fully regular armed forces with only a limited reliance on reservists seemed in line with her insular traditions and requirements. By the same token, however, it made commonality with the rest of NATO Europe hard to work for. All else apart, voluntary recruitment avoids the hidden economic and social costs that conscription must involve; and that alone has made it peculiarly hard to make useful comparisons between Britain's budgetary contribution and everybody else's.

UN and WEU

One respect in which not only Britain but also France are likely long to stand apart, however, is through their being Permanent Members of the Security Council. Obviously, it is vital that the new concert of powers hopefully emerging in the world never lapses into the politics of repressive expediency, post-1815 style. Maybe the best guarantee against its so doing is that it regularly operates through the UN in general and the Security Council in particular. Yet two of the latter's five Permanent Members, the USSR and China, have remained unready for active participation in peace-keeping operations. What this probably means is that, unless Britain and France are prepared to be very contributive, the military burden of keeping or restoring the peace in times of major conflict will redound too heavily on the United States for anybody's comfort.

At some point there will have to be a thorough reconsideration at governmental level of what permanent membership of the Council should entail and who those members should be. Over the years some interest has been shown in Japan in membership as a due accolade.[41] However, the 1990-91 Gulf crisis has concentrated minds wondrously in this respect. At very long last (on 23 January 1991), Tokyo did agree to make a financial contribution equal to one fifth of the burden the alliance had thus far incurred, albeit a contribution subject to rather ambiguous provisos about this money being used only to 'restore peace'. The Japanese government also decided to dispatch transport aircraft from the Self-Defence Force on humanitarian missions in the theatre. Across the country as a whole, however, sentiment waxed strong against any direct involvement, except perhaps via a civil reconstruction corps of the sort the Japan Socialist Party was calling for. Among those who openly doubted whether their military could yet be trusted with overseas responsibilities were some elder statesmen within the ranks of the Liberal Democrats, the long-standing government party.[42] Doubts were also expressed as to whether the state of parliamentary politics was conducive to the flair and resolve required for crisis diplomacy at global level.[43] So were they, too, about the scope of the coalition bombing campaign.

There might, in any case, be some advantage awhile in the Security Council's permanent membership being neatly confined, as currently it is, to what are and likely for some time to remain the only five countries in the 'thermonuclear club': that is to say, those with the capacity to make fusion weapons or 'hydrogen bombs', quite the most potent form of military nuclear power. This might help to expose the futility of others acquiring nuclear fission weapons, at least in so far as these may be sought as status symbols.

From another standpoint, however, a conflict can here be seen with the looked-for evolution of the Western European Union as the European 'twin pillar' for Atlantic security. What is more, this conflict has been rendered the more acute by the interest that emanates from the corridors of WEU in 'out-of-area' military activities as a spearhead of its whole institutional development. Those keen on this have been encouraged by the way the WEU profile in the 1990–91 Gulf crisis extended beyond the precedent set in that of 1987–88. This second time round, Belgium, Britain, France, Italy, The Netherlands and Spain despatched between them over 30 ships; and Britain, France, Italy and The Netherlands deployed forces ashore as well. The British, French and Italians joined in the air offensive at the very outset.

This time round, too, the contributions from WEU countries to the maritime blockade were closely coordinated, this on the spot as well as at Defence and Foreign Minister level. However, every decision on deployment to the theatre has been taken by the country concerned, those by Britain and France respectively involving the provision of a substantial ground-cum-air contingent. The British force was placed under American command early on, the French on the eve of hostilities. Then at the EC Foreign Ministers' meeting on 19 February 1991, those from Britain, France and Germany felt unable to share with their colleagues their privileged access to the Soviet peace initiative.[44]

All of which seems to confirm that the main drive towards WEU unity will have to come from within the European theatre. No doubt European security issues will dominate the agenda of the WEU Institute for Security Studies established in Paris in 1990. Already the WEU Council of Ministers has sought professional guidance on the possible establishment of a verification agency and, later on, a satellite observation system. Actively mooted, too, is the grouping of national brigades into multinational divisions.

Within a few years, however, we will reach a stage at which the further growth of WEU will have to involve major accommodations by both NATO and the EC, even allowing for French and American reservations. Arguably, the WEU should take over and reshape the military command structure in NATO Europe, albeit with due attention paid to what this means for an American presence and all it connotes. At the same time, this much more solid WEU will need to become the lead institution in European foreign policy because of (a) the likely presence within the EC of several nations that adhere firmly to neutrality, and (b) the urgent need at global level for an integrated grand strategy in which both the military and the non-military dimensions will have vital parts to play. In key aspects of economic policy, in particular, this is bound to involve major encroachments by WEU on existing EC preserves. The developing world's debt crisis, for example, is an economic question but also a strategic one.

What one must therefore be talking about is a revision of the several treaties that have respectively shaped the multinational institutions in question. Eventually, too the replacement of the British and French seats on the Security Council with a WEU one may be up for consideration. Meanwhile, one may be looking to several EC neutrals (Austria, Finland, Sweden and Switzerland?) to figure in a new security framework for non-NATO Europe. For Switzerland, in particular, that would involve major adaptation. As for Ireland, if she were to accede to NATO/WEU, her very location would contribute powerfully to sea control in the North Atlantic, much as it could have done in World War Two.[45] However, any such accession is likely to wait upon the cessation of intercommunal strife in Ulster.

Soviet or Russian?

In the face of all these uncertainties, one is tempted to think that, in narrow geopolitical terms, the break up of the Soviet Union could be to the advantage of the West, never mind that it would be a disaster for the Soviet peoples themselves and for the management of this planet in a broader, more holistic sense. In all probability, however, such an expectation would prove grimly illusory. The strategic advantages still inherent in heartland location would not be diminished at all critically by the secession of some peripheral republics. Nor might a Russian republic be by any means too feeble to take advantage of them. So a Kremlin lead not by angrily Marxian 'old believers' but by no less angry Great Russian ones might pose the worst danger since Stalin's time. The apparent failure of the August coup by no means excludes this as a possibility, perhaps within the context of a world more distracted by economic, social and ecological stress than the one we know today.

12

Planetary Horizons

Strategic arms reductions

THE SIGNS still are that, in the course of the next year or two, the superpowers will ratify the new treaty emerging from the Strategic Arms Reduction Talks conducted since 1985 and signed in Moscow on 31 July 1991. Although certain particulars may remain controversial, it does seem firmly agreed that each should reduce to 1,600 strategic delivery vehicles: ICBMs, Submarine-Launched Ballistic Missiles and heavy bombers. Correspondingly, each will have available for delivery 6,000 warheads, this national figure being subject to some technical interpretations. Certain sub-limits have also been agreed.

Yet given the generosity of the main limits, one has to see the START-1 treaty as a holding operation. The big question will come up as and when a START-2 treaty is negotiated as a follow-up. That question will concern the implications for Mutual Assured Destruction (MAD), the regime established between Washington and Moscow during the late 1960s. Might MAD be rendered unstable?

The concept of MAD originated in the 1950s but received keynote promotion from Robert McNamara, as US Secretary of Defense, from 1964 onwards. By then, each superpower was amassing several thousand thermonuclear warheads for contingent use against the homeland of its prime adversary. Yet on almost any reckoning, the utter ruination of either of these essentially urban civilisations could be effected by hits against a very few hundred targets. In principle, the connotations for stability would depend on how well the respective deterrents were protected by hardening, mobility or concealment. As things already were, however, there was little doubt that any strike by Soviet nuclear forces on the United States would leave unscathed enough strategic weapons to allow a quite unacceptable level of retaliation. Around 1967, the converse became as true. Nor did any Ballistic Missile Defence (BMD) available in that generation promise or threaten to alter this situation at all drastically. Then as now, surface-based defence nationwide was a good order of magnitude too costly in relation to likely results. Nor would Space-based defence have been manageable then.[1]

As was well recognised, however, MAD could never rest just on 'minimum deterrence': the retention by each side of enough force to inflict unacceptable damage on the other's urban areas, having ridden out a pre-emptive attack on its own strategic facilities. Both Washington and Moscow have always needed their strategic deterrent to be considerably larger than that and correspondingly diversified. Only then might they effect what the Americans these days call 'extended deterrence': the ability to opt for a duly proportional strategic riposte to some local or regional challenge that might not be countered otherwise. Nor have any changes in the Kremlin yet made that requirement a thing of the past for Washington.

With the continuing improvements in missile accuracy, however,the operational parameters of 'extended deterrence' stand again in need of review. In 1987, the United States Air Force (USAF) reached a 'critical point' in the development, for possible installation in Minuteman 3 ICBMs, of high explosive warheads that could be employed at least against fairly soft targets, such as master radars. Yet the corollary is that by early next century any ICBM emplacements could be far too vulnerable to even low-yield nuclear strikes. Moreover, terminal guidance by means of built-in sensors is already being developed for artillery shells in the USA, the promise being of a standard accuracy on target of around a metre or so. That technology could in due course be extended to strategic missiles. In the light of this gathering trend, Washington has become more attracted than before to the mobile ICBM. In Moscow, the thrust of opinion in that direction has been even stronger. This is why, in December 1988, Ambassador Paul Nitze, speaking as the senior White House aide on arms control, opined that there 'will be no START treaty that bans mobile and transportable ICBMs'.[2] In fact, START-1 seems set to allow for 1,100 mobile ICBMs on each side, all with single warheads. What has therefore to be considered is how eligible for arms control verification such weapons are.

The nub of the current argument is the road-mobile ICBM, the SS-25 the USSR started to deploy in 1985 and the Midgetman the

USA is expected to deploy in modest numbers soon. Analysis of the techniques for satellite surveillance seems to suggest that these could adequately monitor a complete ban because then the discovery of just one mobile launcher would then be clear proof of a breach. Almost certainly, on the other hand, they would be unsuitable as a means of ensuring that an agreed limit had not been exceeded.[3] The problems encountered tracking down Iraq's Scud missiles in the 1991 war amply confirms this view. Nor should one forget how well mobile ICBMs could blend into the Soviet scene, its physical geography and perhaps also its cultural landscape.

Therefore some START negotiators have concluded that the answer must lie in continual checks on the production facilities, many of which would have to be on site. Yet that might not gel with either the Soviet or the American political culture.[4] Correspondingly, any specific provisions might not be rugged enough to withstand a swing towards greater belligerency in Moscow and all the obstructionism this could give rise to. Nor might they, in any case, preclude non-compliance on a scale sufficient to destabilise the situation over, say, several years. Mobile ICBMs are natural instruments of arms control evasion. A complete ban seems the best way to cope with them, something the Reagan administration explicitly favoured.

What should next be admitted is that every argument in favour of retaining the strategic bomber as one element in a 'strategic triad' (the other two being the land- and the sea-based missiles) is open to question. Hopes that they might usefully be employed chasing after mobile ICBM launchers have evaporated.[5] Nor can one well sustain the older argument that, even in the strategic nuclear context, bombers are more flexible than missiles. They are much less well-adapted to the penetration in small numbers of heartland areas. Their established air bases are inviting targets; and dispersal to other airfields may or may not be effected. The alternative, keeping a sizeable fraction of them on continuous air alert, is taxing even for the duration of warlike crises.[6] Nor should one attach too much importance to what has become the classic contention that, during actual confrontation, strategic bombers can be launched, set dissuasively in a holding pattern and hopefully then recalled, the enemy having been deterred. There are many other ways to come visibly to a higher state of readiness and thus to signal nuclear resolve: have naval vessels leave harbour; deploy troops out of barracks; send tactical warplanes up; evacuate civilians; augment surveillance; gear up the command authority.... Nor does the initial use of any strategic weapons have to be more than symbolic.

Meanwhile, an argument in favour of phasing bombers out of strategic deterrence could be that it might assist the reformers in Moscow to press for big reductions in the home air defence command, the PVO-Strany referred to in Chapter 4. One has to admit, however, that this vast organisation has had a strange, not to say perverse, history. Mention has been made of the huge Soviet investment in this sector in the 1950s. A lot of this outlay was for batteries of heavy anti-aircraft guns. Even at that stage, this genre of weaponry was virtually obsolete. Yet some batteries were to be kept in service until a few years ago.

Most anomalous, however, was the way the defence of the Soviet heartland against manned bombers stayed at more or less the same level overall even though, after 1960, bombers conspicuously gave way to long-range missiles as the prime instruments of nuclear retaliation. Again through the 1980s, the size and configuration of PVO-Strany remained remarkably stable at around 500,000–520,000 men and women; 8,500-10,000 Surface-to-Air Missile (SAM) launchers; and 2,500 interceptor aircraft, nearly all of them machines of high aerodynamic performance. At the same time, the air force proper had 3,000-3,500 warplanes operational within Soviet borders, these as the main part of its frontal aviation. That is to say, their formal assignation was the support of the 150 or so divisions of the line also held at home in peacetime. Co-ordination has lately been close between this frontal aviation and PVO-Strany, otherwise known these days as Voyska-PVO. On 28 February 1991, Dimitry Yasov, the Soviet Minister of Defence, and six months later a hesitant coup leader, linked the two organisations together in his candid admission that the Gulf war had shown Soviet air defence to be of little use.

In principle, one should look for action-reaction here, a trade-off between a 'bomber bonfire' in the West and a large reduction in a Voyska-PVO which otherwise may remain perhaps the biggest bulwark of the power and privilege of the Soviet military. However, the fact that Voyska-PVO has regularly been kept at a size far beyond what is rational in terms of national requirements for strategic defence, owes a lot to the evident fact that a lot of military and political 'old believers' are implacably convinced that the pristine virtues of the revolutionary era are best preserved in a garrison state.

Besides which, certain rationalisations can be advanced for keeping Voyska-PVO large, regardless of any bonfires of strategic bombers. One that might persuade a hardline regime in Moscow is that the command could convert from anti-aircraft protection to the engagement of enemy orbital platforms, especially those associated with the Strategic Defense Initiative. The anti-satellite weapon the USSR has already deployed on a limited scale could play a part here. Eligible, too, might be the anti-missile missiles deployed around Moscow, under the terms of the Anti-Ballistic Missile treaty of 1972. Several other types of Soviet surface-to-air missiles have also been cited in the West as perhaps being 'stretchable' for this purpose.[7]

The next complication is that long-range cruise missiles might be used in strategic nuclear strikes, their being dispatched from the land or naval vessels or aircraft. In 1949, J. M. Spaight, a lonely but respected prophet of aerial arms control, felt the notion that 'airliners could be converted into night bombers is no longer of much importance'.[8] In that era of turreted heavy bombers delivering overhead to target large loads of free-fall bombs that was probably true. Nowadays, however, one has to admit that many different types of civil aircraft could be modified for the stand-off delivery, from some of the bigger machines, of dozens of cruise missiles. It is a special case, if you like, of modular adaptation. The inference is that it would never be possible to negotiate a 'bomber bonfire' that also eliminated every potential platform for nuclear-armed cruise missiles. But it would, in any case, be fatuous to seek comprehensive defence against nuclear-armed intruders that can contour-hug the way cruise missiles can. Witness the arrival in Red Square itself in 1987 of the low-flying light aircraft piloted by Matthias Rust, a young West German.

What also has to be reckoned with is the possibility that if PVO-Strany relinquished most of its strategic air defence role, a hardline Kremlin regime would simply see that force as the more available to serve as an aerial reserve for the contingent reinforcement of peripheral theatres: a task to which it is, even as things stand, rather well adapted. All along, indeed, this may have figured quite prominently in its purposes. Although a Brookings study published in 1974 doubted whether the imperatives (as perceived by the Soviets) of strategic air defence would allow of such diversion,[9] there are strong grounds for believing they would have and will do. One has to be the ultimate futility of the drive to give the Soviet heartland an airtight air defence. Another has been the longstanding integration of air defence throughout the Warsaw Pact, west of the Urals, Romania partially excepted. Yet another has been that Soviet strategic bombers have evidently had theatre support as an ancillary function. Yet another has been that, after the Strategic Arms Limitation Talks (SALT) agreement of 1969-72, 'the PVO justified air defence largely in terms of its role in conventional war'.[10] The considerable ability of this force to project itself to Soviet borders and beyond is one of the few ways in which the 'interior lines' of the heartland might be turned to operational advantage. Appreciation of this will have been enhanced in Moscow by a revived interest, in the aftermath of the Gulf war, in strategic mobility and in defence through offence.

Obviously, too, there is some parallelism with the fact that some of us would be prepared to argue that the West has a continuing need for a sizeable echelon of Long-Range Combat Aircraft (LRCA) for distant interventions at theatre level.[11] Soviet anxieties as to whether such machines might have a strategic nuclear role could be met by making it as clear as possible (by means of geographical disposition, command assignment, training schedules and doctrinal declaration) that they are not part of the panoply of strategic deterrence.

Therefore, while this and all aspects of the superpower air balance are extremely important, not least because of the connotations for Soviet internal developments, they are unlikely to be resolved satisfactorily through formal arms control. What may be required instead is using the strategic bomber as a bargaining chip, this with a view to securing informal understandings. Some grounds for hope for a dialogue along these lines can be seen in the recent Soviet decision to convert to civil use the ABM radar complex at Krasnoyarsk, a facility which the West had objected was in breach of the 1972 ABM treaty because it was not located peripherally enough.[12]

The High Seas and Arctic

So what of the insurance against strategic attack provided by naval vessels: the Fleet Ballistic Missile (FBM) submarines of the United States Navy and, of course, their Soviet counterparts, the SSBN? First of all, could the contribution such boats on patrol make to the preservation of MAD be undermined by technical change?

Discussion of this used often to hinge on a comparison with the status of submarines at the height of the Battle of the Atlantic (1939-45). However, in May 1943, a month of triumphant decision for Allied escort forces on North Atlantic stations, the attrition of the U-Boats at sea barely averaged one per cent a day. Yet a pre-emptive strike against an FBM flotilla would have to achieve close to 100 per cent in well under a quarter of an hour. Even in these simple terms, the required advance in Anti-Submarine Warfare (ASW) is well over 10,000-fold.

Nor does adverse comparison stop there. Unlike the U-Boats, the FBMs and SSBNs do not close to action with enemy vessels. Their duty is avoidance, aided by the superior performance afforded by nuclear propulsion and other novel features. Their maximum speed under water is well over twice as great and far more sustainable; and they are able to descend to depths maybe several times as great. Moreover an FBM or SSBN can lie quietly, perhaps at extreme depth. Alternatively, it can glide under an ice sheet. Since 1961, the USSR has tended to group most SSBNs at sea in 'bastion' areas inside the Arctic circle. In the light of all of which, progress in the detection of fully-submerged submarines looks even more modest than it does in relation to theatre war.

The conclusion that emerges is that any sizeable and well dispersed FBM or SSBN flotilla will be immune from a sudden disabling blow, now or indefinitely into the future. Nor is there much in the objection sometimes levelled that an FBM force could never be used against Soviet cities, in reply to a strike against American ICBMs, because that would then leave the USA with no missile forces and hence with her cities exposed to devastating revenge. In scenarios of this sort, all depends on the relative number of weapons available and the pro-portions being released. Admittedly, long-distance communication with submerged submarines is difficult for much the same reason as long-distance surveillance of them is virtually impossible. But nobody need wax too apprehensive on this score either. This is because the command function in a full-scale nuclear exchange could be far less elaborate than might be required in more limited or localised exchanges. Orders could be fewer and briefer. So could responses.

Communications apart, however, FBM boats are acknowledged to be unsatisfactory as instruments of any very selective or slow-motion strategic response. One reason is that the firing of only one or two of a boat's clutch of missiles could betray the vessel's location as the enemy extrapolated backwards each trajectory. Another is that any FBM flotilla depends on but one or two home ports and, albeit less critically, on but several specialist and conspicuous wireless stations. Evidently then, the whole of an FBM fleet could be marooned at sea by a very limited number of low-yield nuclear strikes against its infrastructure ashore. Were such a salvo delivered without warning, indeed, it might also catch roughly a third of all boats in harbour.

Arctic harmony?

A further dimension in the maritime debate is or ought to be that the situation within the Arctic basin affords scope for a singular experiment at regional level in ecological management combined with arms control. It does so because intense greenhouse warming seems bound to aggravate severely the great strain the fragile ecosystems of the far North are already under. Over-fishing in the Barents Sea is one aspect. Acid rain is another. So, too, is 'Arctic haze', the surges of smog that mainly emanate from the erstwhile Soviet bloc.

In essence, the case for embarking on the said experiment might be made as follows:

> It should be possible to stabilise, to an extent, the ecology of the Arctic. However, this would require multinational co-ordination at regional level. Adequate co-ordination would probably require a collateral understanding on arms control. Such an understanding can be arrived at.

What has to be admitted straightaway, of course, is that every link in this chain of argument is open to challenge. Even so, the possibility of such interaction is worth exploring, not least since it could become a signal demonstration of how strategy must and can incorporate ecology. It is mildly encouraging to note that the 1973 pact between the seven Arctic nations to establish a protective regime for polar bears came hard upon the SALT agreement of 1972, a Soviet-American accord that did somewhat constrain the strategic arms race, not least in the Arctic.[13]

Speaking in Murmansk in October 1987, Mikhail Gorbachev invited all polar countries to collaborate through treaty to manage ecologically the Arctic basin.[14] Nevertheless, doubts are sometimes expressed as to whether the USSR was really committed to anything other than bilateral undertakings about ecological control. What is pointed out, however, is that she had already become party to 36 international agreements on environment and conservation, two-thirds of which are multilateral.[15] All the same, everything depends on how much influence the reformers retain in Moscow. But so must it, too, on the other factors that shape the naval balance in this theatre.

Salient among them still is the Concept of Maritime Operations along 'forward strategy' lines approved by NATO's Defence Planning Committee in 1981. The next year, John Lehman, US Secretary of the Navy (1980-87), described the massive Soviet military-cum-naval infrastructure on the Kola peninsula (home of most of the SSBNs) as 'the most valuable piece of real estate on the Earth'. He further averred that the way to keep Soviet naval forces well above the Greenland-Iceland-United Kingdom (GIUK) line was 'to be up there ... forcing them onto the defensive ... to protect their assets'.[16] Even so, the mainspring of this revolution in maritime strategy was not SSBN engagement. Rather it was a conviction that, given the sheer extent of the open ocean, the North Atlantic seaways could only be properly safeguarded if the Soviet fleet (and especially its attack submarine force) could be kept well away from the GIUK line. There was also talk of 'horizontal escalation', if vital but vulnerable sectors like the Gulf or Central Europe came under Soviet-driven threats.[17]

Curiously absent throughout the early 1980s was any incorporation into this forward naval strategy of a recognition that the utility of any arrangement for Ballistic Missile Defence (BMD) could depend on adversary SSBNs being kept a good distance from allied coasts. None the less, American and, even more emphatically, Soviet naval planners had long presumed that SSBNs or FBMs would be fair game in any extensive conflict. Nor would NATO find it easy, in any case, to preserve a distinction between the USSR's attack submarines and her SSBN capability, were its forward deployment pressed far northwards. The awkward topography and hostile climate of the high Arctic makes discrimination all the harder. At longish range, reverberations off the rough undersurface of the ice can attenuate sonar (ie acoustic) waves an order of magnitude more than mere absorption does.[18]

Overlap occurs again in the Pacific. By 1986, a big increase in the United States Navy's year-round presence in the northern Pacific was officially justified largely in terms of the containment of Soviet missile-firing submarines.[19] Twenty-five of the USSR's 62 SSBNs operate from Pacific bases, Petrapavlovsk on Kamchatka and Vladivostok in the Sea of Japan.

Unfortunately, a forward naval strategy cannot be kept in a filing cabinet to be implemented only at a time of warlike crisis. It depends too heavily on familiarity with northern waters for that. Nor would it be easy simply to stand on the GIUK line. Experience in two World Wars suggests that this barrier can be made tolerably secure only by the deployment of a dense mix of systems. Yet that could stimulate the tendencies towards neutralism that are already endemic in Greenland, Iceland and the Faeroes. Besides which, Norway would once again be left too visibly isolated.

On the other hand, it ought to be possible for NATO and the USSR to agree on a thinning out of naval forces in northern waters, thereby easing the ecological strains a bit and generating the right milieu for wider ecological management. Sanctuary areas for SSBNs and FBMs might figure in this process.[20] All the same, it is hard to imagine things proceeding far on that front without some reduction overall in the SSBN and FBM fleets, something the Soviets have intimated will have to figure in a START-2 agreement. In any case, substantive objections remain to having submarines play a larger part proportionally in the respective strategic forces.

Defended deterrence

The general conclusion to be drawn from the above is that there is no satisfactory substitute, within the realm of strategic deterrence, for the ICBMs in static emplacements. Yet the prospect remains that the vulnerability of such systems, a subject of recurrent concern for over 20 years, could become an urgent matter early next century. The only way to square this circle may be to provide the ICBM sites with terminal defence. So far as the United States is concerned, that option is perhaps embraced by the statement on the future of the Strategic Defense Initiative made by President Bush in his State of the Union message of January 1991. Noting the considerable success against the Iraqi Scuds of the modified Patriot surface-to-air missiles, he said he had 'directed that the SDI programme be refocused on providing protection from limited ballistic strikes – whatever their source'.[21]

My own attempt to grapple with the SDI question is expressed in the relevant chapters of *New Strategy Through Space*.[22] Suffice for now to assess how the debate moves on. Nobody doubts that defence against strikes confined to ICBM sites is easier than attempting to cover all the inhabitants and real estate of a large national territory. The basic geometry is favourable for the former task. Also the rate of success against incoming warheads need not approach the 98 to 100 per cent that would be sought were the survival of populations at stake. One would likewise have far less to fear from salvage-fusing, the priming of each descending warhead to explode in the event of its interception. At 18,000 feet, for instance, the density of the Earth's atmosphere is but half what it is at sea level. Nevertheless, the air blast from a five-megaton warhead salvage-fused at that height could still wreck city buildings across a slant range of several miles. In clear weather, paper, curtaining and the like could smoulder and then ignite across 20 miles. An ICBM emplacement, on the other hand, could withstand salvage-fusing much closer in.

All the same, a defence system for missile sites could greatly complicate the strategic nuclear balance if, in fact, its zone of influence – its 'envelope' or 'footprint' – appeared to extend across many other targets. Under those circumstances, the adversary might feel obliged to expand his ICBM force in order to remain able to inflict 'unacceptable retaliation'. However, it should be feasible either to design or to position shield weapons so that the protection they proffer remains strictly 'preferential'. Missiles could thus be utilised. So, against homing sensors, could lasers. So, perhaps most readily, could quick-fire 'gatling' guns. As early as 1961, the United States Air Force considered the latter for silo defence. Lately, the Strategic Defense Initiative Organisation (SDIO) has been examining the Hypervelocity Gun (HVG) concept, for use either in Space or from the ground.[23] A Space-based mode could not, unlike the ground-based, be preferential.

So long as that criterion were met, the terminal defence of hard sites could be decisively stabilising in regard to the risk of a sudden and major disarming blow. Among other things, it could remove any temptation to 'launch on warning'. Introduced on one side but not the other, however, it could still destabilise in regard to the possibility of a slow motion exchange or 'limited strategic war', a form of 'extended deterrence'. Therefore the other side – Moscow, one still presumes – would either have to introduce its own silo defence or else expand its ICBM inventory. Maybe the talk Ronald Reagan and certain colleagues episodically engaged in about sharing SDI knowledge with the Soviets has relevance here.[24]

However, it has never been clear how ready the United States might be to share technical details, given their possible application to other weapons systems and operational capabilities. According to Raymond Garthoff of Brookings, long a leading specialist on Soviet military affairs, a prime cause of Moscow's opposition to SDI has been its concern lest the theatre war weaponry of the West will benefit in a very special way.[25] Nor is there much doubt that Anti-Tactical Ballistic Missiles (ATBM), in particular, are being furthered by SDI, this in collaboration with several European countries, Israel and Japan. What ought to be remembered, however, is that tactical defence against contour-hugging cruise missiles could be almost as important and a sight more difficult. They will continue to travel more slowly than their ballistic counterparts but will bear larger warloads in relation to overall weight.

Space Defense Systems?

An interpretation placed by Pentagon officials on President Bush's pronouncement was that it does make some provision for orbital Space Defense Systems (SDS) as part of a nationwide and alliance-wide defence against (a) missile threats from third parties, probably in the developing world, and (b) the 'accidental' release of isolated missiles.[26] Neither theme is unfamiliar. The former burgeoned strongly in 1985, as the initial enthusiasm for a counter-Soviet SDI ebbed somewhat. That July, Caspar Weinberger even suggested that SDI could police a disarmed world.[27]

But how likely is it that SDI could curb wildcat behaviour by some regime of fascist or fascisto-Marxist adventurers, perhaps operating against a background of internal stress? Would not several factors have to balance finely? The aggressor would be posing a nuclear threat with ballistic missiles, not only cruise missiles or manned aircraft or in some clandestine fashion. No suitable opportunity would have presented itself to abort his preparations by pre-emptive action. He would be too hate-choked or otherwise irrational to be put off by the threat of massive retaliation. His missile force would be strong enough to alarm the USA and friendly countries, yet not of a size and quality SDS could not cope with. Such a combination of circumstances would be problematic, distant in time and transient.

What is more, the only way to provide the requisite SDS cover without destabilising the superpower balance might be to enlist the co-operation of Moscow in adjusting force levels. After all, the geometry of Space-based defence means that hundreds of SDS platforms would be needed to revolve in a low Earth orbit to ensure minimal coverage against even a weak attack. However, such a screen might also have some effect against a Soviet rocket strike, although this could be a lot larger and more sophisticated. Yet were

Moscow and Washington to collaborate to adjust force levels to meet this requirement, this could connote the nuclear condominium with Washington that many people (most notably the late Charles de Gaulle and Mao Tse-tung) have apprehended. At the same time, it could cut across the building up of a multinational regime for the management of Space as a universal common that has become important for a large number of civil activities ranging from DBS television to ecological monitoring;[28] and which has throughout been important, one should add, in a more philosophical and spiritual sense.[29]

Moreover, this solution would be rendered all the more dubious by various other objections to locating Ballistic Missile Defence in orbit against whatever threat. Chief among them are the following. The efficacy of any such 'peace shield' would need to be accurately assessed by each superpower. Otherwise, it would be liable to trigger off a new strategic arms race between them as each sought to insure itself against worst-case assumptions. Yet this assessment would be next to impossible because there would be far too many plausible scenarios, each and every one of them resting on far too many arbitrary assumptions. Then again, even in the absence of hostilities involving the disintegrative attrition of such assets, such a 'peace shield' would aggravate hugely the congestion of near-Space. This would especially apply to the 'brilliant pebbles' concept; the attempt, emanating from the Lawrence Livermore national laboratory, to make a first-generation or front-layer SDS more reactive and effective by going for tens of thousands of mini-platforms, bearing just one small interceptor rocket apiece.[30]

Similar considerations apply in regard to the threat of a nuclear war that is 'accidental' in the sense that it was never intended by any government. Presumably it will have been caused either by a wrong intelligence appreciation or by a technical malfunction or else by unauthorised behaviour by somebody with relevant access.

Inaccurate intelligence may cause a nuclear war as and when two nuclear or chemical powers confront each other, one or both of them being possessed of a deterrent so inferior in its size and configuration that it may have to be used pre-emptively if it is to be used at all. So delicate a situation can no longer obtain as between the USSR and the West. The Near East and South Asia could be another matter, in spite of the curbing of Iraq's ambitions in this regard. However, this hazard is one that might be headed off by anti-proliferation aspects of a grand strategy. If in spite of everything it did present itself, it ought to be containable by external nuclear guarantees. Whether SDS could do anything to reinforce these guarantees is doubtful. A rocket like Scud, say might travel forwards hundreds of kilometres without rising above the altitude of 100 kilometres that is generally accepted to be the upper limit of the atmosphere. The significance of this is that the rocket would thereby remain hard to intercept from Space throughout its flight.

Apprehension of a global war through technical mishap – 'the flock of geese on the radar screen' syndrome – has long been a theme on the Left where it has often assumed lurid and, indeed, apocalyptic forms. Typical was a 1984 admonition by David Brower, a founding father of Friends of the Earth, that 'six minutes from now, based on the failure of a Soviet computer, the end of the world as we know it could be under way'.[31] His unspoken assumption was that the operational detonation of some Soviet nuclear warhead(s) somewhere would inevitably trigger off all such warheads everywhere.

Nor is there much doubt that this notion of the boundless escalation of any nuclear exchange has vaguely been endorsed across a broader spectrum of Western public opinion than anything else the neutralist Left has had to say on defence this last decade. Among its most fervent converts has been Robert McNamara, once the prime architect of flexible nuclear response.[32] Similarly, it was taken as all but axiomatic in the extensive debate some years ago about a 'nuclear winter', the absolute ecological disaster that could be caused by the blockage of the Sun's rays by the skyborne debris from a major nuclear exchange.[33] The fact remains, however, that Mutual Assured Destruction is a regimen that does allow time for the cross-checking of any alarming indications.

The danger of illicit release stems particularly from regimes that are unstable politically as well as deficient in 'fail safe' provisions within their nuclear command and control. Again, the Near East comes to mind. But in the recent as well as the more remote past, either the Soviet military or the KGB have repeatedly been involved in low profile yet highly significant activities that have run counter to their government's declared policies. Examples include those probes by submarines into Swedish territorial waters; the sharp military crackdown in the Baltic states early in 1991; military technical advisers continuing to assist the Iraqi air force after the outbreak of the Gulf war;[34] the murders of several Russian priests, with evident KGB connivance, in the winter of 1990–91; and the infiltration into the US Embassy not long afterwards. What has usually been unclear is how far the officers in question have been acting regardless of their government's wishes (like Japan's Kwantung Army in Manchuria in 1931) or how far with the connivance of all or part of their government (like the Serbian assassins at Sarajevo in 1914 or the Polish troops seizing Vilna in 1920). None the less, it is always possible that an authentic splinter group will wax so desperate as to fire off a missile or two.

However, the worst of the Soviet internal crisis could be over before an adequate SDS canopy was in position. Meanwhile, the fact that this canopy was in prospect would give a strong fillip to the more hawkish elements in the Soviet power structure. In particular, it would provide a rationale for the revamping of Voyska-PVO into a force dedicated to the interception of SDS platforms. In other words, the action-reaction phenomenon would make itself manifest in a very negative fashion. The events of August 1991 have only reduced this possibility.

So one is driven back to the conclusion that the future of SDI should lie in (a) facilitating surface-based anti-missile defence in regional war, (b) underpinning MAD by affording surface-based and close-in defence of fields of ICBMs and (c) protecting those satellites in orbit which are being used for communications, surveillance and so on. The present indications are that the satellite protection might be provided mainly by having available surface-based Anti-Satellite (ASAT) missiles ready to retaliate against enemy assets in orbit. This task, together with the active defence of ICBM fields and the introduction of ATBMs at theatre level, would require the drastic revision if not revocation of the 1972 ABM treaty. Still, this is overdue in any case. The current convention whereby both the shorter-range ATBMs (such as Patriot) and anti-missile gunnery are seen as outside the treaty's constraints is surely too arbitrary to last.[35] Should not the arms control emphasis now swing towards the non-weaponisation of Space? All else apart, the skies above us now stand out as the one 'sacred grove' left to modern man, a grove that he cannot otherwise ruin by high-rise buildings, tourism, pollutants or climatic change. So there would be something gratuitously oppressive about having hundreds or even thousands of weapons-bearing platforms endlessly revolving high overhead. It would be the ultimate 'end of Nature'.

An expedition to Mars?

If the militarisation of Space can be limited to surveillance and communications, the way should be that much more open for international collaboration on manned Space exploration when the time is ripe politically. In July 1989, to mark the 20th anniversary of Neil Armstrong's alighting on the Moon from Apollo-II, President Bush formally designated a manned landing on Mars as an eventual national goal. Addressing graduates at the Texas A and I University the following May, he averred that before the 50th anniversary of Apollo-II 'the American flag should be planted on Mars'. He opined that 'as this century closes, it is in America's hands to help determine the kind of people, the kind of planet we will become in the next. We will leave the solar system and travel to the stars, not only because it is democracy's dream, but because it is democracy's destiny.'[36]

If this presentation was either 'international' or 'planetary', it was so in a very unilateral sense with heavy crusading overtones. Nevertheless, a lot of American thinking, including much from the White House, has been informed by a broader spirit; and this inclination is likely to be ascendant in the aftermath of the Gulf war. In the spring of 1990, a NASA committee reported an 'International Co-operation for Mars Exploration and Sample Return'. Noting the desire of the Soviets for association in this field, the members envisaged that this would begin on the basis of closer co-ordination but with each side 'conducting their own self-contained and independently designed missions'. Hopefully, however, this might lead on 'to missions that involve substantial hardware and software systems interfaces and divided responsibilities'. The report also stressed that collaboration with other parties (particularly Canada, Japan and the European Space Agency) could also be sought.

Still, manned Spaceflight is always in a class by itself. At Lawrence Livermore, ever the home of technological bullishness, one claim has been made that a manned landing could be effected on Mars by the turn of the century for barely $10 billion. But most American and Soviet estimates for a well-found enterprise are in the range of $30 to 600 billion. Granted that, in the USA, at any rate, there is quite a feeling that even the present funding levels for manned flight in Earth orbit are to the detriment of more relevant and cost-effective unmanned Space research. Recent expression thereof can be seen in the Augustin report submitted to NASA at the end of 1990. As a keynote passage put it: 'The Space science programme warrants highest priority for funding. It, in our judgement, ranks above Space stations, manned missions to the planets and many other pursuits which often receive greater visibility'.[37] Nor would anybody deny that a large part of the justification for manned Spaceflight can only be in terms that go beyond inductive scientific enquiry. On the other hand, there are certain experiments in very fundamental physics that could best be carried out in manned observatories in the uncrowded and all but airless environments of the Moon or Mars.[38]

Obviously, multinational collaboration would spread the cost. What may be even more important, however, is that it could be conducive to free-ranging yet scrupulous studies of what is feasible within what time frame. One needs, for instance, much more knowledge of how solar flares may affect long-term Space travellers.[39] One requires, above all, a more comprehensive understanding of how men and women may adjust to the sudden transition from life in a cramped but cosy Space capsule to that on a bleakly hostile planet. Much work has already been done on many aspects of Space medicine. Likewise, a lot of discussion has taken place on the social psychology of life in lunar or planetary outposts.[40] What may yet be lacking, none the less, is a proper integration of these two approaches.

Among other US reports on future Space policy has been the one submitted to NASA in August 1987 by a panel chaired by Sally K. Ride, the first US woman astronaut. It argued for a cautious approach, eschewing any 'human Mars initiative' that 'could escalate into another Space race' and end in 'another one-shot spectacular'.[41] Her panel further concluded that the establishment, as from the turn of the century, of a lunar outpost ought to be a stage in the approach to Mars. By so doing, the report brought itself abreast of a surge of informed American opinion, over the previous year or two, in favour of the Moon as an intermediate step. The reasons adduced were very similar to those that led Winston Churchill to insist as a wartime leader that an active Mediterranean strategy was an essential prelude to a descent on northern France. Voices powerful in Washington in 1942 would have favoured a more 'single-minded' thrust to the main objective.

A lunar staging post would give scope for the involvement of other Spacefaring nations but especially the Europeans and the Japanese. Allowing also for a Chinese Space programme that has already provided training for a cadre of astronauts and envisaged a 22-tonne Space station in orbit by early next century, one can note that the international configuration of what may loosely be termed 'Space potential' corresponds very closely to what are generally understood to be the main nodes, within the modern world, of geopolitical strength. Collaboration in Space research may therefore be singularly valuable as a stimulus to the wider accords among the 'concert of powers' that will have to form up if we are to deal with the awesome ecological and resource crises our world now faces.

To my mind, powerful support for such a view can be drawn from the thought of the great German philosopher, Immanuel Kant. He came to philosophy via the Earth sciences and astronomy. Indeed, he did as much as anybody to popularise the new-found recognition of how all stars are massively grouped into galaxies – 'island universes', as he called them. He enunciated a nebular theory of the origin of the solar system, a theory that paved the way for later formulations along similar lines. He had a strongly holistic perception of the place of everything within the cosmos: 'The starry heavens above me . . . and the moral law within me'. He would have felt immensely refreshed to share the astronaut's view of the oneness of 'Spaceship Earth'.[42]

All of which should encourage us also to reflect well on another strand in his thinking. It is one revealed in his treatise on *Perpetual Peace* published in 1795, at a time when the action-reaction engendered by the French Revolution had started to engulf Europe in war. Here, he called for the formation, in Europe and beyond, of a loose confederation of states. It would lack any power of binding arbitration, its cohesion hopefully being sustained by a collective memory of the awfulness of war. Its author duly admitted that this would leave it fragile, both during inception and subsequently. Nor did he directly address the problem of instability within states.[43] One may fairly surmise that Kant would today have welcomed an international Space programme as a source of extra solidarity as well as a means of extending the frontiers of astronomy.

Of course, the charge that all Space travel is or would be pure escapism is by no means unfamiliar. Among those who have at least insinuated this have been Arnold Toynbee, George Orwell and Leon Trotsky. Likewise Bertrand Russell, in a curious admixture of venom and inanity, justified his antagonism towards the 'silly cleverness' of Neil Armstrong's descent to the lunar surface on the grounds that the wise Immanuel Kant never travelled more than a few miles from his native Konigsberg.[44]

He would have done better to note not only Kant's absorption in astronomy and in peace but also his acceptance of the assessment of Japan made by Engelbert Kaempfer, the German physician who had extensively travelled that country while in the service of the Dutch East India Company (1690-92). Kaempfer had concluded that the philosophical unity of Japan was a mainspring of its peace and progress.[45]

In the future, astronomical research will considerably be conducted from outside our planet's atmosphere; and may eventually be furthered, in certain cardinal respects, by observatories located on the Moon or Mars. It will be important that such research does illuminate those questions within its competence that bear upon the nature of ultimate reality and upon how we humans have customarily sought to make sense of it all. A current exemplar is the doubt now being cast, for several cogent reasons, on what has been, this past quarter of a century, astronomy's cardinal tenet. This is that the entire cosmos was created in one 'big bang', 10 to 20 billion years ago.

By the same token, it is imperative that all belief systems, the humanist or secular ones most certainly included, relate more henceforward to whatever insights astronomers afford. Perhaps one may thus gradually achieve broad convergence of outlook between individuals and between communities, with a corresponding growth of planetary consciousness. The alternative may eventually be that the various adherents retreat into the dark recesses of their respective fundamentalisms and communal affiliations. Such a prospect would be grimly dangerous in an overshrinking world.

Chapter Notes

Chapter 1 – The Quest for Strategy

1. *The Annual Register of World Events, 1988*, Longmans, London (1989), p. 553.
2. *The Annual Register of World Events, 1979*, Longmans, London (1980), p. 497.
3. *The Annual Register of World Events, 1989*, Longmans, London (1990), p. 534.
4. *Ibid.*, pp. 529–30.
5. E. S. Williams, 'Komsomol – a new look', *Armed Forces* 6(7) (July 1987).
6. Miles Kahler, 'Rumours of War: the 1914 Analogy', *Foreign Affairs*, 58(2) (Winter 1979/80), pp. 376–96.
7. Carl Friedrich von Weiszacker, 'Can a Third World War be prevented?', *International Security*, 5(1) (Summer 1980), pp. 198–205.
8. Neville Brown, *Limited World War?*, Canberra Papers on Strategy and Defence No. 32, Australian National University, Canberra (1984), p. 3.
9. Neville Brown, *The Future Global Challenge*, Crane Russak for Royal United Services Institute for Defence Studies, New York and London (1977), p. 215.
10. Adam Meyerson, 'The Battle for the History Books', *Policy Review* (Spring 1990), pp. 2–3.
11. Lawrence Freedman, *The Evolution of Nuclear Strategy*, Macmillan for IISS (1989), p. 418.
12. Thomas S. Kuhn, *The Structure of Scientific Revolutions*, University of Chicago Press, Chicago (1972), p. 68.
13. See, for example, 'Occasional Revolutionary', *Times Higher Educational Supplement* (12 July 1988).
14. Thomas Kuhn, 'Second thoughts on paradigms' in Frederick Suppe (ed.), *The Structure of Scientific Theories*, Urbano (1977), pp. 459–82.
15. Hedley Bull, *The Control of the Arms Race*, Weidenfeld and Nicolson, London (1961), Chapter 1 (v).
16. Professor Neville Brown and General Sir Anthony Farrar–Hockley, *Nuclear First Use*, Buchan and Enright for RUSI, London (1985), p. 30.
17. Nirmal Kumar Bose, 'A Premature Metropolis', *Scientific American*, 213(3) (September 1965), pp. 91–102.
18. This analysis of the subcontinent draws on *The Future Global Challenge, op. cit.*, pp. 22–3.
19. Edward Mead Earle (ed.), *Makers of Modern Strategy*, Princeton University Press, Princeton (1971), Chapter 6.
20. 'A Fjord Too Far', *The Military Review*, Vol. LXVII, No. 4 (April 1987), pp. 51–8.

21. B. H. Liddell Hart, *The Decisive Wars of History*, G. Bell, London (1929), p. 228.
22. J. F. C. Fuller, *The Dragon's Teeth*, Constable, London (1932), p. 183.
23. Captain A. T. Mahan USN, *The Influence of Sea Power upon the French Revolution and Empire, 1793–1812*, Sampson Low, Marston, London (1893), vol. 2 pp. 319–46.
24. Ernest Rhys (ed.), *Orations on the French War to the Peace of Amiens by William Pitt*, J. M. Dent, London, Undated. Chapters I, IV, XIII, XV, XVI and XXI.
25. See Pierre Gallois, *Stratégie de l'âge nucléaire*, Calmann–Levy, Paris (1960) and André Beaufre, *Dissuasion et Stratégie*, Armand Colin, Paris (1964).
26. *Makers of Modern Strategy, op. cit.* p. viii.
27. Daniel Bell, 'The End of Ideology in the West', in Frank Lindenfield (ed.) *Reader in Political Sociology*, Frank and Wagnalls, New York (1968), pp. 545–54.
28. D. C. Watt, Frank Spencer and Neville Brown, *A History of the World in the Twentieth Century*, William Morrow, New York (1968), p. 644.
29 *The Future Global Challenge, op. cit.*, p. 19.
30. D. W. Fryer, *World Economic Development*, McGraw–Hill, New York (1965) Tables 6–3 and 15–4.
31. *The Future Global Challenge, op. cit.* pp. 143–4.
32. For the text see *Survival*, Vol. XVI, No. 4 (July–August 1974), pp. 194–8.
33. e.g. Raymond Vernon, *Multinational Enterprise and National Security*, Adelphi Paper 73, The International Institute for Strategic Studies, London (1971).

Chapter 2 – Indivisible Peace

1. Senator John F. Kennedy, *The Strategy of Peace*, Hamish Hamilton, London (1960), pp. 176 then 53.
2. Neville Brown, Frank Spencer, and Donald Watt, *A History of the World in the Twentieth Century*, William Morrow, New York (1968) Part 3, Chapter XV(i).
3. Interview in December 1959, *The Strategy of Peace, op. cit.* p. 224.
4. *Ibid.* Speech on 14 June 1960 in Addendum p. 8.
5. David Halberstam, *The Best and the Brightest*, Random House, New York (1972) p. 316.
6. *Ibid*, pp. 210–11.
7. *The Strategy of Peace, op. cit.* p. 101.
8. Hugh Sidey, *J. F. Kennedy: Portrait of a President*, London (1964), Chapter 8.
9. See the author's *New Strategy Through Space*, Leicester University Press, Leicester (1990), Chapter 11.
10. Lawrence Freedman, *The Evolution of Nuclear Strategy*, Macmillan for IISS (1989), p. 40.
11. Robert S. McNamara, *Department of State Bulletin*, 47 (9 July 1962), pp. 47–8.
12. See the author's 'Towards the Superpower Deadlock', *The World Today* vol. 22 no. 9 (September 1966), pp. 366–74.
13. Joseph Rotblat, *Nuclear Radiation in Warfare*, Taylor and Francis for SIPRI, London (1981), pp. 47–8.
14. *A Supplement to the Oxford English Dictionary*, The Clarendon Press, Oxford (1986), vol. IV p. 379.
15. Zbigniew Brzezinski, 'The International and the Planetary', *Encounter* vol. XXXIX no. 2 (August 1972), pp. 49–55.
16. Gabriel and Daniel Cohn-Bendit, *Obsolete Communism, the Left–Wing Alternative*, Penguin, London (1968), p. 244.
17. Raymond Williams (ed), *May Day Manifesto, 1968*, Penguin, London (1968), Chapters 16 and 18.

18. Theodore Roszak, *The Making of a Counter-Culture*, Faber and Faber, London (1968), p. xiii.
19. *Ibid.*, p. 265.
20. Theodore Roszak, 'An Autopsy on Science,' *The New Scientist*, vol. 57, No. 830 (11 March 1971), pp. 536–8.
21. Theodore Roszak, *Person/Planet*, Victor Gollancz, London (1979), p. 50.
22. *Ibid*, p. 57.
23. Stewart Boyle and John Ardill, *The Greenhouse Effect*, Hodder and Stoughton, London (1989), pp. 175 and 180.
24. *The Annual Register, 1986*, Longman, London (1987), p. 408.
25. For an outline of the electromagnetic spectrum hopefully appropriate to this mode of interpretation see *New Strategy Through Space, op. cit.* Appendix A.
26. 'Nature's Way to go brown in the Sun' and 'Skin Cancer Vaccine "ready in five years"', *The Times* (11 September 1990).
27. John Gribbin, *The Hole in the Sky*, Corgi, London (1988), Chapter 1.

Chapter 3 – A Globe Distracted

1. For a fuller discussion of the information explosion, especially as engendered by Space science, see the author's *New Strategy Through Space*, Leicester University Press, London (1990), Chapter 7.
2. William J, Broad, *Star Warriors*, Simon and Schuster, New York (1985), pp. 142–3.
3. *New Strategy Through Space, op. cit.*, Appendix A.
4. Secker and Warburg, London (1949).
5. Abraham Friesen, 'The Renaissance' in C. D. Kernig (ed.) *Marxism, Communism and Western Society: A Comparative Encyclopaedia*, Herder and Herder, New York (1973), vol. 7, pp. 192–8.
6. Zbigniew Brzezinski, *Between Two Ages*, Penguin, Harmondsworth (1976), p. 149.
7. Charles E. Ziegler, *Environmental Policy in the USSR*, Frances Pinter, London (1987), p. 154.
8. *The Annual Register, 1989*, Longman, London (1990), p. 445.
9. Vaclav Smil, *The Bad Earth*, Zed Press, London (1984), p. xi.
10. H. R. Trevor Roper, *The European Witch Craze of the 16th and 17th Centuries*, Penguin, Harmondsworth (1969), p. 112.
11. For an interpretation of Sigmund Freud that allows him a full awareness of the cultural factor in human behaviour, see Lionel Trilling, *Freud and the Crisis in Our Culture*, Beacon Press, Boston (1955).
12. Eric Fromm, *Escape from Freedom*, Kegan Paul, London (1942), p. 40.
13. Simone Weil, *The Need for Roots*, Harper and Row, New York (1971), p. 45.
14. 'The New English Empire', *The Economist* (20 December 1986).
15. Special Survey, 'Who speaks for Spain', *The Economist* (11 March 1989).
16. Marianne Heiberg, *The Making of the Basque Nation*, Cambridge University Press, Cambridge (1989), p. 110 and pp. 227–8.
17. Barnet Litvinoff, *A Peculiar People*, Weidenfeld & Nicolson, London (1969), p. 289.
18. William Rees–Mogg, 'The Modern depradations that threaten our cultural heritage', *The Independent* (1 May 1988).
19. Marshall McLuhan, *Understanding Media: the Extensions of Man*, Signet Books, New York (1964), p. 270.
20. Anthony D. Smith, *The Ethnic Revival*, Cambridge University Press, Cambridge (1981), pp. 3–4.

21. Indira Gandhi, *People and Places*, Hodder and Stoughton, London (1982), p. 63.
22. Roslynn D. Haynes, *H. G. Wells. Discoverer of the Future*, Macmillan, London (1980), p. ix.
23. *The Future Global Challenge*, Crane Russak, New York (1976), p. 50.
24. *New Strategy Through Space*, *op. cit.*, p. 198.
25. 'H. G. Wells' in C. P. Snow, *Variety of Men*, Macmillan, London (1967), pp. 47–64.
26. Anthony Storr in A. J. P. Taylor (ed.) *Churchill: Four Faces and the Man*, Pelican, Harmondsworth (1973).
27. Chapman and Hall, London (1902).
28. *The Future Global Challenge*, *op. cit.*, p. 7.
29. 'Crime, Law Enforcement and Penology' in *1989 Britannica Book of the Year*, Encyclopedia Britannica, Chicago (1990), pp. 160–3.
30. Quoted in Dorothy Rowe, *Living With the Bomb. Can We Live Without Enemies?*, Routledge and Kegan Paul, London (1985), p. 146.
31. D. C. Watt in D. C. Watt, Frank Spencer and Neville Brown, *A History of the World in the Twentieth Century*, William Morrow, New York (1968), pp. 114–15.
32. See the author's 'New Paradigms for Strategy', *The World Today*, vol. 46, no. 6 (June 1990), pp. 115–18.
33. Michael Shafir, 'Xenophobic communism – the case of Bulgaria and Romania', *The World Today*, vol. 45, no. 12 (December 1989), pp. 208–12.

Chapter 4 – The Soviet Heartland

1. H. J. Mackinder, 'The geographical pivot of history', *Geographical Journal*, XXIII (1904), p. 421–37.
2. H. J. Mackinder, *Democratic Ideals and Reality*, Constable, London (1919).
3. W. H. Parker, *Mackinder. Geography as an Aid to Statecraft*, Clarendon Press, Oxford (1982), pp. 177–9 and p. 173.
4. Daniel Bell, 'Ten theories in search of reality: The Prediction of Soviet behaviour in the social sciences', *World Politics*, vol. 10, no. 2 (April 1958), pp. 327–65.
5. G. R. Sloan, *Geopolitics in United States Strategic Policy, 1890–1987*, Wheatsheaf, Brighton (1988), p. 210.
6. Senator Daniel Patrick Moynihan, 'For Decades, Washington overrated Soviets', *International Herald Tribune* (13 July 1990).
7. See the author's *New Strategy through Space*, Leicester University Press, Leicester (1990), Chapter 10.
8. Dr Christopher Davis, *Military and Civil Economic Activities of the Soviet Armed Forces: 1975–85*; Paper presented at the Centre for Russian and East European Studies, University of Birmingham (14 November 1986).
9. Neville Brown, *Limited World War?*, Australian National University, Canberra (1984), Chapter 2.
10. Winston Churchill, *The Second World War* (abridged version), Cassell, London (1959), Chapter XXI.
11. *The Daily Telegraph* (23 October 1973).
12. Tibor Szamuely, *The Russian Tradition*, Secker and Warburg, London (1974), p. 101.
13. For a balanced resumé of the different sectoral thrusts see B. H. Sumner, *Survey of Russian History*, Duckworth, London (1947), Chapter VI.
14. Neil Malcolm, 'The "Common European Home" and Soviet European policy', *International Affairs*, vol. 65, no. 4 (Autumn 1989), pp. 659–76.
15. E. Stuart Kirby, *Russian Studies of Japan*, Macmillan, London (1981), pp. 146–7.

16. 'Exodus Revised Version', *The Economist* (23 December 1989).
17. 'Postscript to Chernobyl', *Energy Economist*, 104 (June 1990), p. 10.
18. 'Russia's anti–drink campaign', *The Economist* (23 December 1989).
19. Professor Dr Sava Zivanov, 'Five Years of Soviet *Perestroyka*', *Review of International Affairs*, vol. XLI, 966–7 (5–20 July 1990), pp. 13–14 and 19.
20. Thomas F. Remington, *The Truth of Authority*, University of Pittsburgh Press, Pittsburgh (1988), pp. 17–21.
21. Mikhail Gorbachev, *Perestroika*, Collins, London (1987), pp. 25–6.
22. George F. Kennan, 'America and the Russian Future', *Foreign Affairs*, vol. 69, no. 2 (Spring 1990), pp. 157–66.
23. Seymour Martin Lipset, 'Politics and Society in the USSR: a traveller's report', *Political Science and Politics*, vol. XXIII, no. 1 (March 1990), pp. 20–8.
24. 'The Alternative is Dictatorship', *Time*, vol. 135, no. 16 (16 April 1990), p. 28.
25. Sir Michael Howard, *International Affairs*, vol. 65, no. 3 (Summer 1989), p. 412.
26. H. J. Mackinder, *Britain and the British Seas*, Clarendon Press, Oxford (1907), p. 358.
27. Parker *op. cit.*, Chapter 6.
28. Andrew Lambert, 'Preparing for the Russian War: British Strategic Planning, March 1853–March 1854', *War and Society*, vol. 7, no. 2 (September 1989), pp. 15–39.
29. See the author's 'Trench Gascoigne First Prize Essay', *The Journal of the Royal United Services Institution*, vol. 105, no. 4 (November 1960), pp. 493–509.
30. Alexander Solzhenitsyn, *August 1914*, Penguin, Harmondsworth, London, pp. 124–5.
31. *Democratic Ideals and Reality, op. cit.*, p. 143.
32. See the author's 'The Myth of an Asian Diverson', *The Journal of the Royal United Services Institute for Defence Studies*, vol. 118, no. 3 (September 1973), pp. 48–51.
33. Norman Stone, *The Eastern Front, 1914–7*, London (1975), pp. 23–8.
34. *New Strategy through Space, op. cit.*, p. 161.
35. Herman Kahn, *On Thermonuclear War*, Princeton University Press, Princeton (1960), Chapter 4.

Chapter 5 – Far Beyond Dunkirk

1. Shelford Bidwell, *Modern Warfare*, Allen Lane, London (1973) p. 103.
2. Neville Brown, *The Future of Air Power*, Croom Helm, London (1986) Chapter 4.
3. FM-100–5, *Operations*, Department of the Army, Washington DC (1976), Chapter 2, paragraph 2.
4. Professor Neville Brown and General Sir Anthony Farrar–Hockley, *Nuclear First Use*, Buchan and Enright for RUSI, London (1985), p. 60.
5. B. H. Liddell Hart, *Deterrent or Defence*, Stevens, London (1960) Chapters 10 and 12.
6. B. H. Liddell Hart, 'The Ratio of Troops to Space', *The Journal of the Royal United Services Institute for Defence Studies*, CV, 618 (May 1960), pp. 201–12.
7. F. W. Lanchester, *Aircraft in Warfare: The Dawn of the Fourth Arm*, Constable, London (1916) p. 26.
8. D. L. I. Kirkpatrick, 'Do Lanchester's equations adequately model real battles?', *The Journal of the Royal United Services Institute for Defence Studies* vol. 130, no. 2 (June 1985), pp. 25–7.

9. Lieutenant Colonel Samir Farag, 'Preparation for the War of October 1973', *British Army Review*, 52 (April 1976), pp. 20–2.
10. *Insight on the Middle East War*, André Deutsch, London (1974), p. 83.
11. Robert K. Harkavy and Stephanie Neuman (eds), *The Lessons of Recent Wars*, D. C. Heath, Lexington (1983).
12. *The Future of Air Power, op. cit.* pp. 206–10.
13. 'The Strategic Bomber – A Weapon for the Future', *Air Clues*, 44, 4 (April 1990), pp. 124–9.
14. J. F. C. Fuller, *On Future Warfare*, Sifton Praed, London (1928), p. 202.
15. These figures represent some downward revision of those given in *The Future of Air Power, op. cit.* p. 27.
16. *Soviet Military Power*, US Government Printing Office for Department of Defense, Washington DC (1987), p. 51.
17. Christian Pochhacker, 'German anti-aircraft laser system', *International Combat Arms*, 6, 1 (January 1989), pp. 14–15.
18. W. D. White, *US Tactical Air Power*, Brookings Institution, Washington DC (1974), p. 54.
19. *The Future of Air Power, op. cit.*, p. 235.
20. *Aviation Week and Space Technology*, vol. 120, no. 2, 26 January 1981, p. 18.
21. *Aviation Week and Space Technology*, vol. 120, no. 10, 17 February 1984, pp. 16–18.
22. *Philadelphia Enquirer* (4 April 1990).
23. H. J. Mackinder, *Democratic Ideals and Reality*, Constable, London (1919), pp. 142–3.
24. Christopher Hartley, 'The Future of Manned Aircraft' in *The Implications of Military Technology in the 1970s*, Adelphi Paper 46, International Institute for Strategic Studies (IISS), London (1968), pp. 28–37.
25. Martin Edmonds in John Erickson (ed), *The Military-Technical Revolution*, Pall Mall, London (1966), pp. 28–37.
26. D. Phillips-Birt as quoted in the author's *Strategic Mobility*, Chatto and Windus for IISS, London (1963), p. 143.
27. R. E. Adler, 'In the Navy's future: the small fast surface ship', *United States Naval Institute Proceedings*, vol. 104, 3, no. 901 (March 1978), pp. 102–11.
28. W. J. Ruhe, 'The Nuclear Submarine: Riding High', *United States Naval Instituted Proceedings*, vol. 101, 2, no. 864 (February 1975), pp. 55–62.
29. Francis J. West *et al.*, *Naval Forces and Western Security*, Pergamon-Brassey's for Institute for Foreign Policy Analysis, Cambridge, Massachusetts and Washington DC (1987), p. 19.
30. 'Beyond Invincible', *Navy International*, vol. 95, no. 7/8 (July/August 1990), pp. 348–51.
31. Jonathan B. Stein, 'Anti-Tactical Ballistic Missiles, New threat to the ABM treaty', *Arms Control Today*, 15, 8 (October 1985), pp. 10–12.
32. Neville Brown, *New Strategy Through Space*, Leicester University Press and Columbia University Press, Leicester and New York (1990), pp. 221–2.

Chapter 6 – Crisis Through Climate

1. Richard A. Houghton and George M. Woodwell, 'Global Climatic Change', *Scientific American*, vol. 260, no. 4 (April 1989), pp. 18–26.
2. E. F. Roots, 'Climate Change: High Latitude Regions', *Climatic Change*, vol. 15, no. 112 (October 1989), pp. 223–55.
3. *Executive Summary of Intergovernmental Panel on Climate Change, Working Group I*, United Nations Information Centre, London (August 1990).

4. H. H. Lamb, *Climate, Past, Present and Future*, Methuen (London 1977), vol. 2, pp. 674–7.
5. John S. Hoffman, 'Estimates of future sea level rises', in Michael C. Barth and James T. Titus (eds.), *Greenhouse Effect and Sea Level Rise*, Van Norstrand Reinhold, New York (1984), pp. 79–103.
6. Stewart Boyle and John Ardill, *The Greenhouse Effect*, Hodder and Stoughton, London (1989), p. 12.
7. Nigel Calder, *The Weather Machine and the Threat of Ice*, BBC Publications, London (1974), p. 134.
8. B. J. Mason, 'Man's influence on weather and climate', *Journal of the Royal Society of Arts*, vol. CXXV no. 5247 (February 1977), pp. 150–65.
9. *The Greenhouse Conspiracy*, Channel 4 Television, London (1990), pp. 24–8.
10. See the paper by Ku Qun in *Abstracts of the conference on the variability of the atmosphere on time scales of a month to several years*, Royal Meteorological Society, London (1986), p. 77.
11. Neville Brown, 'Climate, ecology and international security', *Survival*, vol. XXXI No. 6 (November/December 1989), pp. 519–32.
12. *Climate, Present, Past and Future*, op. cit. Chapter 6.
13. S. G. H. Philander, 'General Circulation Models of the Ocean', in Howard Cattle (ed.), *Atmosphere Models and Oceanic Variability*, Royal Meteorological Society, Bracknell (1987), pp. 105–16.
14. W. E. Knowles, *A History of the Thermometer and its use in Meteorology*, Johns Hopkins Press, Baltimore (1966), Chapter X.
15. Editorial, 'Uncertainties about global warming', *Science*, vol. 247, no. 4950 (30 March 1990), p. 1529.
16. For a representative example of this thinking, see S. P. Idso, 'What if increases in atmospheric CO_2 have an inverse greenhouse effect?', *Journal of Climatology*, no. 4 (1984), pp. 389–409.
17. John A. Whitehead, 'Great Ocean Cataracts', *Scientific American*, vol. 260, no. 2 (February 1989), pp. 36–43.
18. Roy W. Spencer and John R. Christy, 'Precise Monitoring of Global Temperature Trends from Satellites', *Science, op. cit.*, pp. 1558–62.
19. *Intergovernmental Panel on Climate Change: Report to IPCC from Working Group I*, World Meteorological Organisation and United Nations Environment Programme, Geneva and Nairobi (1990), Section 11.
20. A. Henderson-Sellers and K. McGuffie, *A Climate Modelling Primer*, John Wiley, Chichester (1987), p. 162.
21. 'Profile: Political Engineer', *Scientific American*, vol. 264, no. 4 (April 1991), pp. 16–17.

Chapter 7 – Climate in History

1. Lyall Watson, *Heaven's Breath*, Hodder and Stoughton, London (1984), pp. 109–10.
2. H. H. Lamb, 'The weather of 1588 and the Spanish Armada', *Weather*, vol. 43, no. 11 (November 1988), pp. 386–95.
3. J. M. Stagg, *Forecast for Overload*, Ian Allan, Shepperton (1971), p. 113.
4. *Ibid.*, pp. 125–6.
5. George Kimble, *The Weather*, Penguin, Harmondsworth (1951), p. 143.
6. Field Manual 100–5, *Operations*. Department of the Army, Washington DC (1976), Chapter 14.
7. Carl Leopold and Robert Ardrey, *Science*, vol. 176, p. 512.
8. The classic work not referred to elsewhere in this section is Emmanuel Le Roy

Ledourie, *Times of Feast: Times of Famine*, Doubleday, New York (1971).

9. John Baines and Jaromik Malek, *Atlas of Ancient Egypt*, Equinox, Oxford (1984), p. 14.

10. H. H. Lamb, *Climate, Present, Past and Future*, Methuen, London (1977), 2 vols, vol. 2, Chapter 12.

11. Edward Gibbon, *The Decline and Fall of the Roman Empire*, W. Strahan and T. Cadell, London (1970), vol. 1, Chapter IX.

12. Thomas Arnold, 'Hannibal's passage of the Alps' in L. Valentine (ed.), *Half Hours With Standard Authors*, The Library Press, London (undated), pp. 133–64.

13. Brent Shaw, 'Climate, environment and history: the case of Roman North Africa', in T. M. L. Wigley *et al* (ed.), *Climate and History*, Cambridge University Press, Cambridge (1981), pp. 379–403.

14. Ellsworth Huntington, *The Pulse of Asia*, Houghton and Mifflin, Boston (1907), Chapter XVII.

15. C. E. P. Brooks, *Climate through the Ages*, Ernest Benn, London (1926), p. 340.

16. H. H. Lamb, *The Changing Climate*, Methuen, London (1966), p. 64.

17. Michael Cole *et al.*, *Atlas of Ancient America*, Equinox, Oxford (1986), pp. 47–8.

18. Jens P. Hart *et al.*, 'The Mummies of Oilakitsoq', *National Geographic* (February 1985), pp. 190–207.

19. Frank Noel Stagg, *North Norway, a history*, George Allen and Unwin, London (1952), pp. 61–2.

20. Michael Hasloch Kirby, *The Vikings*, Phaidon, Oxford (1977), pp. 56–7.

21. P. C. Foote and D. M. Wilson, *The Viking Achievement*, Sidgwick and Jackson, London (1980), pp. 260–1.

22. J. Grace, 'Tree lines' in P. G. Travis *et al.*, *Forests, Weather and Climate*, Royal Society, London (1989), pp. 233–45.

23. Robin Milner-Gaillard and Nikolai Dejesky, *Cultural Atlas of Russia and the Soviet Union*, Equinox, Oxford (1989), p. 24.

24. Huntington, *op. cit.*, p. 287.

25. B. H. Liddell Hart, *The Decisive Wars of History*, G. Bell, London (1929), p. 55.

26. William H. McNeill, *The Pursuit of Power*, Blackwell, Oxford (1983), p. 60.

27. *Scientific American*, vol. 256, no. 4 (April 1987), p. 54.

28. Quoted and annotated in Tibor Szamuely, *The Russian Tradition*, Secker and Warburg, London (1974), Chapter 2.

29. *Ibid*, pp. 19–20.

30. Alfred Guillaume, *Islam*, Pelican, Harmondsworth (1954).

31. *Climate, Past, Present and Future*, *op. cit.*, Tables 13.3 and 13.4.

32. Barbara W. Tuchman, *A Distant Mirror. The Calamitous Fourteenth Century*, Alfred A. Knopf, New York (1978), Chapters 2 and 5.

33. T. H. McGovern, 'The economics of extinction in Norse Greenland' in T. M. L. Wigley *et al.*, *op cit.*, pp. 404–33.

34. F. N. Stagg, *op. cit.*, pp. 75 and 104–20.

35. Frank Emery, *The Oxfordshire Landscape*, Hodder and Stoughton, London (1974), Chapter 4.

36. Irene Scobbie, *Sweden*, Ernest Benn, London (1972), Chapter 2.

37. Shih Ya–feng and Wang Zontai, *The Fluctuations of Climate, Glaciers and Sea Level Since The Late Pleistocene in China*, Langzhou Institute of Glaciology and Cryopedology and Desert Research, Langzhou (1979), quoted in Jean M. Grove, *The Little Ice Age*, Routledge, London (1988), p. 450.

38. Richard Storry, *A History of Modern Japan*, Penguin, Harmondsworth (1960), Chapter 2, section 2.
39. *Kodenska Encyclopedia of Japan*, Kodenska, Tokyo (1983), vol. 6, pp. 222–3.
40. John K. Fairbank *et al.*, *East Asia, Tradition and Transformation*, Allen and Unwin, London (1973), p. 417.
41. *The Economist* (19 September 1987).
42. D. E. Parker, 'The Climate of England and Wales during the past 150 years', *Journal of the Royal Agricultural Society of England*, vol. 149 (1988), pp. 90–101.
43. Cecil Woodham-Smith, *The Great Hunger*, New American Library, New York (1962), p. 96.
44. Cormac O. Grado, 'Irish Agricultural History: Recent Research, 1800–1850', *The Agricultural History Review*, vol. 38, pt. 2. (1990), pp. 165–73.
45. See eg *The Changing Climate, op. cit.*, p. 65.
46. William Miller, *A New History of the World*, George Brazillier, New York (1958), Chapter 9.
47. William E. Riebsame, 'The Dust Bowl. Historical Image, Psychological Anchor and Ecological Taboo', *Great Plains Quarterly*, 6 (Spring 1986), pp. 127–36.
48. Yu L. Rauner, 'Clusters of Drought Years in the Grain Zone of the USSR', *Soviet Geography*, vol. XXVI No. 1 (January 1985), pp. 73–90.
49. Martin van Creveld, *Supplying War*, Cambridge University Press, Cambridge (1980), Chapter 5.
50. *Climate, Past, Present and Future, op cit.*, fig. 18.36.
51. See Bill Forse, 'The myth of the marching desert', *New Scientist*, vol. 121 no. 1650 (4 February 1989), pp. 31–2.
52. John Bartholomew (ed.), *Advanced Atlas of Modern Geography*, Oliver and Boyd, Edinburgh (1949), p. 16.
53. Grove, *op. cit.*, p. 397.
54. *The Changing Climate, op. cit.*, Chapter 3.
55. S. E. Pitovranov et al., *The Effect of Climatic Variations on Agriculture in the Semi-Arid Zone of the USSR*, International Institute of Applied Systems Analysis for United Nations Environment Programme (1987), fig. 6.3.
56. For a discussion thereof see Curt Covey of Lawrence Livermore in *Climate Change*, vol. 14 no. 1 (1989), pp. 103–4.
57. Michael P. Walsh in Jeremy Leggett (ed.), *Global Warming, the Greenpeace Report*, Oxford University Press, Oxford (1990), Chapter 12.
58. *Weather*, vol. 45 no. 9 (September 1990), p. 345.
59. D. E. Parker, *op. cit.*, Fig. 8.
60. Robert N. North, 'The Role of Water Transport in Siberian Development' in Alan Wood and R. A. French (ed.), *The Development of Siberia*, Macmillan, London (1989), pp. 208–27.
61. *Weekend Telegraph* (16 June 1990).
62. Grove *op. cit.*, p. 420.
63. Based on discussions at the international conference on *Climate Impact on Environment and Society* at the University of Tsukuba in Japan, January to February 1991.

Chapter 8 – Ecology and Conflict

1. David Wells, 'Resurrecting the Dismal Parson: Malthus, Ecology, and Political Thought', *Political Studies*, vol. XXX, no. 1 (March 1982), pp. 1–15.
2. Francis Fukuyama, 'The End of History?', *The National Interest* (Summer 1989), pp. 3–18.

3. James Atlas, 'What is Fukuyama saying?', *New York Times Magazine* (22 October 1989), pp. 38–46.
4. Dr Nafis Sadik, *The State of World Population*, 1988, United Nations Population Fund, New York (1988), Figure 1.
5. *Bulletin of the Atomic Scientists*, vol. 42, No. 4 (April 1986), pp. 17–19.
6. Dr Sadik as quoted in *The Daily Telegraph* (22 February 1990).
7. World Commission on Environment and Development, *Our Common Future*, Oxford University Press, Oxford (1987), Table 4.1.
8. eg Desmond Morris, *The Naked Ape*, Jonathan Cape, London (1967), Chapter 5 and *The Human Zoo*, Jonathan Cape, London (1969), Chapter 4.
9. Robert Moss, *Urban Guerrilla Warfare*, Adelphi Paper 79, International Institute for Strategic Studies, London (1972), Appendix.
10. *Our Common Future, op. cit.*, p. 293.
11. Peter H. Gleick, 'The Implications of Global Climatic Changes for International Security', *Climatic Change*, No. 15 (1989), pp. 309–25.
12. *The State of World Population, 1988, op. cit.*, Table I.
13. Masaki Sekino, 'Desalination' in Douglas M. Considine (ed.), *Van Nostrand's Scientific Encyclopedia*, 7th edition, Van Nostrand Reinhold, New York (1989), pp. 857–60.
14. 'Drinking the sea gets cheaper and tastier', *The Economist* (18 May 1987).
15. Johan Gatling, *Environment, Development and Military Activity*, Universitetforlaget, Oslo (1982), pp. 83–4.
16. A. H. Westing, *Warfare in a fragile world: military impact on the human environment*, Taylor and Francis for Stockholm International Peace Research Institute, London (1980).
17. Geoffrey Best, 'The historical evolution of cultural norms relating to war and the environment', in Arthur H. Westing (ed.), *Cultural norms, war and the environment*, Oxford University Press for SIPRI and UNEP, Oxford (1988), pp. 18–28.
18. David Rees, *Korea, the Limited War*, Macmillan, London (1964), Chapter 20.
19. 'The attack on the irrigation dams in North Korea', *Air University Quarterly Review*, vol. VI, no. 4 (Winter 1953–4), pp. 40–61.
20. Neville Brown, 'The Blazing Oil Wells in Kuwait', *The World Today*, vol. 47, no. 6 (June 1991), pp. 93–5.
21. Neville Brown, *The Future of Air Power*, Croom Helm, London (1986), Chapter 7.
22. Air Vice Marshal C. J. Thomson, 'Air Power in Operation Granby – the lessons so far', *Journal of the Royal United Services Institute*, vol. 135, no. 4 (Winter 1990), pp. 25–30.
23. *North-South: A Programme for Survival*, Pan Books, London (1980), p. 13.
24. See the author's 'Palme and Brandt: A World Perspective' in Josephine O'Connor Howe (ed.), *Armed Peace*, Macmillan, London (1984), pp. 95–122.
25. *Our Common Future, op. cit.*, Chapter 11.
26. Published at the White House, Washington DC (March 1990).
27. Official Text as released by United States Information Service, London (21 February 1990).
28. Michael J. Dziedic, 'The transnational drug trade and regional security', *Survival*, vol. XXXI, no. 6 (November–December 1989), pp. 533–48.
29. 'World Environment Is Source of Conflict, Nunn Warns', *International Herald Tribune* (30 June and 1 July 1990).
30. Crispin Tickell, *Climatic Change and World Affairs*, Harvard Studies in International Affairs No. 37, Harvard University, Cambridge (1977), Chapters 1 and 3.

31. Edward Teller and Albert L. Latter, *Our Nuclear Future . . . Facts, Dangers and Opportunities*, Secker and Warburg, London (1958), p. 167.
32. *New York Times* translation of Andrei D. Sakharov, *Progress, Co–existence and Intellectual Freedom*, New York Times Book Service, New York (1968), p. 49.
33. Douglas H. Strong, *Dreamers and Defenders* University of Nebraska Press, Lincoln (1988), Chapter 7.
34. Charles Lindbergh, *An Autobiography of Values*, Harcourt Brace Jovanovich, New York (1976), pp. 349 and 31–2.
35. Peter Scott, *Observations of Wildlife*, Phaidon, Oxford (1980), pp. 73–81.
36. Daniel Deudney, 'The case against linking environmental degradation and national security', *Millennium*, vol. 19, no. 3 (Winter 1990), pp. 461–76.
37. *The Japan Times* (5 January 1991).
38. *Supplement to Oxford English Dictionary* (4 vols.), Oxford (1976), vol. 2, p. 120.

Chapter 9 – Strategy Unbound

1. eg Herman Kahn, *On Escalation, Metaphors and Scenarios*, Praeger, New York (1965).
2. Lawrence Freedman, *The Evolution of Nuclear Strategy*, Macmillan for IISS, London (1989), p. 217.
3. Professor Neville Brown and General Sir Anthony Farrar-Hockley, *Nuclear First Use*, Buchan and Enright for RUSI (1985), pp. 50–1.
4. Theodore White, *China: the Roots of Madness*, BBC, London (1970), p. 11.
5. *The Military Balance, 1990–91*, Brassey's for The International Institute for Strategic Studies, London (1990), pp. 38–43.
6. Harold Pinter, 'The Catastrophe Culture', *The Independent* (3 February 1987).
7. E. P. Thompson, 'Notes on Exterminism: the Last Stage of Civilisation', *New Left Review*, 121 (May–June 1980), pp. 1–31.
8. *Ibid.*
9. Bill McKibben, *The End of Nature*, Viking Penguin, New York (1990), Chapter 2.
10. Thomas C. Schelling, *Arms and Influence*, Yale University Press, New Haven (1966), Chapter 2.
11. *Ibid.*, Chapter 3.
12. *The Evolution of Nuclear Strategy, op. cit.*, pp. 244 and 254–6.
13. Albert Einstein, *The World as I see it*, Watts and Co., London (1940), pp. 96 and 105.
14. Merle Lipton in Godfrey Morrison (ed.), *Change in Southern Africa*, Miramoar Publications, London (1975), p. 17.
15. *Weekly Hansard. House of Commons Official Report*, vol. 99, no. 129, HMSO, London (June 1986), column 907.
16. Transkei, Ciskei, Bophuthatswana and Venda.
17. Neville and Yu-Ying Brown, *South Africa: Sanctions or Targetted Aid?*, Muirhead Foreign Policy Papers No. 1, University of Birmingham, Birmingham (November 1986), p. 35.
18. Martin Parry, *Climate Change and World Agriculture*, Earthscan, London (1990), Table 7.1.
19. *The Guardian* (4 April 1986).
20. *The Guardian* (27 May 1986).
21. Jeffrey D. Dillman, 'Water Rights in the Occupied Territories', *The Journal of Palestine Studies*, vol. XIX, no. 1 (Autumn 1989), pp. 46–71.
22. Jeremy Leggett (ed.), *Global Warming. The Greenpeace Report*, Oxford University Press, Oxford (1990), Chapter 13.3.1.

23. *The Independent* (4 September 1990).
24. Martin Parry, *op. cit.*, pp. 127–8.
25. Jon MacNeill, 'Strategies for sustainable economic development', *Scientific American*, vol. 261, no. 3 (September 1989), pp. 105–13.
26. Herman Kahn, *The Next 200 Years*, Associated Business Programmes, London (1977), Chapter 3.
27. D. J. Kessler, 'Orbital Space issues', *Advanced Space Review*, vol. 5, no. 2 (1985), pp. 3–10.
28. Barbara Wood-Kacmar, 'The junkyard in the sky', *New Scientist*, vol. 128, no. 1738 (13 October 1990), pp. 36–40.
29. Neville Brown, *Limited World War?*, Australian National University, Canberra (1984), p. 9.
30. René Albrecht-Carrie, *The Meaning of the First World War*, Prentice Hall, Englewood Cliffs (1965), pp. 42–3.
31. John K. Fairbank, *et al.*, *East Asia. Tradition and Transformation*, Allen and Unwin, London (1973), p. 242.
32. Neville Brown, *New Strategy Through Space*, Leicester University Press, Leicester (1990), p. 190.
33. Geoffrey Weston, 'Pragmatism tones down socialist dogma', *Tanzania, A Special Report* in *The Times* (13 September 1978), p. 1.
34. Jonas Widgren, 'International migration and regional stability', *Internatinal Affairs*, vol. 66, no. 4 (October 1990), pp. 749–66.
35. John Andres, 'Privatisation as an emerging force', *1987 Britannica Book of the Year*, Encyclopedia Britannica, Chicago (1987), pp. 194–5.
36. 'Eastern Europe Moves Right', *The Economist* (24 March 1990).
37. 'Blacks attend formerly all-white schools in parts of South Africa for the first time', *The Japan Times* (11 January 1991).
38. For a fuller discussion of this attitude, see *New Strategy Through Space, op. cit.*, p. 195.
39. Henri Focillon, *The Year 1000*, Harper and Row, New York (1969), p. 60.
40. Norman Cohn, *The Pursuit of the Millennium*, Paladin, London (1972), p. 282.
41. David Hoey, 'The Green Movements' Collectivist Roots', *The European Freedom Review*, vol. 2, no. 3 (Autumn 1990), pp. 000–00.
42. Marjorie Mazel Hecht, 'The Soviet disaster: accident – or war push?', *Executive Intelligence Review*, 13, 20 (16 May 1986), pp. 34–5.
43. 'Messianic Mission', *Far Eastern Economic Review*, 44 (1 November 1990), pp. 24–31.

Chapter 10 – Geopolitics and Beyond

1. Saul B. Cohen, *Geography and Politics in a Divided World*, Methuen, London (1964), pp. 83–90.
2. 'The bleak continent', *The Economist* (9 December 1989).
3. *Documents on American Foreign Relations, 1966*, Council on Foreign Relations, New York (1967), pp. 251–4.
4. P. B. Cove, *Websters Third International Dictionary*, G. and C. Merriam, Springfield (1961), p. 1510.
5. L. E. Seltzer (ed.), *The Columbia Lippincott Gazetteer of the World*, Columbia University Press, New York (1952), p. 1293.
6. Cohen, *op. cit.*, p. 234.
7. This exercise in definition derives from the author's *Limited World War?*, Australian National University, Canberra (1984), pp. 33–5.

8. See the author's *New Strategy Through Space*, Leicester University Press, Leicester (1990), pp. 20–2.
9. Doubts are sometimes expressed as to whether the Egyptians did use mustard gas in the Yemen. Visiting Aden and the Radfan as a journalist, 1966–67, one heard convincing reports that they had.
10. Alan J. Day (ed.), *The Annual Register, a Record of World Events, 1989*, vol. 231, Longman, London (1990), pp. 371–2.
11. See the author's 'Cyprus: a study in unresolved conflict', *The World Today*, Vol. 23, No. 11 (November 1967).
12. *New Strategy Through Space, op. cit.*, pp. 142–3.
13. 'Invasion Plan Ideological Feud Among Republicans', *The Times* (10 September 1990).
14. Frank L. Klingberg, 'The historical alternation of moods in American foreign policy', *World Politics*, 2, 1 (January 1952), pp. 239–73.
15. Arthur M. Schlesinger, *The Cycles of American History*, André Deutsch, London (1987), p. 45.
16. 'Thinking ahead, a survey of Japanese technology', *The Economist* (2 December 1989).
17. Yoshio Nagata, 'Poll: US leads Japan in research', *The Japan Economic Journal* (11 March 1989).
18. 'Can Japan make Einsteins, too?', *The Economist* (11 August 1990).
19. Michael Grubb, *The Greenhouse Effect: Negotiating Targets*, Royal Institute of International Affairs, London (1989), Figure 5b.
20. Juichi Inada, 'Japan's Aid Diplomacy: Economic, Political or Strategic?', *Millennium*, vol. 18, no. 3 (Winter 1989), pp. 399–414.
21. 'Japanese Crash?', *The Economist* (18 August 1990).
22. R. Taggart Murphy, 'Power without Purpose: the crisis of Japan's Global Financial Dominance', *Harvard Business Review* (March–April 1989), pp. 71–83.
23. Martin Parry, *Climate Change and World Agriculture*, Earthscan, London (1990), p. 57.
24. B. Santer, 'The use of general circulation models in climate impact analysis – a preliminary study of the impacts of a CO_2-induced climate change on Western European agriculture', *Climate Change*, vol. 7, no. 1 (1985), pp. 71–93.
25. Professor Michael Porter, 'Don't collaborate, compete', *The Economist* (1 June 1990).
26. Michael L. Nash, 'The European Economic Space', *Contemporary Review*, vol. 257, no. 1498 (November 1990), pp. 237–40.
27. *Ibid.*
28. Jack Snyder, 'International Leverage on Soviet Domestic Change', *World Politics*, Vol. 48, No. 3 (October 1989), pp. 3–30.
29. Robert Conquest, 'I told you so', *Encounter*, vol. LXXV, no. 2 (September 1990), pp. 24–5.
30. Jacob Bronowski and Bruce Mazlish, *The Western Intellectual Tradition*, Harper and Row, New York (1975), p. 494.
31. Neville Brown, *The Future Global Challenge*, Crane Russak, New York (1977), p. 49.
32. J. A. Hobson, *Imperialism*, George Allen and Unwin, London (1938 edition), p. 302.
33. George Watson, 'Were the intellectuals duped?', *Encounter*, vol. XLI, no. 4 (December 1973), pp. 20–30.
34. The author's 'New Paradigms for Strategy', *The World Today*, vol. 46, no. 5 (June 1990), pp. 115–18.

35. Eric Hobsbawn, 'Goodbye to all that', *Marxism Today* (October 1990), pp. 18–23.
36. Michel Garder, *A History of the Soviet Army*, Pall Mall Press, London (1966), p. 111.
37. Malcolm Mackintosh, *Juggernaut*, Secker and Warburg, London (1967), p. 159.
38. C. J. Dick in J. P. Harris and F. N. Toase (ed.), *Armoured Warfare*, B. T. Batsford, London (1990), p. 123.
39. R. Wagner (ed.) and L. Fetzer (trans.), *The Soviet Air Force in World War Two*, David and Charles, Newton Abbot (1974), Appendix 3.
40. Zhores A. Medvedev, *Soviet Science*, Oxford University Press, Oxford (1979), Chapters 2 and 3.
41. Yuri Orlov, 'How we can help open up Soviet society', *The Scientist*, vol. 1, no. 19 (10 August 1987), p. 11.
42. *New Strategy Through Space*, op cit., pp. 256–7.
43. *The Future Global Challenge*, op. cit., Chapter 7(b).
44. *The Greenhouse Effect: Negotiating Targets*, op. cit., Figure 2a.
45. Kwame Nkrumah, *Towards Colonial Freedom*, Heinemann, London (1942).
46. Muammar Al Gadafi, *The Green Book*, Public Establishment for Publishing, Advertising and Distribution,Tripoli (undated), pp. 110–11.
47. *The Annual Register of World Events, 1977*, Longman, London (1978), p. 256.
48. Steve Biko, *I write what I like*, Penguin, Harmondsworth (1988).
49. A. James Gregor, *The Fascist Persuasion in Radical Politics*, Princeton University Press, Princeton (1974), p. 408.
50. Ian Roxborough, *Theories of Underdevelopment*, Macmillan, London (1979), Chapter 1.
51. Eric R. Wolf, *Peasant Wars of the Twentieth Century*, Faber and Faber, London (1971), pp. 288–9.
52. *The Future Global Challenge*, op. cit., pp. 9–10.
53. R. G. Wilkinson, *Poverty and Progress: An Ecological Model of Economic Equilibrium*, Methuen, London (1973).
54. Takeshi Umehara, 'Shinto and Buddhism in traditional Japanese culture', *The Japan Foundation Newsletter*, XV, 1 (July 1987), pp. 1–7.
55. eg The address to the US President famously made by Chief Seattle of the Duwamish League in 1854. For text see *Wildlife* (March 1976), pp. 113–15.
56. Indira Gandhi, *Peoples and Problems*, Hodder and Stoughton, London (1982), Chapter 17.
57. See Arthur Koestler, *The Heel of Achilles*, Hutchinson, London (1974), pp. 221–4.
58. Roland Dallas, 'Will Latin American democracy last?', *The World Today*, vol. 43, no. 4 (April 1987), pp. 70–2.
59. Jacques Barzun, 'Is democratic theory still for export?', *Ethics and International Affairs*, no. 1 (1987), pp. 53–71.
60. 'United Nations Agencies, a case for emergency treatment', *The Economist* (2 December 1989).
61. Bruce Rich, 'The Emperor's New Clothes: the World Bank and Environmental Reform', *World Policy Journal*, Vol. VII, no. 2 (Spring 1990), pp. 305–29.
62. eg David Lilienthal, *TVA. Democracy on the March*, Penguin, Harmondsworth (1944).
63. *Bahrein: Violations of Human Rights*, Amnesty International, London (May 1991).
64. Ruskin was referring to the illusion that the weather reflects our mood.

Chapter 11 – Defended Peace

1. *The Economist* (12 December 1970).
2. *The Economist* (29 July 1978).
3. R. W. Amann *et al.*, *The Technological Level of Soviet Industry*, Yale University Press, New Haven and London (1977), Chapter 8.
4. *Soviet Military Power*, US Government Printing Office for Department of Defense, Washington DC (1982), p. 74.
5. *Soviet Military Power*, Washington, DC (1987), p. 112.
6. Paul Snell, 'Inquest on Soviet computing', *New Scientist*, vol. 128, no. 1745 (8 December 1990), pp. 46–9.
7. Philip Hanson, Discussion Paper I, *Soviet Industrial Espionage: Some New Information*, Royal Institute of International Affairs, London (1987), pp. 17–19.
8. Snell, *op. cit.*, p. 46.
9. Dr. Christopher Davies, *Military and Civil Economic Activities of the Soviet Armed Forces, 1975–85*, Paper presented at the Centre for Russian and East European Studies, University of Birmingham (14 November 1986).
10. 'Converting Soviet Arms Factories', *The Economist* (15 December 1990).
11. W. W. Rostow, 'The Coming Age of Regionalism', *Encounter*, vol. LXXIV, no. 5 (June 1990), pp. 3–7.
12. E. Jantsch, *Technological Forecasting in Perspective*, OECD, Paris (1967), pp. 156–63.
13. Richard Falk, *A Study of Future Worlds*, North-Holland, Amsterdam (1975), p. 139.
14. Gerrit van Roon, 'Historians and Long Waves', in Christopher Freeman (ed.), *Long Waves in the World Economy*, Butterworth, London (1983), pp. 237–43.
15. Erol Yagci, *The Quest for Strategic Sufficiency: Turkey and her Defence Industry*, Master's thesis at the University of Birmingham. Unpublished, held in the university library (1990), Chapter 4.
16. Speech by William Webster, US Information Service, London, London (1 April 1989).
17. Speech by Richard Clarke, US Information Service, London (2 November 1989).
18. Michael T. Klare, 'Growing firepower in the third world', *Bulletin of the Atomic Scientists*, vol. 46, no. 5 (May 1990), pp. 9–13.
19. Ron Matthews, 'Dangerous New Twists in the Middle East's Arms Race Spiral', *The Journal of the Royal United Services Institute for Defence Studies*, vol. 135, no. 4 (Winter 1990), pp. 31–8.
20. *The Military Balance, 1990–91*, Brassey's for The International Institute for Strategic Studies, London (1990), p. 99.
21. The CEP is the radius of a circle centred on the target and within which half the shots can be expected to fall.
22. David Rubenson and James Bonomo, 'The role of ATBM in NATO strategy', *Survival*, vol. XXIX, no. 6 (Novembe–December 1987), pp. 511–27.
23. Neville Brown, *The Future of Air Power*, Croom Helm, London (1986), p. 109.
24. Dr Martin S. Navias, 'Is There an Emerging Third World Ballistic Missile Threat to Europe?', *The Journal of the Royal United Services Institute for Defence Studies, op. cit.*, pp. 12–18.
25. 'Arming the IRA. The Libyan Connection', *The Economist* (31 March 1990).
26. Richard Clutterbuck, *Terrorism, Drugs and Crime in Europe after 1992*, Routledge, London (1990), p. 76.
27. Tim Zimmermann, 'The American bombing of Libya. A success for coercive diplomacy?', *Survival*, vol. XXIX, no. 3 (May–June 1987), pp. 195–214.

28. For a thorough discussion of this vexed matter, see Philip Towle, '*Should the West arm guerrillas?*', Faraday Discussion Paper, no. 11, The Council for Arms Control, London (February, 1988).
29. Chapter 11, 'The Future of Intelligence' in *The Future Global Challenge*, *op. cit.*
30. Thomas Paine, *Common Sense*, Peter Eckler, New York (1891), p. 43.
31. William R. Arkin et alia, *On Impact*, Greenpeace, Washington, DC (May 1991), p. 90.
32. See the author's *European Security*, Royal United Services Institute for Defence Studies, London (April 1972), Chapter 5(3).
33. Quoted in *The Guardian* (13 April 1960).
34. S. G. Gorshkov, *The Sea Power of the State*, United States Naval Institute, Annapolis (1977), pp. 100–101.
35. Jonathan B. Stein, 'Anti-Tactical Ballistic Missiles. New Threat to the ABM treaty', *Arms Control Today*, vol. 15, no. 8 (October 1985), pp. 10–12.
36. Hedley Bull, *The Control of the Arms Race*, Weidenfeld and Nicolson for the Institute for Strategic Studies, London (1961), Chapter 12.
37. Graham Norton, 'The terrorist and the traveller', *The World Today*, vol. 47, no. 5 (May 1991), pp. 80–1.
38. Charles J. Gross, 'A different breed of cats. The Air National Guard and the 1968 Reserve Mobilisation', *Air University Review*, vol. 34, no. 1 (January 1983), pp. 92–9.
39. *Australian Defence*, Australian Government Publishing House, Canberra (1976), p. 24.
40. Peter Berger, Chapter 7, 'The Obsolescence of the Concept of Honour' in Michael J. Sandel (ed.), *Liberalism and its Critics*, Basil Blackwell, Oxford (1984), pp. 149–58.
41. eg Kei Wakaizumi, 'Japan's role in a new world order', *Foreign Affairs*, vol. 51, no. 2 (January 1973), pp. 310–26.
42. Editorial, 'Poor Public Confidence in Politics', *Japan Times* (7 January 1991).
43. Yukio Suzuki, 'Diplomacy means Strategy', *Japan Times* (5 January 1991).
44. 'Privileged EC trio keep the nine in the dark', *The Daily Telegraph* (20 February 1991).
45. Winston S. Churchill, *The Second World War*, vol. 1, Cassell, London (1948), p. 583.

Chapter 12 – Planetary Horizons

1. Neville Brown, *New Strategy Through Space*, Leicester University Press, Leicester and Columbia University Press, New York (1990), pp. 4–5.
2. Paul Nitze, 'Security and arms control. A number of good beginnings', *NATO Reviews*, 36, 6 (December 1988), pp. 1–6.
3. Michael Brower, 'Targetting Soviet mobile missiles. Prospects and implications', *Survival*, vol. XXXI, no. 5 (September–October, 1989), pp. 433–45.
4. Robert C. Gray, 'The Bush Administration and mobile ICBM', *Ibid*, pp. 415–31.
5. Brower, *op. cit.*
6. See the author's *The Future of Air Power*, Croom Helm, London (1986), p. 213.
7. See the author's 'A Soviet SDI', *The World Today*, vol. 43, no. 12 (December 1987), pp. 212–14.
8. J. M. Spaight, *Air Power and War Rights*, London (1949), p. 10.
9. Richard Lawrence and Jeffrey Record, *US Force Structure in NATO*, The Brookings Institution, Washington DC (1974), p. 44.
10. Jeanette Voas, *Soviet Attitudes towards Ballistic Missile Defence and the ABM*

Treaty, Adelphi Paper 255, International Institute for Strategic Studies, London (Winter 1990), p. 54.

11. Jacquelyn K. Davis and Robert L. Pfaltzgraff, *Power Projection and the Long-Range Combat Aircraft*, Institute for Foreign Policy Analysis, Cambridge in Massachusetts (1981).

12. *Nuclear and Space Talks: US and Soviet Proposals*, Arms Control and Disarmament Agency, Washington DC (3 July 1990), p. 10.

13. See the paper by Anne Fikkan delivered at the International Studies Association 31st Annual Convention in Washington DC (April 1990).

14. Jeff Ballot, 'Northern vision', *The Toronto Globe and Mail* (10 October 1987).

15. Gail Osherenko, 'Environmental co–operation in the Arctic: will the Soviets participate?', *International Environmental Affairs*, vol. 1, no. 3 (Summer 1989), pp. 203–21.

16. Michael Getler, 'Lehman sees Norwegian Sea as key to Soviet naval strategy', *The Washington Post* (29 December 1972).

17. Colin S. Gray, *Maritime Strategy, Geopolitics and the Defense of the West*, National Strategy Information Centre, New York (1986), p. 75.

18. *Technical Report 8089*, Naval Underwater Systems Centre, Newport (1 September 1987), p. 1.

19. See the author's 'SDI revisited', *The World Today*, vol. 43, no. 4 (April 1987), pp. 57–8.

20. George Lindsey, Adelphi Paper 241, *Strategic Stability in The Arctic*, International Institute for Strategic Studies, London (Summer 1989), pp. 75–6.

21. As quoted in *The Japan Times* (31 January 1991).

22. The more techical appraisals are mainly in Chapters 5, 6, 12 and Appendix A.

23. *1989 Report to Congress on the Strategic Defense Initiative*, US Government Printing Office for Strategic Defense Initiative Organisation, Washington DC (March 1989), sections 5.5.2 to 5.5.10.

24. *Star Wars Quotes*, Arms Control Association, Washington DC (July 1986), pp. 48–50.

25. *Scientific American*, vol. 255, no. 6 (December 1986), p. 64.

26. *The Japan Times, op. cit.*

27 Quoted in *Los Angeles Times* (9 July 1985).

28. For a valuable overview of the legal situation, see David Whitehouse, 'Law in orbit', *New Scientist*, vol. 119, no. 1620 (7 July 1988), pp. 41–3.

29. Chapters 3 and 16, *New Strategy Through Space, op. cit.*

30. 'In Space, America plans a Star Wars defence to protect itself from Third World missiles', *The Sunday Times* (11 March 1990).

31. *The Baltimore Sun* (28 August 1984).

32. In correspondence, Mr McNamara now insists that he never did believe in limited nuclear war; and that he told President Kennedy as much.

33. Dr. A. Barrie Pittock, *Beyond Darkness*, Macmillan, Melbourne (1987), Chapter 8.

34. *Mainichi Daily News* (27 January 1991).

35. Jonathan B. Stein, 'Anti-Tactical Ballistic Missiles. New threat to the ABM treaty', *Arms Control Today*, vol. 15, no. 8 (October 1985), pp. 10–12.

36. Text as issued by United States Information Service, London (14 May 1990).

37. 'White House endorses plan for Shuttle, Station cutback', *Aviation Week and Space Technology*, vol. 133, no. 25 (17 December 1990), pp. 18–20.

38. *New Strategy Through Space, op. cit.*, p. 214.

39. 'Cold Water on Mars', *The Economist* (10 March 1990), pp. 132–4.

40. See, for example, Philip R. Harris, 'Living on the Moon', *The Futurist*, vol. XIX, no. 2 (April 1985), pp. 46–50.

41. Sally K. Ride quoted in *Aviation Week and Space Technology*, vol. 127, no. 8 (24 August 1987), p. 27.
42. Neville Brown, 'Planetary geopolitics', *Millennium*, vol. 19, no. 3 (Winter 1990), pp. 447–60.
43. W. B. Gallie, *Philosophers of Peace and War*, Cambridge University Press, Cambridge (1979), Chapter 2.
44. Bertrand Russell, 'Why men should keep away from the Moon', *The Times* (15 July 1969).
45. A British Library exhibition on Engelbert Kaempfer was held in Tokyo in the winter of 1990–91 before moving elsewhere in Japan. The official catalogue noted that *On Perpetual Peace* quoted Kaempfer three times. Santory Museum of Art, Tokyo (1990).

Index